Sarah's
DAUGHTERS

KITTY JONES CULWELL

For nearly 50 years Mrs. Culwell has been a wife and mother. In four decades she has found time to teach hundreds of children and grown-ups, in public school and church. Her 15 grandchildren attest the wisdom and kindness of their "Mimi."

Throughout the Magic Valley of Texas where the Culwells call home, she is known as an authority on Bible themes. She teaches groups of women how to be better homemakers by patterning their lives after the Bible examples.

Scattered among the lessons are warnings of what not-to-be, gleaned from the stories of Jezebel, Lot's wife, and Sapphira.

These are the narratives she has written in "Sarah's Daughters"—a collection of true stories drawn from women of Bible times and applied to the women of modern times.

Convincing because of the inner beauty of her character, the author of "Sarah's Daughters" inspires today's Christian woman to live closer to God.

Study suggestions follow each chapter. They will be helpful to groups of students who follow the lessons in an organized class.

All ladies' groups will benefit from this accurate, scriptural survey of Bible women.

Through character studies of women who have made sacred history, the spiritual descendants of Sarah are portrayed in this informative book.

Sarah's DAUGHTERS

by
Kitty Jones Culwell

DeHoff
Christian Bookstore

GOLDEN RULE SERVICE

749 N.W. Broad Street • Murfreesboro, TN 37129
Phone 615.893.8322 • Fax 615.896.7447 • 1.800.695.5385
Email dehoff@bellsouth.net • www.dehoffbooks.com

2006

Acknowledgment is made to Harper & Brothers for
permission to reprint five poems from the book *Songs
of Faith* by Grace Noll Crowell, copyright 1939.

Printed in the United States of America

Dedicated

to

MY CHILDREN

and

MY CHILDREN'S CHILDREN

Foreword

One of the great encouraging signs in the church today is the increasing interest in Christian womanhood. It has long been my contention that the work of the church cannot succeed anywhere without the support of Christian women—women who fulfill their God-given responsibility of "keepers at home" and thus stabilize church, state and civilization.

We are glad to see this new study of priceless womanhood by Kitty Jones Culwell of McAllen, Texas. Mrs. Culwell is well known in the Rio Grande Valley for her consecration, faithfulness, and teaching ability. Her book will contribute further to the advance of understanding the important role which women played in Bible times. It will offer to the student a greater appreciation, and to women of the church today a greater inspiration.

THOMAS L. CAMPBELL

Contents

Introduction

G ENESIS is a book of beginnings. It tells us of the beginning of the world and all things therein—the beginning of the family and the family's relationship to God.

It was the sixth day of creation. The world was very new. God had spoken order and beauty out of darkness and chaos. The earth was ready for its inhabitants. Vegetation preceded animal life. Fishes were in the water. Birds were in the air. The mammals and the lower order of animals had been given life. On the sixth day the beasts of the field were created. Then . . . "the Lord God formed man of the dust of the ground, and breathed into his nostrils the breath of life; and man became a living soul" (Gen. 2:7). This is the story of man's beginning. God made him. God gave him life.

Before Adam, God brought all the animals, birds and fishes. Adam gave to each creature his name. Yet in all this great company of God's creatures there was no true companion for Adam. "And the Lord God said, 'It is not good for man to be alone; and I will make an help meet for him' "(Gen. 2:18).

God caused a deep sleep to fall upon Adam. While the first man was in slumber, Jehovah took from his side a rib and made woman. Thus the Holy Scriptures make a vivid picture of the creation of the first husband and wife . . . "male and female created he them."

THE FIRST MARRIAGE

This is the sacred story of the first marriage. "And God blessed them, and God said unto them, 'Be fruitful and multiply and replenish the earth.' " God honored woman by placing her by man's side and giving her the privilege of helping him. Here we see God's purpose and plan for marriage. Eve was Adam's companion and partner in the work assigned them by their Maker. The husband and wife relationship is from God.

It has been perpetuated under the laws of God. Jesus taught that it should always be as it was from the beginning.

THE FIRST HOME

The Lord God provided a home for these two. This beautiful garden-home was adaptable to their every need. God provided beauty in this first home by giving every tree that was pleasant to the sight. There were gold and precious stones. God gave them good things to enjoy: fruit of the trees and water from a beautiful river. And God himself walked and talked with them in this Paradise. There was work to be done; the garden must be cultivated and the trees must be pruned. How happy was their lot!

9

THE THREE AGES

The Bible depicts for our study the woman, her family and her home during three periods of time. From the creation until the giving of the Law to Moses is the first age. Next we see the children of Israel and their drawing nearer to God, and third, the perfect dispensation of Christianity. All of God's children, however, imperfect might have been their culture, had a faith that was the same as ours—looking forward to an eternal city whose builder is God. The Bible naturally divides itself into three histories of the family:

1. The Starlight Age

2. The Moonlight Age

3. The Sunlight Age

The Starlight Age

Starlight represents the Patriarchal Dispensation. We understand that this period of the patriarchs is the interval between Genesis 1 and Exodus 20. The account of early worship gives us a picture of the father and mother kneeling before a crude altar of stones, God's ordained institution for worship. Animal sacrifice was required; the smoke of their offering ascends heavenward. The father is the head of the family; he is the priest for the family. Women reign as queens in their tent-homes. As she lives in harmony with God's laws she makes an important contribution to the era; the bad women who do not fulfill God's purpose serve to paint the tragic result of sin.

The Moonlight Age

More light concerning God's purpose and plan for man is revealed during the next period. Along with civil and moral laws, God on Sinai gave to Israel an educational system; and this plan of education for the family was effective until A.D. 33 (Acts 2). He laid upon the fathers and mothers a serious responsibility: "Take heed to thyself . . . and teach them thy sons, and thy sons' sons." The very nature of this law gave a quality of stability to the family and national life of Israel. Moses built the tabernacle to replace the stone altar. Faith and obedience characterized the true worshipper according to the Law of Moses. The women of this period fulfilled their destiny by bearing and training good men. Respect and sacredness attached to the family developed noble and heroic elements in the Jewish woman. Motherhood was highly esteemed because of the age-old promise that some Judean mother would give birth to the Savior of the world. Every cradle was made sacred by the thought of that holy child who was to be the "seed of the woman."

The Sunlight Age

Faith passed as a legacy through the families of the Old Testament. The inspiring motive of their lives was the invisible God. The promise of the Messiah, given first in sumbolic language in Eden (Gen. 3:15), was repeated to Abraham and each succeeding generation until its consummation in the Christian era. Faithful women of the Bible made patterns of light; the unfaithful left patterns of darkness.

The sunlight of God's complete revelation burst forth in the splendor of the gospel of the Son of God. In this Spirit-illumined age, woman's position is clear and unmistakable.

The mechanisms of living change; the world changes; but God's design for woman has not changed. This is clearly shown when the Holy Spirit through two New Testament writers paid great tribute to Sarah, the wife of Abraham. She is held up as an example to Christian wives who would please the Lord and have happy homes. She is commended for her faith; this faith was manifested in her function as a wife and mother. She is represented as the forebearer of all Christian women. "Even as Sarah obeyed Abraham, calling him lord; whose daughters ye are, as long as ye do well . . ." (1 Pet. 3:6).

The mother of our Lord "found favor with God." She was the product of the Hebrew family who had nurtured the ideals of an obedient faith through the ages. It is an honor to womanhood that among Jesus' most ardent believers and followers were women. His gospel message found a ready acceptance in feminine hearts.

". . . Ye Do Well"

Many were the women who recognized Christ as the "promised seed" and the end of the law. The Holy Spirit testified that he "took it out of the way, nailing it to the cross" (Col. 2:14). They followed and ministered unto him of their substance during his earthly ministry. Among the great multitude of people who went with Jesus to the cross were women who bewailed and lamented him. Faithful women witnessed his death; they were first to see the empty tomb. It was women who heard the sweetest message ever told, "He is not here; he is risen."

The daughters of Jerusalem were among those who saw the Savior ascend into the heavens. They heard the glorious message that he would come again as they had seen him go. Loyal and steadfast, they continued with the disciples; with wonder they beheld the Holy Spirit descend on the day of Pentecost. They were among the multitude who heard the death, burial and resurrection of the adored Jesus proclaimed. We know with assurance ". . . they continued steadfastly in the apostles' doctrine, in fellowship, and in breaking of bread, and in prayers." As these noble women ministered to our

Lord while he lived upon this earth, now they centered their ministry
in his church.

> *"I love thy kingdom, Lord,*
> *The house of thine abode;*
> *The church our blest Redeemer saved*
> *With His own precious blood."*

Eve

Gen. 3:20; 4:1
2 Cor. 11:3
1 Tim. 2:13

"Therefore shall a man leave his father and his mother, and shall cleave unto his wife, and they shall be one flesh" (Gen. 2:24).

THE STORY OF EVE as the mother of all living is the story of the first woman. Early in the record of creation, God's purpose relative to woman is made clear. "So God created man in his own image, in the image of God created he him; male and female created he them" (Gen. 1:27). And Adam called his wife's name Eve because she was the mother of all living (Gen. 3:20). In the instant of creation she stood before Adam a full and complete woman—never a child, never a daughter, never a maiden. She was perfect. She was the product of divine creation. God created her to be a help meet for Adam. He was lacking, and she was the help he needed. He was the head and root from which she sprang.

"Therefore shall a man leave his father and his mother, and shall cleave unto his wife, and they shall be one flesh." Here the oneness of husband and wife in the marriage relationship comes to its complete meaning. Marriage is a divine institution.

In the Genesis account of Eve is the complete story of every woman: the picture of her marriage, her family, and her home with their attendant joys and sorrows. Marriage and homemaking were a part of God's purpose for his children from the beginning. The happy marriage is the marriage that follows the divine pattern. Thus marriage originated with God and not with the plans of men; our Lord has said, "What God has joined together let not man put asunder" (Matt. 19:6b).

We do not know how long Adam and Eve enjoyed their beautiful garden home, but a sad thing happened. Sin crept slyly into this home. The subtle serpent approached Eve instead of her husband. He knew that only through Eve would he be able to seduce Adam. "Adam was not deceived, but the woman being deceived was in the transgression" (1 Tim. 2:14).

Woman is more sensitive than man. She is more alert to the attractive. The love of the beautiful is in her to a greater degree than it is in man. Satan approached Eve; she had never known fear. She listened to the tempter, intrigued and fascinated. Satan made the temptation three-fold and very alluring. Had she discussed these things with her husband, together they could have resisted the devil. But Eve failed to let her higher and better nature control.

13

She "saw that the tree was good for food; it was pleasant to the eye, and a tree to be desired to make one wise." It appealed to the imagination, a mystery that captivated curiosity. It appealed to her vanity; she would come into possession of a marvelous knowledge. Had not the subtle one said, "Ye shall be as God"? She saw; she desired; she took. Lust conceived and sin was born. She did not transgress alone, "but she gave also unto Adam and he did eat." Instead of rescuing her from Satan, Adam permitted himself through Eve to be attracted to him. Fear, cowardice and shame caused them to hide themselves from the once welcome presence of God.

"And they heard the sound of the Lord God walking in the garden in the cool of the day: and Adam and his wife hid themselves from the presence of the Lord God amongst the trees of the garden." Sin had separated them from God, the source of all life. No doubt they now realized the full import of those words, "In the day thou eatest thereof thou shall surely die." This dreadful separation from God was not all. God said to Eve, "I will greatly multiply thy sorrow and thy conception: in sorrow shall thou bring forth children; and thy desire shall be to thy husband" (Gen. 3:16).

Because of this, Eve's happiness did not last long. She was driven from the beautiful Eden to enter a world of thorns and thistles. She found herself thrust into a world in which nothing had been provided for woman. How weary and exacting must have been her days! No doubt her very being was ravaged in anxiety and the anguish that is in childbirth. She had brought herself to a very low state by her willful sin. Her feminine perfection was completely marred.

But in tender pity and great mercy, God looked down upon this woman and sowed the seed of a glorious faith in her soul. The seed of this tempted woman was to bruise the head of the Tempter (Gen. 3:15). Eve saw God's mercy as he spoke these words to the serpent, and she fixed her whole life to that promise. When Cain was born, she exclaimed, "I have gotten a man from the Lord," thinking this child was the promised seed. How bitter must have been her grief and disillusionment when after some years her first-born son murdered his own brother. After many epochs Paul writes an account of the fruition of this prophecy: "But when the fulness of time was come, God sent forth his Son, made of woman, made under the law, to redeem them that were under the law, that we might receive the adoption of sons" (Gal. 4:4).

Paradise was lost to Eve of her disobedience. The beauties of Eden were exchanged for thorns and thistles. Cain her first-born became a murderer and a fugitive. Abel was the victim of his brother's jealousy. How poignant must have been her grief.

Adam and Eve lived a long time. Other sons and daughters were born to them. When Adam was one hundred and thirty years old Eve gave birth to Seth. "God hath given me another seed, instead of

Abel, whom Cain slew," said Eve. Seth is named in the lineage of Jesus our Lord. Eve's name is mentioned twice in the New Testament (2 Cor. 11:3) as a warning that Christians be not led away from the simplicity of Christ's teaching by the "subtility of the serpent."

Again the apostle Paul states woman's position; her position is secondary by the fact of her creation. "Woman was deceived in the transgression. Notwithstanding she shall be saved in child bearing, if they continue in faith and love with sobriety" (1 Tim. 2:14, 15).

THE AFTERMATH

After Eve's transgression Genesis plainly records the degradation of womanhood and God's ordinances profaned. For 1,625 years in the pages of God's Holy Word there is recorded the name of only four women. The Scriptures have painted for us a picture of the woman marred by sin. Adah and Zillah are the next women to be introduced to us by name. They were the wives of one and the same man, Lamech. By yielding to such polygamous arrangement they degraded the dignity of womanhood, profaned marriage and the home. The names of these suggest their character. Adah means a "gorgeously adorned woman" and Zillah, "one whose approach can be recognized at a distance by a jigling of her jewelry." There seems to be no piety nor modest virtue attributed to these two. They have surrendered inner beauty for external adornment:

"Thy desire shall be to thy husband and he shall rule over thee." In this decree from God is expiration and a new dignity for woman. Contrary to God's will and purpose, Adah and Zillah have become the wives of one man. Thus begins the history of polygamy and concubinage. As a result they have become even more miserable than Eve. They have become slaves. Their sons are Tubal-cain and Jubal-Cain. These sons are workers in metals. They are materialists, the physical being emphasized to the neglect of the spiritual.

The sad story continues: "The sons of God saw the daughters of men . . . they took them wives of all which they chose . . . they bare children to them. And God saw the wickedness of man was great in the earth . . . And it repented the Lord that He had made man on the earth . . . And the Lord said, I will destroy man whom I have created from the face of the earth" (Gen. 6:2-8).

NOAH'S WIFE

There seems to be no woman worthy of mention in the Scriptures until the time of Noah. Noah's wife must have been a wonderful woman, though her name is not given. She is the mother of three righteous sons, whose wives were worthy to go into the ark. Their lives were to be miraculously and providentially preserved. Through these godly women, the cleansed and purified world was repopulated.

The Divine Pattern

The home of our first parents was divinely appointed—one wife for one husband, one husband for one wife. The great career of motherhood and homemaking is God's purpose for woman. There is nothing the world needs more today than good Christian homes. While homemaking can be dreary, it may also be made a fine and beautiful art. It is a cooperative business of unseen values, a producer of the Christ-like personality. The home is the foundation unit of society. No nation can rise above the faith and ideals of the home.

"Lo, children are a heritage of Jehovah and the fruit of the womb is his reward. As arrows in the hand of a mighty man, so are the children of youth. Happy is the man that hath his quiver full of them." A house dedicated to God becomes a home. In this first home there was one husband and one wife. Children were born to this union. There was work to be done; the garden must be kept; the earth replenished and subdued.

"I will therefore that the younger women marry, bear children, guide the house . . ." (1 Tim. 5:14). Through the wife's labors a house becomes a home. It is a peaceful shelter. There is no fear, doubt or division. The wife is the Queen of the home. She sets the moral and spiritual tone of the home.

> . . . These queens who have no scepter in their hands
> and yet reign upon a firmer throne
> Than any that the earth has ever known.
>
> Rulers of life itself, with love as pure
> and selfless as the old earth knows,
> Their trust in God unshakable and sure,
> Their faith implanted in their children grows,
> Into a living, lifting, shining thing
> That through life's stress can know no conquering.
>
> —Grace Noll Crowell[1]

Every normal girl dreams of a husband and a home of her own. This is a high and holy ambition if God's plan is understood and honored.

"In the home she is one of two senior members, with all the demands, privileges and opportunities that implies. She has the chance to make the place where she works reflect her own taste and personality. She has the chance to be creative. In the home she can be a womanly woman. She is making a home for a man and working with him, instead of competing against him" (Ruth Millet).

The home is the foundation unit of society. No nation can rise

[1] Taken from *Songs of Faith* by Grace Noll Crowell. Copyright 1939, Harper & Brothers. Used by permission.

above the ideals and standards of its homes.

How can we know God's purposes for women, and can we harmonize our lives with His plan? God's plan is revealed in His word. In order to know that great purpose, we must study.

The home of our first parents was divinely appointed—one wife for one husband, one husband for one wife. The great career of motherhood and homemaking is God's purpose for woman. There is nothing the world needs more today than good Christian homes. While homemaking can be dreary, it may also be made a fine and beautiful art. It is a cooperative business of unseen values, a producer of the Christ-like personality. The home is the foundation unit of society. No nation can rise above the faith and ideals of the home.

> We would but know God passed this way
> When he let mothers come to stay.
> He glimpsed our need though near or far
> And left the gates of heaven ajar.
> The greatest job among all others—
> God passed this way and gave us mothers.
>
> —VIRGINIA CONWAY

STUDY SUGGESTIONS

In whose image was Eve created? (Gen. 1:27)

What does this mean? (2 Cor. 4:16, 1 Thess. 5:23; Gen. 2:7, Ecc. 12:7)

Physically whose image do we all bear? (1 Cor. 15:45, 49)

What was lacking at the climax of creation? (Gen. 2:20)

Give the account of Eve's creation. (Gen. 2:21-22)

Discuss the first marriage. (Gen. 2:22-24)

Discuss *leaving father and mother, cleaving to companion and becoming one flesh.*

Who instituted marriage and what did Jesus say about it? (Matt. 19:4, 5)

Name four purposes of marriage. (Gen. 2:28; Gen. 1:28; 1 Cor. 7:2; Heb. 13:4; 1 Tim. 5:13, 14)

What would the Apostle Paul have us know? (1 Cor. 11:3)

Is a woman's subjection twofold? What of the wife's subjection and its limitation? (Eph. 5:22)

Discuss the first home: its beauty, privileges, obligations and restrictions. (Gen. 2:8-17)

Why did Satan approach Eve first in the temptation? (1 Pet. 3:7)

When convinced of three things, what did she do? (Gen. 3:6)

Whom did she involve in her fall? (Gen. 3:6b)

Could this have been different had Eve talked it over with her husband?

Use your imagination to picture her anguish and suffering after leaving the garden-home.

What promise was made to her? (Gen. 3:15)

How is woman to be saved? (1 Tim. 4:15)

Name her sons. (Gen. 4:2)

How did Cain break his mother's heart? (Gen. 4:8)

What is the significance of the lives of Adah and Zillah relative to marriage?

Name some evils of polygamy and concubinage.

What do their lives teach regarding personal adornment? (1 Pet. 3:3, 4)

Discuss 2 Peter 1:5-11.

Does your home conform to God's plan?

Do we today recognize God's purpose for women?

Sarah

Gen. 11:29-31; 12:5-17; 16:1-8;
18:6-15; 20:2-18; 21:1-12;
23:1, 2, 9; 25:10-12
1 Pet. 3:6

"Through faith also Sarah herself received strength to conceive seed and was delivered of a child when she was past age, because she judged him faithful who had promised" (Heb. 11:11).

S ARAH is the first woman commended for her faith. This faith finds expression in her function as a wife and mother. In this role she contributes much to the history of man's spiritual growth.

The Scriptures introduce her as the wife of Abraham (Gen. 11: 29b). This is the beginning of the story of the lovely Sarah and the faithful Abraham. In all literature both sacred and secular there is no story more beautiful and revealing than that of this woman and her family and their relationship to the Lord God.

The writers of the New Testament instruct women of today to observe the faith of Sarah. The Apostle Paul points out that she became a mother by faith. And Peter pleads with all Christian women to become "daughters of Sarah who obeyed Abraham, calling him Lord" (1 Pet. 3:6).

Sarah's name, among the long list of the honored ancients named by Paul, is there because of her victorious life through faith. All of her life her faith was continually tested by the promise of God made to Abraham, "And I will make of thee a great nation" (Gen. 12: 2a). And as this promise included Sarah, it became the very warp and woof of her life.

"But Sarah was barren; she had no child" (Gen. 11:30). These were the most tragic words in the days of Sarah. The hope of every woman was to be the mother of the promised seed (Gen. 3:15). This great tragedy of Sarah's life was the supreme trial of her faith. Her faith triumphed when Isaac was born. "Through faith also Sarah herself received strength to conceive seed, and was delivered of a child when she was past age, because she had judged him faithful who had promised."

Abraham, a descendant of Arphaxad the son of Shem, lived with his father, Terah in Ur of the Chaldees, in southern Babylonia. Here he heard the voice of God calling him to leave the land of his boyhood to journey unto a land that God would show him. By faith Abraham began the trek up the great river Euphrates. Sarah accompanied her husband from Ur. The Bible says that Abraham was seventy-five and Sarah was sixty-five when they began their wanderings at the call of God.

It has been said that Abraham married well. Terah was the father of Sarah; she was her husband's half sister. This was not at all uncommon at this time. All of her life Sarah had known this man who was to become the "Friend of God." They possessed the very characteristics that the Lord desired in a family and eventually a great nation.

PIONEERS

"Now the Lord had said unto Abram, Get thee out of thy country and from thy kindred, and from thy father's house; unto a land that I will shew thee: And I will make of thee a great nation, and I will bless thee, and make thy name great; and thou shall be a blessing" (Gen. 12: 1-3). It might truly have been written, "That the Lord said unto Abram and Sarai," for where Abraham went, Sarah went. She willingly left the old home; she broke with the old familiar ties, and by his side she began the journey to the unknown country.

The journey was fraught with many dangers and hardships, but Sarah was a pioneer of great fortitude. This nomadic life was surely one of feminine self-denial. Yet in the sacred narrative, there is not to be found one word of complaint or reproach made by this lovely Sarah.

Together they took all their possessions, the tents in which they lived, large flocks of sheep and herds of cattle. Driving their flocks and herds they journeyed southwest toward the land of Canaan. Every experience of Abraham was Sarah's as well, and as she shared the dangers and heartaches she also shared in the great promise that she would be "the mother of nations."

Many weeks and months passed and at last they came to the Plains of Moreh, and there God spoke to Abraham saying, "This is the land that I will give to you and your children forever." And there he builded an altar and the Lord appeared unto him (Gen. 12:7). He continued his journey unto a mountain on the east of Bethel twelve miles north of Jerusalem. He built an altar there and later another in Mamre. There is every reason to believe that Sarah worshipped at these altars with Abraham. The Lord God said, "Thy desire shall be to thy husband." She fulfilled all the demands of this precept. Peter says, "They were heirs together of the grace of life" (1 Pet. 3:7b).

Submission

Sarah is an example for all ages of the faithful constant help-meet of her husband. She was steadfast and uncomplaining in days of famine. She was content and unspoiled when her husband became a rich man. Her desire was unto her husband under all circumstances.

When kings desired her for her beauty, and on two occasions took her into their harems, she was still a loyal and faithful wife. Through providential intervention she was returned to her home and was still content to abide in the black tents. There is not recorded that she ever made any unfavorable comparison between her surroundings and those she might have had in the kings' palaces.

After awhile because of delay and her age, Sarah's faith wavered; there was despair in her heart. It must have required a great sacrifice of vainglory, when she said to Abraham, "Behold the Lord has restrained me from bearing; I pray thee go in unto my hand maid; it may be that I may obtain children of her. And Abram hearkened to the voice of Sarah" (Gen. 16:2).

Sarah believed with all her heart that the Messiah was to arise from her husband and she would be the mother of the promised seed (Gen. 3:15). If God had denied her the ability to bear a child, she was willing to acquiesce this honor to another. The child would be regarded as Sarah's according to the ancient custom. This was an unholy state of affairs. She was guilty of abetting the sin of concubinage introduced by Adah and Zillah before the flood. In the beginning God ordained one wife for one husband. Add to this the fact that jealousy breaks out between her and Hagar; intense misery and anguish became the lot of this child and his mother.

Neither did Sarah escape the consequence of her lack of faith. For as soon as Hagar was sure of her pregnancy, she forgot the generosity of her mistress who had exalted her from the position of bond-woman to that of a secondary wife. Hagar became proud and arrogant and no doubt often belittled Sarah's barren state. The situation was unendurable to Sarah and she severely upbraided Abraham, "I have given my maid into thy bosom; and when she saw that she had conceived, I was despised in her eyes; the Lord judge between thee and me" (Gen. 16:5).

Prestige of the Wife

Abraham recognized Sarah's rights as a wife. His answer to her complaint showed clearly the strength of their marriage. "Behold thy maid is in thy hand; do to her as it pleaseth thee" (Gen. 16:6). Thus Sarah was reassured of her position in the household, and of her husband's love and affection. Sarah had put too much into the building of this union for it to be destroyed by this one sinful mistake.

Sarah had the assurance of her husband that she still had authority over her maid. Hagar refused to remain a servant to Sarah. And upon an occasion of rebuke, she fled into the wilderness. There the Lord found her and through an angel said unto her, "Return to thy mistress; and submit thyself under her hands" (Gen. 16:9).

This is a wonderful example of the wife's position in the home. Sarah's sin is not camouflaged in the Scriptures.

So Hagar returned to Sarah's tent. Possibly, never again was their relationship the same. It is very likely that Sarah loved Ishmael and perhaps with Abraham considered him as the promised Son.

God gave to Abraham the rite of circumcision, which was a sign of His covenant to him and his seed.

Abraham, Ishmael and all that were born in his house were circumcised on the self-same day. But on this occasion it was revealed to him that Ishmael was not to be the heir according to promise. The covenant was to be continued and confirmed in a son of Sarah.

No doubt this was ever in Sarah's mind, and her faith was quickened again by the visit of three men. Abraham saw the approach of these men as he sat in the door of his tent in the plains of Mamre. Abraham felt perfectly free to offer hospitality to these travelers before consulting Sarah. He knew that he could depend upon her. This mutual hospitality in their home has been urged upon the Christian home. She joined her husband in hospitality and entertained angels unaware (Heb. 13:3).

HOSPITALITY

The Lord Himself was a guest in the home of this faithful couple. He had come to tell again that Sarah would have a son. And Sarah heard it in the tent door which was behind him. "Therefore Sarah laughed within herself saying, After I am waxed old, shall I have pleasure, my lord being old also?" And when the Lord inquired of Abraham why Sarah had laughed, Sarah denied her laughter (Gen. 18:15).

"Is anything too hard for the Lord? At the appointed time I will return unto thee, according to the time of life, and Sarah shall have a son" (Gen. 18:14).

The triumph of Sarah's faith is recorded in Genesis 21:1-8. That this birth was a miracle is attested in the first verse. "And the Lord did unto Sarah as he had spoken." No longer does she deny having laughed. She confessed that God had made her to laugh and that all who heard would laugh with her. Besides the birth of our Savior, there is not a sweeter story told than the birth of Isaac.

She even nursed him at her breast, marvelling and exulting,—for herself? No, for her husband: "I have borne him a son in his old age."

The birth of Isaac must have been a bitter blow to Hagar's hopes. Soon again there was friction between the two women. The relationship was restrained. Isaac's birthday was celebrated. This was a celebration of his weaning, possibly his third birthday. There were many guests, feasting, and rejoicing. The breach between the two mothers was brought into the open when Sarah saw Hagar and Ishmael mocking. For the second time Sarah took a positive stand for her rights. She demanded of Abraham, "Cast out this bondwoman and her son; for the son of this bondwoman shall not be heir with my son, even with Isaac" (Gen. 21:10).

This at first glance seems to be a very harsh decision that Sarah made. But God gave his approval and there was more wisdom than cruelty in this decision.

"Let it not be grievous in thy sight because of the lad, and be cause of thy bondwoman; in all that Sarah hath said unto thee, hearken unto her voice; for in Isaac shall thy seed be called" (Gen. 21:12). Thus God commanded Abraham.

Abraham and Sarah had regarded Ishmael as a son for at least thirteen years. They must have had a great deal of love for this boy. It was hard to turn him and his mother out. Hagar's grief and distress must have been pitiful to see. She did not go out unseen and alone. Relief came to her and her son after a time from God. God gave to Hagar proof of his presence and his mercy was extended to her.

Again love and devotion one for the other and faith in Israel's God held this marriage through another crisis. There have been many criticisms for both Sarah and Abraham in this incident of Hagar and Ishmael. They deserve our sympathy rather than our censure.

Sarah had a great responsibility placed upon her as the mother of this child. The rivalry, mockery and bickering that would have prevailed was not the proper atmosphere for Isaac's rearing and training.

FAITH'S REWARD

The supreme testing of Abraham was when he offered up Isaac (Heb. 11:17). And shall we not say it was Sarah's too? Had she not shared every experience of her husband? And met every trial valiantly? Surely in this, she was there to lend encouragement to Abraham. Her heart must have been breaking as she watched these two leave for Mount Moriah. Sarah's faith never wavered after the birth of Isaac. She could with full assurance face this ordeal because "she judged him faithful who had promised" (Heb. 11:11b).

Her faith was rewarded and a ram was offered instead of Isaac. Sarah died at the age of one hundred and twenty-seven. She holds the honor of being the only Biblical woman whose age is recorded at her death.

Abraham and Isaac mourned for her, and it is said Isaac was not comforted in the loss of his mother until his marriage. Abraham purchased the cave of Machpelah, near the oak of Mamre. This was the beloved Sarah's burial place. How clearly the life of Sarah shows to all women of all times that true happiness is achieved when God's plan is understood and honored. She was true to her marriage vow and today after four thousand years, women are urged to obey their husbands, "Even as Sarah obeyed Abraham," (I Pet. 3:6); "I will therefore that the young women marry, bear children, guide the house" (1 Tim. 5:14). "The aged women are to teach the young women to love their husbands, to love their children" (Titus 2:4).

The picture of Biblical women becomes brighter. Through faith in God and submission to his will, woman slowly climbs to the place for which she was created. When Christ, "the seed of woman," came into the world, he elevated true womanhood. He placed a great value upon the family and the home.

There are five functions of marriage; biological, educational, moral social and religious. Marriage is honorable (Heb. 13:4; 1 Tim. 4:1-3). Marriage is to propagate the race (Gen. 1:28; Rom. 7:14). Marriage is to prevent immorality (1 Cor. 7:2). Marriage is to be a union for life, "until death do us part" (Rom. 7:2; 1 Cor. 7:39). The biological fact of motherhood within itself does not mean noble motherhood. Neither does motherhood transform the girl's character. How often do we hear the desperate cry, "I wish she would marry and settle down." The frivolous, pleasure-mad girl will never be changed into a steadfast daughter of Sarah. There must be training for marriage and motherhood. God's plan must be taught and emphasized. The functions of marriage when taught and understood, foster a proper relationship, physically, mentally, socially and spiritually. When these are brought into a wholesome relationship, marriage is a real success. A successful marriage is a successful life. All the successful endeavors of the world can never be comfort for the home that fails.

The Bible faces motherhood frankly. There are mothers, good and bad. Delinquent parents have delinquent children. Lord Shaftesbury said, "Give me a generation of Christian mothers, and I will undertake to change the face of society in twelve months." How important for the happiness of the human family and for society that marriage and home be regulated by the principles of God.

How clearly do the lives of Biblical women show all women of all times that true happiness is achieved when God's plans are understood and obeyed. When man begins to change that which was originated by God he defeats its purpose and destroys its honor.

"Marriage is the nursery of heaven . . . It lies under more burden (than does the single life), but is supported by all the strengths of love and charity, and these burdens are delightful. Marriage is the mother of the world, and fills cities, and churches and heaven itself."—Jeremy Taylor

Much time and emphasis should be placed upon the essential elements toward a successful marriage. There are many fine reference books to be studied, but let us take the Bible as the most important textbook on every human relationship.

> O happy home, where each one serves Thee lowly,
>   Whatever his appointed work may be,
> Till every common task seems great and holy,
>   When it is done, O Lord, as unto Thee.
>
> —CARL J. P. SPITTA

STUDY SUGGESTIONS

How old was Sarah at her death? (Gen. 23:2a)

Tell of her death and its effect upon Abraham. (Gen. 23:2b, 17, 19)

Who was Sarah and Abraham's son? What nation descended from them? (Isa. 51:2)

Discuss the promise fulfilled to Sarah. (Gen. 17:16)

Discuss God's promise to Abraham. (Gen. 12:2; 13:15-17; 22:17-18)

Read Gal. 4:24-26. Repeat the allegory. What covenant did Sarah represent?

What sin did Sarah commit? (Gen. 15:1-3)

Read 1 Peter 3:1-6. What lessons should wives and mothers learn from this?

Did Abraham rule his house? (Gen. 18:19)

Was Sarah in subjection to her husband? (Quote 1 Cor. 11:3)

When was man made head of woman?

Discuss "head" and "helper."

Read Gen. 3:15 and Gal. 4:28 and tell Sarah's greatest contribution to the world.

How was Sarah signally blessed?

How did God recompense her faith?

Hagar

Gen. 16:1-16; 21:9-17; 25:12

"And also of the seed of the bond-woman will I make a nation, because he is thy seed" (Gen. 21:13).

HAGAR was an Egyptian. Some say that she had been stolen from Egypt as a girl. And she had come from Ur of the Chaldees with Sarah. There is also the explanation that when Abraham made the sojourn into Egypt because of the famine in Canaan, he brought back the intelligent little slave girl by the name of Hagar. The Bible introduces her as Sarah's maid. Disaster and sorrow became her lot. As a part of Sarah's and Abraham's family she must have heard much about the God of Abraham. If she lived with them in Ur, she knew of the call that came from God. She became a very vital part of that great journey. She was of great assistance to her mistress on that long and tiresome trek. She saw this man of God and his wife leave their native land in answer to the divine summons. They looked to God for daily guidance. They trusted Him to bring them to the land they had not seen. As time went on, the promise included land, a numerous posterity and a great nation. This promise of a son was the very fiber of their lives. Hagar soon learned that Abraham and Sarah could talk about little else than this high hope. Perhaps Hagar herself began to share their expectations. Yet the days, the weeks, the months and the years passed by and nothing happened. No child came to fulfill the blessing.

In their quiet tent home under the oak trees near Hebron, Abraham was growing old. Although he had great riches and many servants, yet he had no children. Sarah's faith had burned low; fearful that there should be no heir to carry on the line, they agreed that Abraham shall have an heir through the Egyptian slave. No doubt Sarah must have held Hagar in very high esteem. She thought she was bestowing the highest honor upon a bondwoman. Hagar herself thought that now she, the bondwoman, and not Sarah would be the mother of the son through whom all nations of the world would be blessed. She had been honored beyond her wildest dreams. When Hagar knew that she was with child, her mistress was despised in her eyes (Gen. 16:1-16). No longer was she the meek and submissive slave. The situation became unbearable. Both women were wretchedly unhappy. And when Sarah "dealt hardly" with her, the expectant mother fled into the wilderness.

The Runaway

As Hagar hastened along the sandy, desert road, she grew very tired. She stopped to rest by a fountain of water along the roadside. In this lonely place, in the deep wilderness, an angel of the Lord found her. The angel instructed Hagar to return to the tents of Abraham and be submissive to her mistress. She was told that her child would be a son. He would be a strong man and his name should be called Ishmael. Hagar knew this message was from God. She knew now that she could never run away from the God of Abraham. She obeyed the angel's words and returned to her mistress.

Soon after Hagar returned to Sarah's tent home, God gave her the child he had promised. Abraham named him Ishmael which means "God hears." At Beerahai-roi, the angel of the Lord told Hagar, "I will multiply thy seed exceedingly, that it shall not be numbered for multitude." She was told, besides, that Ishmael's people would be a fighting people. His hand will be against every man, and every man's hand will be against him. And to Abraham, God said he would make

Ishmael prosperous because he was Abraham's seed.

Mohammed claimed to be the descendant of Ishmael, son of Hagar, and so do all Arabs. Out of this unholy union of Abraham and a slave girl came the false faith of Islam. The Mohammedans have used the sword to propagate their false religion. They reject Christ and place Mohammed above him. In Gal. 4:22, Paul compares Sarah as a free woman with Hagar as a bondwoman. Again one is impressed with the terrible consequence in all cases of polygamy. God's ordinances cannot be profaned without the most awful degradation, and the sin reaches into the centuries.

Hagar Is Rebuffed

Hagar was no doubt supremely happy when her son was born and through the years when Sarah bore no children for Abraham. Then something happened to change her joy to sorrow, her hope to despair. God at last fulfilled his promise to Sarah. Isaac was born. Then were living in Gerar when God gave to Abraham and Sarah the child of promise. Trouble begins; each mother is jealous for her son. Two women quarreling, two children listening. There are strife and contention in the tents of Abraham.

When Isaac was about four years old, there was a celebration in his honor. During this celebration Sarah observed Ishmael mocking Isaac. This was more than the jealous mother could bear. She demanded that Abraham cast out the slave woman and her son. This demand was a grievous blow for Abraham because he must have loved Ishmael as any father loves a son. God told Abraham to comply with Sarah's demand. God recognized Sarah as the wife of Abraham (Rom. 7:3) (Gen. 21:12, 13). Hagar and Ishmael were sent away, cast out with a small provision of bread and water. Hagar, no doubt blinded by tears of grief and anger, became hopelessly lost. "Let me not see the death of my child." And she sat over against him, and "lifted up her voice and wept" (Gen. 21:16).

It is heartbreaking, even now, as we hear her sobs and witness her grief at the loss of all she held dear. How clearly the Scriptures teach by precept and example, that not one blessing ever accrues to the human arrangement over the divine. But He who takes note of the sparrow's fall and knows every heartache and every tear is listening. Hagar was not lost; neither was she alone. The second time in the life of Hagar the Lord God sustained and comforted the bondwoman. "What aileth thee, Hagar? Fear not; for God hath heard the voice of the lad" (Gen. 21:17). And he opened her eyes, and she saw a well of water. What a beautiful picture of our Heavenly Father! God is near, God sees, God hears and He cares.

E'en the hour that darkest seemeth,
Will his changeless goodness prove;
From the gloom his brightness streameth,
God is wisdom, God is love.
                    —JOHN BOWRING

In Hagar's black despair, she closed her ears to the voice of her son. She gave him up to die. But God listened to the cry of a dying lad. Here is the Father's care for the little child. Centuries later the same attitude characterized the Christ who took the little children in his arms and said, "Suffer little children to come unto me and forbid them not: for of such is the kingdom of heaven" (Matt. 19:13). The finale in this poignant story is very tender and beautiful. "She went and filled the bottle with water and gave the lad to drink." A true picture of a mother's love!

They dwelt in the wilderness of Parani. Hagar took Ishmael a wife out of the land of Egypt.

There lies an eloquence of praise
Imprisoned in a tear
And crushed within a broken heart
That God bends low to hear.
                    —EDITH DALEY

STUDY SUGGESTIONS

Discuss the slave's relationship to the owner.
Was Hagar bound to acquiesce to this polygamous arrangement?
Do you think Hagar was pleased and honored to be known as the wife of Abraham?
Whose was the greatest sin of the three who perpetrated this unholy alliance?
Discuss the two women in this triangle. Was Sarah justified in her treatment of her maid? (Gen. 16:6)
Tell of Hagar's flight; the angel finding her and his words to her. (Gen. 16:7-12)
Whose child was born to her? (Gen. 16:15)
What was prophesied about this child? (Gen. 16:10-12)
Is the unceasing feud between Jews and Arabs a fulfillment of this prophecy?
Discuss the final separation in the family. (Gen. 21:19-21)
What is the message in Hagar's life for Christian women?
What covenant does Hagar represent? (Gal. 4:24b, 25)
How is the end of the covenant typified? (Gal. 4:26, 30)
In the light of these Scriptures, Gen. 2:24; Matt. 19:4, 5; Gen. 2:18-23, discuss marriage as God ordained, and how it was profaned by Sarah and Abraham.
Do you think "quick marriages, easy divorces" a rejection of the sacredness of marriage? (1 Cor. 7:11; Rom. 7:1-3)

Lot's Wife

Gen. 19:26
Luke 17:32

"But his wife looked back from behind him, and she became a pillar of salt" (Gen. 19:20).

JESUS handed down immortality of fame to two women. One was the woman who anointed his head and feet with costly ointment and dried his feet with her hair. The other woman is Lot's wife who turned back from behind him and became a pillar of salt.

In the midst of one of Jesus' sermons, when he was teaching of the separations and the sacrifices which true discipleship requires, He uttered this solemn warning, "Remember Lot's wife." Of all the women of the Old Testament, Christ singles out Lot's wife as one whose fate is to be studied and remembered. The story of this woman cannot be separated from the story of her husband.

Abraham and Lot journeyed from Ur of the Chaldees to Canaan, to Egypt when famine came. Leaving there they came back to Bethel. Here they prospered materially. Their flocks multiplied rapidly; their herdsmen began to quarrel. They decided to separate. Lot was given first selection as to district. He chose the well-watered Jordan Valley, "even as the garden of the Lord" (Gen. 13:5-11). "And he pitched his tents in the direction of Sodom." He made the wrong choice, and that choice led him in the wrong direction. Probably his wife joined him in this decision, though the Scriptures do not say. Having set out in the wrong direction, certainly he arrived at the wrong destination. He had not really intended to move to Sodom. Not only, however, did he settle in this wicked city with his family; in Gen. 19:1 we read that Lot sat *in the gate of Sodom*. We find him in a capacity similar to that of the mayor. For a number of years he lived and prospered in Sodom. These could have been years of moral and spiritual enrichment to Lot and his family and to the city in which they lived. They could have changed Sodom, but Sodom changed them.

LOVE OF THE WORLD

Is the world the general direction in which our homes are drifting today? Do we have more friends, business and social, of the world than in the church? Abraham's prayer revealed that not ten righteous men could be found in these exceedingly wicked cities. We read of Lot (2 Pet. 2:6-8) that the evil men of the city vexed his righteous soul from day to day. He had been with Abraham too long to forsake the faith he knew.

The city was doomed, but Lot and his wife were urged to escape. They were offered the opportunity to begin life anew in the mountains. Two angels went to Sodom and Lot sat in the gate of the city. He arose up to meet the two men and with very warm hospitality insisted they spend the night in his home. There is every reason to believe that his wife joined him in this invitation. The Scriptures relate their very generous hospitality.

The guests delivered the message of doom. They offered to Lot and his family deliverance from the city. Lot told his sons-in-law the mission of his guest, and urged them to leave before the awful destruction came. Lot's influence was a lost influence. To his daughters' husbands he was as one who mocked. Surely this was a joke that Sodom was a city of destruction. He had no influence with his family —therefore no influence in the town where he had lived for years.

A Wife's Failure

"Remember Lot's wife"—her lost influence, her failure as a wife and a mother. Remember the influence of evil association upon herself and her family. Remember the tragedy of a divided heart. "Take your family and leave this city of doom." How loathe she was to leave. How slowly and reluctantly she turned to go. "Love not the world, neither the things that are in the world." Life in Sodom had been more pleasant than the nomadic life in the black tents, following the herds and flocks. "Escape for your life; look not behind, tarry not in the plains, but flee to the mountains (Gen. 19:1-17). She lingered and delayed, until the angel took her by the hand and led her out of Sodom.

If Lot's wife cooperated with him, as evidently she did to the extent of accompanying him outside the ill-fated Sodom, it is evident she believed the angels' predictions. Then, as a mother who could be trusted to give safe advice she should have been able to convince her children to flee.

Lot and his wife and only two daughters were providentially guided from the destruction that was to befall this wicked city. "But she looked back from behind" speaks volumes. Her feet were heavy. She had no heart for this hurried departure. "Do I have to go; must I leave my children, home, and all that I have labored to obtain?" "Do not look back behind." (Surely one last look at the place that has been home so long could not possibly be wrong.) "Where the treasure is, there the heart is also." "You cannot serve two masters."

A man once said to Jesus, "Suffer me to bury my father, and I will follow you." Another said, "Let me say good-by to my family." Not so. "No man having put his hand to the plow and looking back is fit for the kingdom." "And she looked back from behind him." She became a pillar of salt. A half-hearted obedience is no obedience at all. Her heart was in Sodom. "Remember Lot's wife," said our Savior. The role of wife and mother has not been bestowed upon woman that she may achieve a place in elite society for her family. The wife, as the husband's helper, should seek for the very best environment in which to establish a home and rear a family with primary emphasis on spiritual rather than physical values.

PROFIT AND LOSS

When the Lot family decided to move to Sodom, the financial problem was the deciding factor in their move. They sacrificed spiritual values for the lesser values in life.

How often we see the counterpart of Lot's wife in the wife and mother. They have a misguided desire for wealth, thus becoming so burdened and so anxious that there is little time in their lives for Bible study and prayer. There seems to be no joy or conviction or desire in living for Christ. The family seldom attends worship together. The children are sent only occasionally to Bible class. The mother seldom if ever attends a class. She is forever "looking back from behind," How this world needs mothers whose thoughts are centered on things above! How the child needs the divinest home that this earth can offer! How the Church needs devout, consecrated families!

STUDY SUGGESTIONS

What did the Lord tell Abraham about Sodom and Gomorrah? (Gen. 18:20-22)

For what did Abraham pray? (Gen. 18:23-33)

How did this environment affect their children? (Gen. 19:12-14)

What did Peter say of Lot's distress? (2 Pet. 2:7, 8)

Discuss their hospitality. (Gen. 19:1-3)

Discuss their lack of influence. (Gen. 19:14)

How were they forced to leave the city? (Gen. 19:16)

What strange death did Lot's wife die? (Gen. 19:26)

Why did she disobey? Do you think that she intended to leave Sodom some day? What lesson did Jesus make of Lot? (Lk. 17:28-31)

Discuss the heart and its treasure. (Matt. 6:21; Lk. 12:34)

Would Lot's wife be an example of the halfway Christian?

How did she fail as a wife; as a mother?

Rebekah

Gen. 24:15-67; 25:20-28;
26:7, 8; 27:5-46

"Upon me be thy curse, my son"
(Gen. 27:13).

*"And Rebekah took goodly raiment
of her eldest son, and put them
upon Jacob, her younger son"*
(Gen. 27:15).

W HEN Sarah was one hundred and twenty-seven years old, she died. Abraham buried Sarah in the field in the cave of Machpelah. Abraham and Isaac were very lonely after the death of Sarah. Isaac now was grown to manhood, and Abraham thought he was old enough to be married. He wanted a good wife for his son. This is a commendable attitude. This should be the desire of every father for his son. Too often Christian parents think that to "fall in love" is inevitable, and when this falling in love occurs, there is nothing else to be considered.

Someone has said, "There is no such thing as *'falling in love'*; rather, true marriages are based on *'climbing in love.'"*

The parents usually chose wives for their sons in those countries. Abraham knew that the women who lived in Canaan were idolworshippers, and they would not teach their children to love the true God. Because he wanted Isaac's children to serve God, he would not choose a woman of Canaan to be Isaac's wife. Christian parents who desire Christian grandchildren must teach their sons to marry Christian women.

Eliezer, his trusted servant, was called and asked to journey back to Haran and try to find a God-fearing wife for Isaac. We see two old men, Abraham and Eliezer in very earnest conversation. They are deeply concerned about the selection of a wife for Isaac. The great need of the world today is a deep and powerful concern that our young people marry well. Every child has the right to be well-born. The Christian home is the best background into which a child can be born.

God had made great promises to Abraham. He had clearly made known that through Isaac and not Ishmael was the promise to be fulfilled. So Abraham worked with God and not against God to bring this about. He knew that this would be impossible if his son married a pagan woman of Canaan. So the two old men talked, the one exacting a solemn promise and the other faithfully agreeing that Isaac shall have a wife who will share his faith in God.

If parents could see and teach how hard it is for a man to stand loyal to his faith when he does not have a wife of like precious faith! With a Christian companion, the road to heaven is made easier.

Rebekah Appears

The faithful steward made the long journey to Haran. He reached the city at eventide. They stopped outside the city and the tired camels knelt down near a well. The girls of the city were coming to this well to fill their pitchers with water. Eliezer had learned to trust in Abraham's God. Now he lifted up his heart and prayed God to send out to this well a young woman who would be a suitable wife for Isaac. "Let it come to pass, O Lord, he prayed, that the young woman of whom I shall ask a drink will offer to draw water for my camels also!" He seemed to be asking God to direct him to a girl who is generous and kind and willing to serve. No sooner had he finished praying than a beautiful young girl with a pitcher on her shoulder came to the well. Her name Rebekah indicates "an amiable and lovely maiden." Eliezer waited until she had filled her pitcher with water; then he hurried forward and asked for a drink. He was a stranger; he was an old man. Here was a test; Rebekah did not fail. She spoke kindly to him and offered to draw water for his camels also, ten in all.

She was the answer to his prayer. Eliezer gave her some of the gifts he had brought; jewelry, golden bracelets, earrings. They must have been of unusual value. Then he inquired whose daughter she was and whether her people could supply lodging for him and his camels. When she told him she was the granddaughter of Nahor, Abraham's brother, Eliezer knew again his prayer was answered, and he bowed his head and worshipped God. Rebekah assured him that there was room for him and his camels at her father's home.

When her brother Laban heard his sister and saw the beautiful gifts which Eliezer had given to Rebekah, he ran eagerly to meet the stranger at the well and extended to him royal hospitality. He invited him in, brought water to wash his feet and set food before him.

But Eliezer could not eat. He told his errand. He related that under the blessings of God, Abraham had become a great man. He was a rich man. He had a son of his old age, Isaac, who was heir to this great estate. And it was in quest of a "wife for Isaac that I have been sent." And he told them how Rebekah had offered to draw water for his camels in answer to his prayer. Together the assembled believers in God felt the planned providence of the great I AM in arranging this marriage. They felt the hand of the Lord was with them.

Her Decision

When Rebekah's father and brother heard this, they decided to leave the decision to the one most vitally concerned. They called the beautiful girl and put to her this question: "Wilt thou go with this man?" She answered promptly, "I will go." Not only was Rebekah kind and generous, but she was brave and well able to make decisions.

What motivated this brave decision? Was it possibly because her future husband was one of the richest men in the land? Did she know that God had promised to bless all nations of the earth through the family of Abraham? Perhaps she was eager to be a part of this beautiful promise. Too, romance and appeal were in this decision, "I will go." It was to a man unknown to herself that she was committing her life, but with trust and confidence that Jehovah wished it to be so.

Through all ages women have made this courageous declaration, "I will go." Women have followed their men, as did Sarah, Rebekah and Rachel, to new and unseen lands, to far flung frontiers. Every young woman who has broken the old familiar ties of home to become a wife has answered that age-old question, "Wilt thou go with this man?" And her answer has been, "I will go." And thus God's purpose is fulfilled, marriages are made, homes established and children born.

ISAAC MEETS REBEKAH

So the family said good-bye to Rebekah and sent her away with her nurse and other attending maids. Rebekah and her maids rode the camels and Eliezer led the way to Canaan. As she traveled farther away from loved ones and her home, she was doubtless at times thrilled and happy, and there were other times when she was uneasy and a bit fearful. At last they drew near to the home of Abraham and Isaac. The evening shadows were stealing through the trees. Isaac was alone in the fields meditating when he saw the camels coming. He hurried out to meet them. Rebekah seeing him asked who he was. "This is Isaac." Rebekah alighted from her camel and covered her face with her veil. Isaac took her to his mother's tent, and she became his wife. He loved her and did not grieve more because of his mother's death.

They were strangers to each other, but little more so than many who marry today. This marriage should have been a happy marriage; this marriage was through the providence of God; they had the same family and religious backgrounds. Rebekah was a comfort to Isaac. Surely this should have had a "they lived happily ever after" ending. But such was not the case.

PLAYING FAVORITES

After some years a change took place in Isaac's home life. After long waiting Rebekah became a mother. She gave birth to twins, Esau and Jacob. These were Rebekah's boys. These were the sons of Isaac; the mother and father had shared with God in their creation. Children are the link that binds parents closer together. Not so in this case; Isaac and Rebekah were pushed apart. Not because of the boys, but because each parent picked a favorite. What a foolish and sinful mistake!

Esau, the older son, was Isaac's favorite. His hair was red. He was very fond of hunting. Not only did he know how to kill the deer, he also knew how to dress and cook the meat that he brought home from his hunting trips. This pleased Isaac very much. The apostle describes Esau as "a profane person, who for one morsel of meat sold his birthright" (Heb. 12:16). It has been said that Esau thought more of his stomach than he did of his soul. Even in his marriage he allied himself with idolatory and godlessness. Rebekah said, "I am weary of my life because of the daughters of Heth," indicating Esau's choice of women was from the heathen tribes. Esau repudiated things spiritual for things material.

Rebekah observed the difference in her two sons. She observed Esau's secular disposition, and the spiritual mold of her last-born, Jacob. She saw that Esau spent his time hunting, while Jacob's time was spent in spiritual meditation. Full well she realized that Esau lived for today, while Jacob shared her dreams of the future. She recalled how lightly Esau esteemed his birthright had he not sold it for a mess of pottage? She remembered the Lord had said to her, "The elder shall serve the younger." Rebekah thought Esau was not worthy of the blessing. He despised his birthright; he had two wives who were Canaanitish women. She wanted Jacob to be the heir of God's promise.

One day she heard Isaac say to Esau, "Bring me venison, and make me savoury meat, that I may eat and bless thee before the Lord before I die." This was a death blow to Rebekah's hopes. Rebekah was a woman of decision. She took immediate action. She began to plot and scheme to obtain for her favorite son the blessing.

She remembered Isaac's failing vision; "I will send Jacob to him instead of Esau. I will cook tender meat of two young kids, and season the food as Esau seasons it. I will clothe Jacob in Esau's raiment." Jacob feared to try to deceive his father. He was afraid they might be caught and he would receive a curse instead of the blessing. "Upon me be thy curse, my son. Only obey my voice." The scheme was a success, and Jacob stole the blessing. He secured the blessing, but the sin of his deception fell upon his own head, in spite of his mother's willingness to bear it for him. "Whatsoever ye sow—that shall ye also reap."

Esau's Plan

After this time Esau's heart was filled with hatred toward his brother. And he purposed to kill Jacob after the death of his father. Thus he would have all the possessions and power which belonged to the first born. With these wicked thoughts he consoled himself.

When Rebekah heard of Esau's intention to kill Jacob, she called Jacob to her and told him he must go to Haran and stay with his Uncle Laban until Esau's anger had passed. "Then you can come back to me, for why should I lose both of you in one day?" Deception came easy for Rebekah and again she deceived her husband. She did not tell him of Esau's wicked intentions. But she planned for Isaac to send Jacob away, "If Jacob take a wife of the daughters of Heth, such as these which are of the daughters of the land, what good shall my life be to me?"

So Isaac called his son to him, counselled him not to take a wife of the daughters of Canaan. His advice is to go back to Padan Aram and there take a wife from his mother's relatives—and "God's blessings be upon you, and he shall give you the blessings of your grandfather Abraham."

REBEKAH'S REWARD

"Upon me be thy curse." The specter of Rebekah's treachery must have been between her and her husband all their days. She was forever separated from Esau. Her twin sons were separated by hatred brought about by their own mother's deception. And then one day her beloved Jacob must flee for his life. Thus she lost her beloved favorite.

"Go away for a few days till Esau forgets." Jacob bade his father and mother good-bye and started on his long, lonely journey, and it is not for a "few days only," as his mother fondly thought. The days became weeks, the weeks months and the months twenty long years. Never again did Rebekah see her beloved son. She died before his return and was buried in Machpelah. Thus not only was the curse upon Rebekah, it was upon Jacob, upon Esau and even Isaac bore a part of the curse.

Esau was the father of the Edomites, a nation that was a thorn in the side of Israel for centuries to come. Those near and dear to Rebekah bore the curse; countless thousands who never saw her face suffered because of her sin. Rebekah's motives were high and good. Had she not left her home in Padan Aram to journey to Canaan to become a part of the promise God made to Abraham? Had not God said that Esau should serve Jacob? She was seeking a high spiritual destiny for her son. Instead of yielding herself to God and waiting upon the Lord for the fulfillment of this destiny, she thought to bend God to her purpose.

STUDY SUGGESTIONS

Study carefully Genesis 22-28.

Discuss Rebekah's family background. (Gen. 22:23; 22:20; 24:15; 24:29)

Narrate the plans and prayers that went into this marriage. (Gen. 24:1-27)

Point out the things that we of the Christian dispensation would do well to imitate.

What traits of character do we see in Rebekah?

Discuss the significance of her answer, "I will go."

Name four reasons why this should have been a highly successful marriage.

Do you think this marriage failed? Give your reasons.

Would you consider a vivacious, decisive character like Rebekah should
marry a man with Isaac's quiet and peaceful disposition?

Would Isaac be considered a henpecked husband? Or was Rebekah a helpmeet?

Discuss the personalities of the twin boys. What great factor contributed
to these personalities?

Point out the dangers of partiality of parents.

Name the sins of which Rebekah was guilty in her plot to obtain the blessing for Jacob. (Gen. 27:5-16; Deut. 27:18)

With all her faults, Rebekah was a great woman and a great mother. What
promise of God was fulfilled in Rebekah? Were the means justified?

Do you think Rebekah was a good cook? (Gen. 27:3, 4, 7, 9, 25) Seam-
stress? (Gen. 27:15, 16)

Was Rebekah in subjection to her husband?

Do you think the home of Rebekah was according to God's plan in the
second chapter of Genesis?

Does your home conform to God's plan?

Is there one husband and one wife?

Is the husband the head? (1 Cor. 11:3)

Is the wife suited to his needs?

Rachel

Gen. 29:6-31; 30:1-25;
31:4-34; 35:16-25

*"And they seemed unto him but a
few days for the love he had to
her"* (Gen. 29:20).

To study the life of Rachel is to see and appreciate the truly
feminine woman. To her motherhood was everything. The story
of Jacob and Rachel is a beautiful story of love and marriage. Rachel
felt joy in motherhood even to the going down into the valley of
death that a child might be born. Christian women can learn to appreciate the great honor God conferred upon them.

To save Jacob from Esau's anger, Rebekah had urged her son to
go to the home of her brother, Laban, in Mesopotamia. There she
had thought he would find refuge and oasis for a few days.

"Yonder is Jacob starting on his long journey to Mesopotamia with
his staff and his bundle on his shoulder. Take a long look, Rebekah,
for it is not for just a few days. Never again wilt thou see his face,
Rebekah. Yonder he goes, now he stops, turns and looks back at
the encampment of Isaac and waves to his mother who waves back
to him. Now his form is lost on the distant horizon. Morning will
dawn about your black tents, Rebekah. The tinkling of the goats'

bells and the bleating of the sheep will be heard tomorrow as of old. The sun will rise in splendor and in splendor go down again, but Jacob thou will never see again, for when Jacob returns, thou Rebekah, will be sleeping in Machpelah's lonely cavern." (McCartney's *The Woman Who Married the Right Man*)

We do not know Jacob's thoughts as he walked along the dusty road. Lonely though he may have felt, he was not alone—God was with him. By and by the sun went down. Jacob was tired—he chose a stone for his pillow and lay down on the ground to sleep. While he slept he saw a wonderful ladder reaching into heaven. He saw angels ascending and descending the ladder. Sanding at the top he saw God.

And behold the Lord said, "I am the God of your grandfather Abraham and of your father Isaac. The land upon which you are lying I will give unto you and your descendants. The descendants shall be many . . . and in thee and thy seed shall all families of the earth be blessed."

Jacob rose up early in the morning and took the stone he had used for a pillow and set it upright, poured oil upon it and called the name of the place Bethel, "The House of God." He made a vow and promised to give back to God a tenth of all God should give him, if he would feed and clothe him and return him again to his father's house.

After this wonderful dream, Jacob's heart must have felt lighter as he hurried on his way. With his bundle and staff over his shoulder, Jacob arrived at the well in Mesopotamia at eventide . . .

He saw some men at the well. Round about them three flocks of sheep were waiting to be watered. He came near and spoke to the men, inquiring for his Uncle Laban.

"Yes, we know him, and here comes his daughter, Rachel, with his sheep."

Jacob saw a beautiful young girl approaching, and he hurried to meet her. He rolled the stone from the well and watered the flock of Laban, his mother's brother. Tears came into his eyes as he kissed his cousin. And he told Rachel that he was Rebekah's son. She hurried to tell her father that his sister's son had arrived from Canaan.

Love at First Sight

Thus begins another romance at the well. It was love at first sight for Jacob, and it remained love beautiful unto the end. So great was his love that 2,555 days (7 years) seemed but a few days while he worked and waited for Rachel. Rachel too manifested patience, perseverance and a wisdom that caused her to wait seven years for the right man.

Laban drove a cruel bargain; Jacob was to serve him seven years for Rachel. Think of all the changes that can occur in seven years; changes in the world, in the family, in the body and heart. But no change was seen in Jacob's love, constant and true until death. The seven years of labor, labor of love, did not seem long to him.

So the years went by and at last the marriage day arrived. Friends and neighbors gathered to the wedding. The vows were spoken, gifts were exchanged, the festivities began. He took Rachel to his tent; the wedding veil was removed; it was not Rachel! Not his beloved for whom he had labored seven years! It was the ill-favored, weak-eyed Leah. He had not wanted to marry Leah. How unhappy he must have felt when he realized his uncle had deceived him. Perhaps he remembered how he had cheated his own brother. Now he was suffering from the same kind of sin he had committed against others.

The marriage feast lasted seven days. It would not have been proper to interrupt the marriage festivities and solemnities to which many guests were invited. Too, Laban did not wish his fraud to be made public, so he informed Jacob if he will fulfill the marriage week with Leah, he will give him Rachel at the end of it on condition of his serving seven other years. The necessity of the case caused Jacob to agree, and Laban received fourteen years service for Rachel, and gained settlement for both his daughters.

"What a man soweth, that shall he also reap." No doubt Jacob's conscience said to him, "Thou art the man."

Two Unhappy Women

Soon there was discord in the tents of Jacob in spite of the beautiful love of Jacob and Rachel. God's order can never be cast aside and ignored without untold misery and heartaches. The customs of any dispensation can never change God's laws.

Both wives were unhappy. Leah had six children, but Rachel had none.

"And when Rachel saw that she bare Jacob no children, Rachel envied her sister; and said unto Jacob, Give me children or else I die."

This unholy state of affairs led the kind and patient Rachel to make a most reprehensible statement. She displayed envy and jealousy and a complete lack of dependence upon God. This seemed to be the only time that even a suggestion of a cloud came between Jacob and Rachel. And Jacob's reply is one of anger, "Am I in God's stead, who hath withheld from thee the fruit of the womb?" The Scripture clearly states that his love for Rachel was more than his love for Leah.

We feel that the gentle Rachel was sorry for this outburst of jealousy and a temporary loss of faith. And God remembered Rachel, and God hearkened unto her. No doubt after Jacob's reproof she turned to God in prayer, and He heard her. So her prayer and faith obtained what her envy and impatience prevented.

And Joseph was born to her, a wonderful son, a child worth waiting for. He was Jacob's eleventh son. He was the kind of boy that can be trusted to do right. It has been said that Joseph was the noblest man in the book of Genesis. Certainly God was with him in his dreams, in Egypt, in prison, and later when he became a ruler. His love was beautiful beyond understanding; his forgiveness was Christlike. What a wonderful gift to the world was Joseph, the son of Rachel! What greater thing can any woman do than to give to the world a great and good man?

> God send us men whose aim will be
> Not to defend some worn out creed,
> But to live out the laws of Christ
> In every thought, and word and deed.
>
> God send us men alert and quick
> His holy precepts to translate
> Until the laws of Christ become
> The laws and habits of the state.
>
> God send us men! God send us men!
> Patient, courageous, strong and true
> With vision clear and mind equipped
> His will to learn, His work to do.
>
> God send us men with hearts ablaze
> All truth to love, all wrong to hate
> These are the patriots the nations need,
> These are the bulwarks of the State.
> —F. J. GILLIAM

Men of sincere and exalted spirits must come from mothers of sincere and exalted spirits. Perhaps it might be said that the women of Israel were more desirous of being a part of the great promise of Abraham, a longing to be the mother of the "promised seed," rather than for the sake of motherhood alone. The biological fact of motherhood alone is not sufficient within itself to commend one to God. The neglected, forsaken children in institutions today are the tragic outcome of parenthood with no purpose above the immediate biological urge. The desire to be the mother of the Messiah was a noble aspiration. And Rachel's cry to Jacob, "Give me children, or else I die," was perhaps the longing of a hungry heart, a longing more intense because her husband was shared with another woman. Jacob was a father; Rachel had no child. Joseph was an answer to deep and sincere prayer. He lost his lovely mother when still a youth, but what seeds of character were planted in his heart in those few short years!

After twenty years in the service of Laban, Jacob was deceived as well as deceiving. He was a rich man. God had prospered him. He had camels and asses and owned many servants. God gave him eleven sons and one daughter. There was envy on the part of Laban and his sons. They felt very unkindly toward Jacob.

The angel of God spoke to Jacob in a dream and comforted him.

"I am the God of Bethel," the angel said, "where you anointed the stone, and where you made a vow to me. The time has come for you to return again to your people in Canaan. I will be with you."

"Our Father Sold Us"

He called Leah and Rachel out into the field and counseled with them. He told them he feared Laban would try to prevent their departure. And he told them also, God had charged him to again return to Canaan. And their reply was, "We will go; our father hath sold us."

One may well cry out against Laban—what an unnatural father! Many Christian parents, so-called, are selling their daughters today. The emphasis is placed upon the desires of the flesh. The daughter is clothed or "unclothed" so that her body attracts attention. Her future happiness is being sold in order to make the present hour a little more exciting and stimulating. Fashions and customs come and go, but principles never change. Daughters are sold for popularity, for pleasure, for a place in so-called "society." When the physical, mental and spiritual growth of a child has been neglected, the mother has sold her child to insecurity and often delinquency.

A Christian mother will say, "Give me light that I may tread softly into the unknown." The voice of wisdom will reply, "Go out into the darkness and put your hand into the hand of God. That shall be to you a light that is safer than any known way."

"Our father hath sold us and whatsoever God hath said unto thee, do."

The Journey

Busy days followed in which Jacob and his family prepared to start out over the long road which he had traveled twenty years before. The herds were all collected from the fields where they had been grazing. The servants drove the animals while Jacob's wives and children rode on camels.

When Jacob's departure was made known to Laban, he was angry. He took several men and hurried in pursuit of Jacob's company. At last he overtook Jacob's company at Mt. Gilead where they had camped. Before reaching the place, Laban had been warned by God not to harm Jacob. This warning caused Laban to feel less angry toward Jacob, and soon their quarrel was ended. Afterward Jacob set up a stone for a pillar; the men gathered together stones together in a heap. Laban called the heap of stones, "Mizpah," which means a watch tower. And he said to Jacob, "May God watch over us while we are absent one from another." After an affectionate farewell, he returned to Haran. Jacob and his family continued their journey to Canaan.

"And Jacob went on his way and the angels of God met him." This must have been a thrilling, a wonderful experience to Jacob. God was continually watching for his welfare.

That night after he had passed his families and flocks and herds over ahead of him, Jacob tarried on the other side of Jabbok. "And there wrestled a man with him until the breaking of the day." Jacob wrestled earnestly, but neither of them prevailed. When morning began to dawn, Jacob saw he had been wrestling with an angel of God. Jacob emerged from that contest a changed man with a new name, Israel. which means, "A Prince of God." When the angel departed, Jacob was crippled in his thigh, for the angel had struck his thigh. And Jacob called the name of the place Peniel, which means, "The Face of God," because there he saw God face to face and received the blessing he had sought.

Rachel who waited seven years while her lover labored for her, waited for a man upon whose life was the touch of God.

> Come, O thou Traveler unknown,
> Whom still I hold but cannot see.
> My company before is gone,
> And I am left alone with thee.
> With thee all night I mean to stay
> And wrestle till the break of day.
>
> I need not tell thee who I am
> My sin and misery declare;
> Thyself hast called me by my name—
> Look on thy hands, and read it there:
> But who, I ask thee, Who art thou?
> Tell me thy name, and tell me now.
>
> Yield to me now for I am weak,
> But confident in self-despair;
> Speak to my heart, in blessing speak;
> Be conquered by my instant prayer.
> Speak, or thou never hence shall move
> And tell me if thy name be Love!
>
> 'Tis love! 'Tis love! Thou diedst for me!
> I hear thy whisper in my heart;

The morning breaks, the shadows flee;
Pure, universal Love thou art:
To me, to all, thy mercies move;
Thy Nature and thy Name is Love.
—CHARLES WESLEY (Hymn)

This was a critical night in the life of Jacob. It seemed that his
all was at stake. How careful and concerned he was for the safety
of his beloved Rachel. How different was his conduct from that of
his father and grandfather. Abraham and Isaac both at one time
passed their wives off as their sisters in order that they might
protect themselves! It seemed that they had little care for what might
happen to their wives.

All the great company was sent first, Leah and her children next,
Rachel and Joseph in the rear, the farthest from the point of danger.
His love was ever deep and tender for Rachel.

Jacob journeyed on to Canaan. At Shechem he bought a field,
where he built an altar and worshipped God. It seems that he forgot
Bethel and the vow that he had made there in the long ago. Later he
moved to Bethel at God's command, and built another altar in
memory of the promise God had given to him when he slept at that
place while fleeing from Esau. God again appeared to him and en-
larged the promise that he had made concerning Jacob's descendants,
and told him that kings should be born among them in the coming
years.

"CHILD OF GRIEF"

From Bethel, Jacob and his family moved southward toward his
old home at Hebron where his father, Isaac, still lived. Before they
arrived at Hebron, a sad thing happened. When Joseph was born,
Rachel had said, "The Lord will add another son to me." Now the
hour of her travail was upon her—it was time for her to go down again
into the valley of the shadows. "Give me a child or else I die,"
cried Rachel. The Scriptures say, "And Rachel had hard labor."
Rachel died, but before her passing she heard the midwife say that
she had borne a son. With her last breath she called the baby Ben-oni,
"Child of grief." There was a tragic sadness in that last, "My child,
but a child of grief."

Jacob could not understand this, and he called the child Benjamin, "Child of my right hand." Jacob buried her at Bethlehem,
and set a pillar upon her grave.

She left Joseph and Benjamin, but she lived again in her two
boys. Perhaps Jacob could see in Joseph a likeness to his mother,
her eyes, a smile, the shape of his face brought memories of the
beloved Rachel. He loved Joseph so tenderly.

And when the jealous brothers came to him one day and said,

"Is this thy son's coat?" He knew this was the coat he had given Joseph. His grief was intense and he mourned bitterly. And Jacob knew this sorrow until Pharaoh's chariots took him into Egypt and he found that Joseph was still alive.

This was a wonderful thing in the life of Jacob, this reunion with Joseph. What tender care and love Joseph bestowed upon his father until the day of his death!

"Behold I die," said Israel, now an old man, and he called his sons and his grandsons to him. Before Joseph's sons were brought to him, he told of God's appearing to him and repeating the promise. As his mind goes back to the past, he told Joseph: "Rachel died by me in the land of Canaan in the way when yet there was but little way to come unto Ephrath: And I buried her there in the way of Ephrath; the same is Bethlehem."

She was ever in his heart, and with his dying breath he talks of Rachel.

STUDY SUGGESTIONS

Genesis 24 through 50 is the Scripture background for this study.
Who was Rachel's family? (Gen. 24; 15; 29:12)
What relation were Jacob and Rachel? (Gen. 24:29; 29:12b)
Contrast her beauty with her sister's looks. (Gen. 29:17)
Tell of their meeting at the well. (Gen. 29:4-12)
Relate the marriage contract between her lover and her father. (Gen. 29:15-20)

Leah

Gen. 29:16-32; 30:9-20;
31:4, 14, 33; 35:23-26.

"*Leah was tender-eyed; but Rachel was beautiful and well-favored*" (Gen. 29:16-35).

God does not look upon the outward appearance, but he judges the heart. With God's Holy Book before us as a picture gallery, we see that Biblical women were frequently "fair to look upon." Leah seems to be one of the few women of whom it was written that she was not particularly attractive. In fact, compared to Rachel, her sister, it might be said she was downright ugly. Yet there is much about Leah to be admired.

The desire for personal beauty is a common desire, and is not sinful. Yet there is a danger in being beautiful. "Favor is deceitful, beauty is vain" (Prov. 31:30). Favor is something withdrawn from us, and beauty disappears with age. How pathetic to see an aged woman striving to be youthful in appearance! Youthful in heart, yes, in love and service.

Leah was a daughter of her environment, and as truly as Laban sold Rachel he also sold Leah. She was, too, a victim of her father's deceit. How sad must have been her lot! No beauty of face and form, not chosen by Jacob as was Rachel. True, Rachel mourned because she had no children, but she exulted in the love of her husband. Leah mothered Jacob's sons, but mourned because he never loved her. Perhaps Jacob might have thought her as guilty as Laban in the marriage trick. She might have been often reproached for this trickery.

When Eliezer went for Rebekah, her parents said, "Wilt thou go with this man?" The decision was Rebekah's. The moral tone of family life had so degenerated that we find nowhere did Laban give his daughters a choice. He was the master and the daughters were his to be bartered as chattel.

LEAH'S FRUIT

There was a consolation of faith in the heart of Leah. There was a great compensation for the lack of beauty. As her sons were born, and the names given, we see an inward beauty in Leah. When Reuben was born, she praised God because he had favored her showing a rather self-centered gratitude. Simeon was a source of comfort and Leah was grateful for this comfort in hate of which she was a victim. Levi brought great rejoicing to her heart, because now surely her husband would love her. When Judah was born, Leah has defeated the hate and selfishness in her heart, "Now I will praise the Lord; therefore she called his name Judah," a confessor, one who acknowledges God, from whom all good comes. God is praised.

Next to Joseph, Judah was the most admirable of Jacob's twelve boys. It was Judah who persuaded the brothers not to murder Joseph, but to sell him to the Ishmaelites. It was Judah who stood as a surety for the safety of Benjamin on the second trip into Egypt. It was Judah who was the pleader and judge before the governor of Egypt in behalf of Jacob. Hear him, "We have a father, an old man, and a child of his old age, a little one." Joseph wept at this beautiful and tender plea. It was Judah who so carefully took the old Jacob into the land of Goshen. This was Judah, son of the tender-eyed Leah.

It was of Judah and his descendants that his old father prophesied, "The scepter shall not depart from Judah nor a lawgiver from between his feet, until Shiloh come; and unto him shall the gathering of the people be." This was the tribe of our Lord and Savior; and thus Leah and not beautiful Rachel was the one through whom the Christ came.

Leah lies buried in the family tomb, with Abraham, Sarah, Isaac, and Rebekah in the cave of Machpelah.

There are two kinds of beauty: the external and the internal. The external beauty as a flower fades. It is vain. The beauty of the soul and spirit is a beauty that never fades.

"But let it be the hidden man of the heart, that which is not corruptible, even the ornament of a meek and quiet spirit which is in the sight of God of great price" (1 Pet. 3:4).

Her Daughter

Before we turn away from the Biblical picture of Leah and her family, let us look at Dinah, her only daughter.

As is too often the case, Leah's whole life seems to have been dedicated to her sons. And her only daughter, Dinah, was left to follow her own inclinations. How modern does the story run: "And Dinah . . . went out to see the daughters of the land."

The tents of her father were pitched near Shechem. No doubt she saw the daughters of Shechem walking outside the city walls. They were beautiful and attractive as most oriental girls are. Did Leah give her permission to go, or did Leah remind her of some trouble that her grandmother and great-grandmother had in the matter of Abimelech and Pharaoh? Perhaps she reminded Leah she was fifteen years old, perfectly able to take care of herself; and besides the girls of Shechem were so friendly and charming. So she goes, and goes alone. How many mothers follow the line of least resistance where the desire of a child is concerned.

Prince Shechem, son of King Hamor, saw Dinah; and she must have been as beautiful as her famous grandmothers. Perhaps she was pleased and flattered at the attention of the Prince. "Surely," she thought, "no harm can come of one little visit to the palace of a king." And the end of the adventure was that Dinah was seduced and held a captive in the palace. We feel sure that Dinah was forced and did not surrender her virginity willingly. What a price she paid for her longing to be with the daughters of the land!

Vengeance

Her brothers in anger sought to avenge the great wrong to their sister. Hamor and his son offered the honorable solution, the only solution to be offered since the sin was done. How much wiser to avoid even the appearance of evil!

Her brothers deceitfully destroyed the inhabitants of Shechem while they suffered from the pain of circumcision. Simeon and Levi violated every principle of justice as they took the women and children as their spoil. They vindicated their treachery and bloodshed by saying, "Shall he deal with our sister as a harlot?"

Her desire for the friendship of the world enticed Dinah to Shechem and robbed her of her purity. And Jacob cries that he as her father was "caused to stink among the inhabitants of the land." There is no sadder sight than disgraced parents—children who have brought shame and dishonor.

Today the youth of Christian homes are seeking the friendship of the world. They do not ask for much—they only want to be like other girls and boys. And too often worldly pleasures and the association of worldly friends involve the morale and spiritual death of our youth. This is a serious indictment against Christian parents as it was of Jacob and Leah.

STUDY SUGGESTIONS

Read 1 Pet. 3:1-4. Contrast the two adornments. Discuss "a meek and quiet spirit."

Does Peter forbid outward adornment? Or is he denying the *one* in order to emphasize the more important?

Read 1 Tim. 2:9-10. Does modesty forbid style and good taste?

Read Jno. 6:27. Discuss external beauty and inward beauty.

Seek ye first the kingdom of God. On what are you placing *emphasis?*

How do you evaluate personality?

Would you take issue with this statement: that it is a must of the Christian woman to be attractive physically as well as spiritually?

Name some dangers of being beautiful. (Gen. 34:1-31)

What is God's lesson to us as we read it from the life of Leah?

What does the lesson of Dinah teach concerning the world? (1 John 1:15-17)

Tamar

Gen. 38:6, 11, 13, 24
Ruth 4:12; 1 Chron. 2:4

"*She hath been more righteous than I*" (Gen. 38:26).

TAMAR's story reveals the low ideals of morality of the era in which she lived. Tamar was the daughter-in-law of Judah. Twice married and twice widowed, she was childless. The law of Moses demanded that the brother of a man who died, having a widow but no children, must marry the widow (Deut. 25:5). She was refused Judah's younger son. So Tamar took positive and legitimate action to obtain her rights to motherhood. The first we hear of Tamar was when she

married Er, the first-born son of Judah and Shuah, the Canaanite.
"And Er, Judah's first-born was wicked and the Lord slew him" (Gen.
38:7). According to law she became the wife of his brother, Onan
"And the thing which he did displeased the Lord, wherefore he slew
him" (Gen. 38:10).

Judah advised Tamar to remain a widow in her father's house until
Shelah his son was grown: "for he said lest peradventure he die also,
as his brethren did" (Gen. 37:11). So Tamar went to her father's
house. Judah gave not the slightest indication of fulfilling his promise
to Tamar.

After the death of Shuah, Judah's wife, he went to Timnath. It was
sheep shearing season. His friend Hirah the Adullamite was with him.
When Tamar heard that her father-in-law was at Timnath, she too
planned to be there. "For she saw that Shelah was grown up and
she was not given him to wife" (Gen. 38:14).

Her plan was bold and shocking, but her courage and ingenuity are
to be admired. She was not wicked. She was denied a lawful marriage.
"Remain a widow at thy father's house," advised her father-in-law.
She was also denied the right to be the mother of Judah's heir.

Tamar means "slender one." The same name is used in the Scripture
to designate a palm tree. Her name suggests a tall, graceful young
woman. She was no doubt very attractive. She would attract attention
in any attire.

TAMAR'S PLAN

She removed her garments of widowhood, put on a veil and
"wrapped herself." The veil would disguise her. The garment that
she wrapped about herself was to attract attention, no doubt very
colorful and becoming. Thus adorned "she sat in an open place."
Many guests would come to Timnath at this season. The place
where she sat, was one where she could see and be seen.

How shrewdly and wisely she planned! How well did she know the
disposition and the weakness of her husband's father. He had deceived her. Now she through foul means or fair would outwit this
man and be the mother of his heir, according to law.

Her disguise was so perfect, Judah thought her a harlot. So he
approached her and said "Go to, I pray thee, and let me come in unto
thee" (Gen. 38:16). Everything had worked just as Tamar planned.
With shrewd forethought, she said, "What wilt thou givest me, that
thou mayest come in unto me?" (Gen. 38:16) When Judah promised
her a kid from the flock, she demanded a pledge until he sent it.
By this clever suggestion she obtained his signet, bracelets, and his
staff. "And he gave it to her, and came in unto her, and she conceived
by him" (Gen. 38:17-18). Tamar returned to her father's house, taking
with her Judah's pledge. She wore her widow's garments. Promptly
Judah sent the kid by his friend the Adullamite, and instructed him

to bring his pledge from the woman. His friend couldn't find her. He inquired of the men of that place concerning the harlot. They assured him there was no harlot in this place. This is proof that Tamar was no prostitute. Her motive was not one of lust. But her scheme was not becoming to the dignity and honor belonging to Noble Womanhood.

TAMAR IS ACCUSED

About three months later tongues began to wag. And "it was told Judah saying, Tamar thy daughter-in-law hath played the harlot; she is with child by whoredom" (Gen. 38:24). Self righteously Judah demanded that she be brought forth and burned. The sin of adultery was punishable by burning (Lev. 21:9). In the patriarchal era the father possessed the power of life and death over members of his family. How ironical that he who was guilty of the same sin was quick to pronounce the sentence of death upon her. She was confident and assured when she was brought before Judah. He would not be able to deny the ownership of the signet, bracelet and staff. "By the man whose these are I am with child," she said.

Then we hear Judah say, "She hath been more righteous than I; because I gave her not to Shelah my son" (Gen. 38:26). And the Scripture gives further evidence that Tamar was not a promiscuous woman in the statement, "And he knew her again no more" (Gen. 38:26).

She became the mother of twin boys, Pharez, the elder; and Zarah was born with the "Scarlet thread upon his hand." The first-born son of Tamar became an ancestor of David and of Christ. Three times in the Scripture we find worthy mention made of Tamar.

A COMPARISON

The tale of Tamar parallels John's story of the adulterous woman who was presented to Jesus (John 7:53ff). When Tamar was accused of being with child by whoredom, Judah was quick to condemn her. He believed in abiding by the letter of the law. Two thousand years later as the adulterous woman stood silent while Jesus heard her accusers, the Pharisees took the law into their own hands. They considered no avenue of mercy. A conviction of conscience caused Judah to repent; he was made to realize that he had brought Tamar to her present state. Jesus pricked the Pharisees into dropping the matter of adulterous woman's guilt by telling them, "If you are not guilty, throw stones at her."

God did not condone the sin in Tamar; neither did Christ condone sin in the woman. But God's tender mercy was extended to Tamar and she received his approval. Similarly, the gracious words of Christ shed mercy to the woman as he said to her, "Go thy way; sin no more."

Though we are repulsed by Tamar's conduct in obtaining her just rights, there is an honest simplicity in the narrative. She had a natural desire to become a mother. All women, even the Canaanites who had married Jews, longed to share in the promise made to the family of Sarah and Abraham. They dreamed of becoming the Mother of the Savior.

STUDY SUGGESTIONS

1) Consult a Bible dictionary about the Canaanites, their idols and lewd cults.
2) Contrast with Israelites.
3) Discuss the evils of these mixed marriages.
4) Why was Tamar's action more righteous than that of Judah? *He lied to her.*
5) Would you say the plan followed by Tamar was justified?
6) Can sin ever be condoned? *no.*
7) Does the Bible present a single or double standard of morals? *Sin can be forgiven.*
8) Why did all women want to be mothers?
They dreamed of becoming the mother of the Savior

Jochebed

Ex. 2:1-10; 2:20
Num. 26:59

"*Take this child away and nurse him for me, and I will give thee wages*" (Exodus 2:9).

JACOB, the last of the patriarchs, died in Egypt—a grand old man who had much to overcome in his life, but in the end died the death of the righteous.

Jacob and his sons numbered seventy when they went into his Egypt. His dearly beloved Joseph was a ruler in that great nation.

The Israelites lived in the Land of Goshen 230 years. They became a strong nation. "And Joseph died, being one hundred and ten years old." With his last breath he reminded his people that God would visit them and take them back to Canaan and give them the land promised to Abraham. And his last request was that his bones be carried when the exodus began.

At last another Pharaoh came to the throne, who did not look with favor upon the fast-growing Israelites. He felt a great fear of these people who lived apart and worshipped none of the gods of the Egyptians. He resolved to hold them in Goshen for his slaves.

They set over the children of Israel taskmasters to afflict them with their burdens. And they built for Pharaoh treasure cities, Pithom and Raamses.

DROWN THE BABIES

But the greater their affliction, the greater was their growth. The hard-working Israelites were horror-stricken when one day the message came to them from the king's house, "Every boy baby that is born among you must be thrown into the River Nile." This cruel edict was an added grief and sorrow to their bitter slavery and bondage.

The King of Egypt called the Hebrew mid-wives to him and gave them command to enforce this cruel law. "But the mid-wives feared God." What a glorious tribute to be paid to any woman. "The mid-wives feared God and did not as the King of Egypt commanded them, but saved the men children alive."

Shiphrah and Puah were God-fearing women, defying even the jealous wicked king. They saved their people from extinction, perhaps not for Israel's sake alone, but because these mid-wives feared God.

"And there went a man of the house of Levi and married a daughter of Levi." In spite of bonds, labors and fears, marriages are made and children are born.

MOSES' PARENTS

Amram married Jochebed. And upon the pages of the Holy Bible, God's Book, a great and lasting tribute is paid to Amram and Jochebed. Their faith is recorded for eternity, "By faith, Moses when he was born was hid three months of his parents." "Faith comes by hearing, and hearing by the Word of God."

Three children were born to this marriage: Miriam, Aaron and Moses. The cruel command to slay the male children of the Israelites was in force when the third child, Moses, was born.

Jochebed loved her baby as tenderly as any true mother. The parents by faith hid Moses for three months.

The mid-wives feared God; the faith of Amram and Jochebed made them fearless, too, in the very face of death.

> Something of God is in a Mother's love,
>   Something of his tenderness and care.
> I never see a mother bent above an ailing child
>   But I can see God there.
>
> _____
>
> And I can feel him in a mother's touch:
>   Across the widening years her shielding hands
> Will still reach out as if to keep from harm
>   Her little child—how well God understands.
>   —GRACE NOLL CROWELL[1]

[1] Taken from *Songs of Faith* by Grace Noll Crowell. Copyright 1939, Harper & Brothers. Used by permission.

Moses was saved from the King's decree. Jochebed made the little ark of bulrushes. She placed her precious baby in it. She took the basket to the river and there among the tall reeds that grew by the water's edge, she placed her precious burden and went away. No doubt the prayer was in her heart, "Guard him, God, guard him safely."

A faith and a fear of Jehovah God outweighed the fear of an earthly king.

Miriam, about twelve years old, was left to watch. How carefully she must have been instructed by her mother. How often she must have said, "Now, tell me what you are to do and say. Miriam, my child, don't forget."

The conduct of Miriam on this occasion speaks well for this woman of faith, this slave woman in Egypt whose name has been included on the Honor Roll of the Book of Hebrews among "that great cloud of witnesses."

A Nurse

God rewarded Jochebed's courageous faith. Miriam hurried home with the heart thrilling news that Pharaoh's daughter had rescued the baby and had sent her to find a nurse for the child. Mother and daughter hastened to return to the princess. "Take this child and nurse him for me and I will give thee wages." Pharaoh's daughter had chosen a Hebrew woman for the Hebrew child. She did not realize it was his natural mother.

So Jochebed took her own precious child to nurse for the princess? No, to train him for the great destiny for which he was born. She was working for God, not for the princess, not for the weekly wages that Pharaoh's daughter may have sent. She was receiving wages of vastly more importance than the wages from the king's house. Let us look at Jochebed's wages: She received wages rich beyond her fondest dreams. She had the privilege of loving. She had the reward of self-sacrifice. She offered her life, a willing sacrifice upon the altar of her home. She became the mother of a good man. Her faith became his faith. She made a great life. Perhaps she never saw his greatness in this life, but she beholds it from the heavenly side. She is among the great "cloud of witnesses" by which we are compassed about.

Her Wages

"Take this child and nurse him, and I will give thee wages."

This mother had a sincere conviction that she must give an account to God for this child. "I will give thee wages." God gives to every mother wages who accepts willingly the role of motherhood and trains her children for His glory.

God had great plans for Moses. He was born for a great work. He was intrusted to God-fearing parents. He was placed in a home whose parents were willing to accept the responsibility. He was not committed to a hired servant. He was not committed to a heathen nurse, even though it might have been in a king's palace. God committed him to his mother. It has been said when God wants to train a child for achieving the best and highest in life, he sends his to school to a godly mother.

Jochebed was a willing mother.

> They tie you down, a woman said
>   Whose cheeks should have been flaming red
> With shame to speak of children so.
>   When babies come, you can not go
> In search of pleasure with your friends,
>   And all your happy wandering ends;
> The things you like, you can not do
>   For babies make a slave of you.
>
> I looked at her and said: "'Tis true
>   That children make a slave of you
> And tie you down with many a knot
>   But have you never thought to what
> It is of happiness and pride
>   That little babies have you tied?
> They tie you down to laughter rare,
>   To hours of smiles and hours of care.
>
> Sometimes they tie you down to tears
>   To nights of watching, and to fears;
> And then repay you with a smile,
>   And make your trouble all worth while.
> They tie you fast to chubby feet
>   And cheeks of pink and kisses sweet.
> They fasten you with cords of love
>
>   To God divine, Who reigns above.
> They tie you down, whereso'er you roam
>   Unto the little place called home;
> And over sea or railroad track
>   They tug at you to bring you back.
>
> Oh, go your selfish way and free
>   But hampered I would rather be;
> Yes, rather than wear a kingly crown
>   I would be, what you term, tied down,
> Tied down to dancing eyes and charms
>   Held fast by chubby dimpled arms
> The fettered slave of girl and boy,
>   And win from them earth's finest joy.
>   —Edgar A. Guest

Trained Her Children

Jochebed was a faithful mother. This slave woman mothered and trained one of the greatest men that ever walked upon this earth. She had Moses for a little while, but her teaching was through the plastic years of early childhood. Here a little, there a little, line upon line, precept upon precept, she filled his mind with love for his people and a reverence for Jehovah God.

Then he went away to the big university. He went to be schooled in all the wisdom of the Egyptians. He became Pharaoh's heir. But he stood true to the teaching of the slave woman, Jochebed, "Choosing rather to suffer affliction with the people of God than to enjoy the pleasures of sin for a season, esteeming the reproach of Christ greater riches than the treasures in Egypt."

This younger son of Levite parents became a law-giver, deliverer and a prophet. Forty years in Egypt, forty years in the desert, shepherding the flocks of Jethro—here God calls him back to Egypt and assigns the greatest commission a single man ever received. He was magnificent; no man ever had more to contend with as he welded this race of slaves into a nation.

His education began at home, and Jochebed was his teacher. Jochebed also gave to the world Aaron and Miriam. Three children were born to Amram and Jochebed—their lives are read and studied and will be as long as the world stands. And when time is no more, they will be waiting to welcome the faithful to the celestial land of eternal day.

They lived in days of darkness when the light was dim, but the mother's hand was in the hand of God.

Jochebed's Other Children

Aaron was the first high priest, and that great honor was handed down to his sons until the "Christ being come a high priest of good things to come. . ."

Miriam was the oldest child of Jochebed. She saved the life of Moses, and restored him to their mother.

After the crossing of the Red Sea, being miraculously and dramatically delivered from Pharaoh, she led the women in a song of praise, thanksgiving and exultation.

Prophetess, poet and musician, she is the first woman in the Bible to have a career outside the home. As far as we know she was an old maid. She was divinely called as were her brothers. There is one blot upon an otherwise beautiful character. She persuaded Aaron to join her in rebellion against Moses: "Hath the Lord indeed spoken only by Moses?" She was stricken with leprosy and remained without the camp seven days. Moses prayed God to forgive and heal his sister. She was healed and restored in favor. She died at Kadesh,

"Where there was no water for the congregation."

What a wonderful contribution this home gave to the world! Truly the child is the center and hope of all our responsibilities.

STORY OF THE LITTLE PALACE BEAUTIFUL

"The first is a room called Fancy; in this room sleeps a child, a beautiful baby. It is called the Child-That-Never-Was. It was longed for, hoped for, but never came.

"In the West room, looking out toward the North, in the room of experience, is the Child-That-Is. He is the child that now plays in our homes. He is in our Sunday School classes.

And in the room looking out toward the sunrise, the room called Hope, is the Child-That-Is-To-Be.

We think tenderly of the child that never was. We think sadly of the child that was. We give love and devotion to the child that is, and think hopefully of the child that is to be.

The future of the church and the nation is in our cradles, homes and nurseries today." (From Chappel's *Book of Biblical Characters*)

Just as surely was the future of national Israel in the little ark among the bulrushes.

STUDY SUGGESTIONS

Read Exodus 1 and 2:10; Ex. 2:11-25; Ex. 3-4; Ex. 5:1-7, 24; Ex. 14:1-15, 21.

Discuss the teaching program of the Old Testament (Deut. 4:5-11).

Discuss the teaching program of the New Testament (Eph. 6:1-4).

Discuss the value of early training. A certain church says, "Give me your child until he is seven."

Essential elements in child training:

  a. Precepts

    (1) Commands—Gen. 18:19.

    (2) Instruction—Deut. 4:9-10; 6:9; 18:8-9; Psalms 78:1-8.

  b. Examples

    (1) Children are great imitators.—Ezk. 16:44.

    (2) Solomon admonished to follow David's example.

        1 Kings 3:14; 8:25; 9:4; 11:38; 11 Chron. 7:17.

    (3) Precept without example worth little.

Discuss the potential of a truly Christian home.

Discuss Jochebed's influence.

Discuss Miriam's sin.

Name the kinds of wages Jochebed received.

Apply Prov. 22:6 to Jochebed's children.

Rahab

Joshua 2:1-22; 6:17-25

"By faith the harlot Rahab perished not with them that believed not, when she had received the spies with peace" (Heb. 11:31).

O N THE WEST SIDE of the Jordan River was located the high walled city of Jericho. A gate in the wall permitted the people of Jericho to go in and out of the city. When the Israelites made their camp near the Jordan River, the people of Jericho heard about it. They became afraid. They were a wicked people, governed by a clever and wicked king. They had for their protection iron chariots, and warriors with the latest and most improved weapons in their hands.

For forty years strange and wonderful things had been told about this vast army of people who were led and protected by Jehovah God. The crossing of the Red Sea; cities captured, and land taken;—these were victories that were well known.

"I will send my fear before thee, and will destroy all the people to whom thou shalt come, and I will make thine enemies turn their backs unto thee." Exodus 23:27.

Thus God had promised his people. All Jericho was living in terror of invasion when the spies sent out by Joshua entered the city.

THE HOUSE ON THE WALL

In those days there lived in a house built over a gap between the two walls of Jericho, a woman identified in both the Old Testament and New Testament as Rahab the harlot. It was to Rahab's door that the two spies of Joshua came and asked for lodging. While they talked with her, some one hurried to tell the king of Jericho that two strange men had come inside the City, and were stopping at Rahab's house. They believed these men were from the camp of Israel. So the king sent his officers to Rahab's house to capture the spies.

Suddenly there came a fierce knocking at Rahab's door, the soldiers of the king striking the panels with their spears. Realizing the gates of the City would now be closed against their escape, the spies with lowered voices asked Rahab to hide them.

RAHAB'S CHARACTER

There is a difference of opinion as to the real character of Rahab. Some have denied she was a harlot. Others have described her as one who would have carnal traffic with any and all who came to her with cash in hand. However, the spies were on a secret mission and the woman's character was of no consequence.

It is recorded in the Book of Joshua (6:23) "that Rahab, her parents, her brethren and all that she had" were brought out of Jericho and left without the camp of Israel." The camp of Israel was holy and no unclean person was allowed to enter. This is considered strong evidence that Rahab was a harlot.

Now the king's police were at her door. The spies were in her house. There was an army on the other side of the river ready for an attack. The God of that army was all-powerful and always to be counted upon. And she hid them with the stalks of flax which she laid upon the roof. She admitted to the soldiers that two men answering the descriptions had been in her house; she did not know the direction they had gone, but if they would hurry they would overtake them.

THE BARGAIN

She exacted a promise from the two spies, that in return for the kindness that she had shown them, that when they came with a great army to take Jericho, they would save Rahab and her family. And a truce was made between them. She dropped a scarlet cord out of her window and over the wall, and the spies slid down to safety.

The Israelites under the leadership of Joshua took the City. All the inhabitants were destroyed; only Rahab and her family were spared; a piece of scarlet cord hanging from her window was the signal.

"And Joshua saved Rahab the harlot, and her father's household and all that she had; and she dwelleth in Israel even unto this day; because she hid the messengers which Joshua sent to spy out Jericho."

It is generally agreed that Rachab (Matt. 1:5) and Rahab, the harlot are one and the same. This being true, she married Salmon, became the mother of Boaz and is included in the maternal lineage of Christ. Not Rahab only, but Tamar and Bathsheba were other sinful women, and yet in a sense they were the mothers of our Lord. God did not approve, nor did he ignore their sins:

"For all have sinned and come short of the glory of God; being justified freely by his grace through the redemption that is in Christ Jesus" (Rom. 3:23-24).

The law of Moses forbade harlotry. Its social evil was known to Jesus. When the woman taken in adultery was set before Jesus by the scribes and Pharisees, he exposed their own self-righteousness— a sin as great as the sin of this victim of commercialized vice (John 8:1-11).

Again Jesus said that even harlots would enter the kingdom of heaven before those self-righteous individuals (Matt. 21:31). This was a stinging rebuke to those who professed to know and did not, and encouragement to those who have sinned and repented.

Rahab did not hesitate to lie. When the king ordered her to bring out the men that were seen to enter her house, she said, "There came men unto me, but I wist not whence they were" (Joshua 2:24). And she pointed out the direction which they might have taken. But they were hiding under the flax upon the roof of her house.

When the apostle Paul made out the great honor roll (Heb. 11), Rahab is enrolled with the faithful along with Sarah. The Apostle James mentions her as one who is worthy because of her good works. (Jas. 2:25).

We hear this woman of faith declare to those seeking the spies, "The Lord your God, he is God in heaven above, and in earth beneath" (Josh. 2:11).

She is commended for her faith and for her works—whatever she might have been, she was surely pardoned.

"Though your sins be as scarlet, they shall be as white as snow" (Isa. 1:18).

HER VIRTUES

The Bible gives us a complete picture of Rahab. She was an industrious woman. She wove fine linen and dried the flax on her roof top. Her faith in Israel's God made her a courageous woman. She was ready to risk her own life to protect the lives of the enemy spies. And she feared them because she believed fervently that they had been sent from the Most High God. Their flight from Egypt through the Red Sea; their entrance into the promised land by the parting of the Jordan River caused her to believe strongly in the Israelites' cause. She confidently tells the spies, "I know the Lord hath given you the land, and that your terror is fallen upon us, and all the inhabitants of the land faint because of you." This was repeated to Joshua by the spies, and the people were greatly encouraged.

Israel's army completely surrounded Jericho. In the whole city none but the harlot recognized the approach of God in that army.

And too, we have a glimpse of compassion in this woman whose faith is active and decisive. She is tenderly solicitous for her family. She and all her family agreed to remain indoors during the attack.

"By faith the harlot Rahab perished not with them that believed not, when she had received the spies with peace" (Heb. 11:31b).

STUDY SUGGESTIONS

Do you see any reason why the two young spies might have chosen a house of prostitution as a place of safety?

How do you account for Rahab's faith?

How did she receive the spies? (Heb. 11:31b)

How and why was she justified? (Jas. 2:25)

How was she saved? (Heb. 11:31)

Where did she dwell; why? (Joshua 6:25)

Whom did she marry? (Matt. 1:5a)

Who were her son and daughter-in-law? (Matt. 1:1-5)

Name another harlot in the genealogy of Christ. (Matt. 1:3a)

With what other Gentile was she listed? (Matt. 1:5b)

What claim through Rahab may Gentiles have on Christ? When does this claim become effective? (Acts 10:34, 35)

Deborah

Judges 4:4-14; 5:1-15

"Until that I Deborah arose, that I arose a mother in Israel" (Judges 5:7).

A ND THE children of Israel again did evil in the sight of the Lord." This tragic thing is said time after time about God's people.

In the early life of the Hebrew nation while they were yet on the east side of the Jordan, Moses, before his death, prophesied their worship of gods, "the work of men's hands, wood and stone, which neither see, nor hear, nor smell."

And the Lord sold them into the hand of Jabin, King of Canaan. King Jabin had a large army and many of his soldiers rode in iron chariots. The Israelites feared these chariots more then they feared a host of men. The oppression was heavy, and the children of Israel cried unto the Lord.

AN OUTSTANDING WOMAN

There was a homemaker and "mother in Israel" who had not turned away from God to worship idols. This brave woman loved and worshipped the true God.

Deborah, the wife of Lapidoth, lived under a palm tree between Ramah and Bethel. She was a prophetess and poet. People from over all the land came to this "mother of Israel" for advice and counsel during the dark days of slavery. Deborah was the fourth judge of Israel. She served not only in religious affairs, but also in civil affairs. God made known his will to her. So she sent for Captain Barak and delivered God's message to him. He was told to gather 10,000 men of the tribes of Naphtali and Zebulon and march toward Mount Tabor to meet the chariots of Jabin commanded by Sisera. God promised victory that day to Barak and his little army.

Barak was a brave man, but the Israelites were discouraged, and he said to Deborah, "If thou wilt go with me I will go; but if thou wilt not go with me then I will not go." Deborah, the prophetess said, "I will surely go with thee." Not only Barak, but the entire army was encouraged and inspired by this godly woman. She was the woman of her time, doing and serving in whatever field she saw an opportunity. Deborah was ready to go with Barak. Her faith in God so filled her heart there was no room for fear of Sisera and his nine hundred chariots.

"I will surely go with thee, notwithstanding the journey that thou takest shall not be for thine honour; for the Lord shall sell Sisera into the hand of a woman."

Thus she makes one last appeal to Barak, to assume the *command and authority*. He was supposed to be the leader. She appealed to him to fill his place.

From Mount Tabor, Deborah and Barak could see the little river of Kishon winding like a silver ribbon into the valley below. This is where God had told Deborah he would draw the army of Jabin. Presently they saw a swarm of people and hundreds of iron chariots, and the men of Israel feared greatly. Deborah said unto Barak, "This is the day when the Lord hath delivered Sisera into thy hands. Already the Lord has gone out to battle; now go down at once."

The two armies met in the plains of Esdraelon. The battle was fierce, but not for long. God sent a great fear unto the hearts of the enemies, and they began to run away. A driving storm broke from the east; flood waters swept down the little river and overflowed its banks. Many of Sisera's men were drowned in the flood, and all the others were killed. Sisera himself left his iron chariot and ran away only to lose his life at the hand of Jael as he sought refuge in her tent. "For the Lord shall sell Sisera into the hands of a woman," said Deborah. Barak found him in Jael's tent, nailed to the floor.

"This is the day Jehovah hath delivered Sisera into thy hands." Israel won a glorious victory as Deborah had declared.

She and Barak joined in singing the song she had composed. It was a song of praise and thanksgiving unto the Lord God of Israel. She took none of the honor unto herself.

Of Barak she sang:

"Awake, awake, utter a song,

Arise, Barak, and lead away the captives."

Deborah taught Barak his duty; she was his helper through teaching and encouragement; nowhere did she usurp authority over man.

She respected God's order. "Jehovah will deliver Sisera unto *thy* hands," not *our* hands. Through her counsel and aid she assisted Barak in going to battle with him—she kept herself in the background. She assumed no authority and stayed well within her God-given sphere. She was no Joan of Arc. Women who love the Lord and long to be well pleasing in his sight strive to know his purpose and plan for her, and to stay within those limitations.

There are those who will insist that a woman can never teach a man: that to teach a man is to usurp authority. It is altogether possible for the woman to assist and teach a man in any work God has assigned him, and yet maintain her God-given position. Deborah is an example.

What do you think of Jael? Deborah said, "Blessed shall she be above women in the tent."

One of the most dramatic lines in Deborah's song is the picture of Sisera's mother looking out the window and waiting for him to come home:

> "The mother of Sisera cried through the lattice,
> Why is his chariot so long in coming?"

The "Song of Deborah" is said to be a masterpiece in literature.

STUDY SUGGESTIONS

Discuss Israel's plight at this time. (Judges 4:1-3)
What promise had God made? (Deut. 4:29-31)
Who was Deborah? (Judges 4:4)
Where did she live? (Judges 4:5)
Locate the place relative to Jerusalem.
Locate the plain of Esdraelon.
Describe Jabin's army. (Judges 4:3, 13)
Who was Sisera? (Judges 4:1)
Whom did Deborah direct to assemble Israel's army? (Judges 4:5)
Discuss Deborah, as a *judge*, as a *prophet*, as a *mother in Israel*, and as a *song writer*.
Did Deborah show a desire to lead the army? Did she seek glory for herself?
Discuss her opportunity to usurp authority had she so desired.
Read Matt. 28:18-20; Mark 16:15, 16; 2 Tim. 4:5. Are these Scriptures addressed to women?
Read and discuss her only restriction. (1 Tim. 2:12)
Name ways in which a "mother in the church" can be helper to the evangelist. (1 Cor. 9:14; 1 Thess. 3:1-2; Titus 1:8; 1 Pet. 4:9; Heb. 13:2; Acts 18:26)

Jephthah's Daughter

Judges 11:34-40

"My father, if thou has opened thy mouth unto the Lord, do to me according to that which proceedeth out of thy mouth; for as much as the Lord hath taken vengeance for thee of thine enemies, even of the children of Ammon" (Judges 11:36).

F ORTY YEARS had passed since Deborah's great victory. The people again did evil in the sight of the Lord.

During the leadership of Joshua, Israel remained true to Jehovah. After that they lapsed into idolatry for which they were punished by being brought under the servitudes of six idolatrous nations. When they cried in their distress unto Jehovah, judges were raised up for their deliverance.

The Israelites were again in great trouble. They did not go to the Tabernacle at Shiloh to worship God. Everywhere in the land they were bowing down before the gods that other nations worshipped. And the very nations whose gods they were serving began to trouble them. They began to make war against the Israelites and take away their riches.

The Ammonites came from the East and the Philistines came from the West and ruled over the Israelites. The Ammonites even threatened to take away their homes and drive them out of their land. This was an unhappy time indeed for a people who had once enjoyed God's blessings. So they cried to God for help, and they expected Him to send them a deliverer just as he had done at other times. The Ammonites oppressed them for eighteen long years.

The Israelites became very sorry for their sins. They realized the gods they were serving could never help them. They tore down their idols and began to serve the Lord. The time had come now for a new champion to save their people from extinction.

In this era of national darkness, a father and a daughter became the providential agents of restoration.

There was a man among them whose name was Jephthah. A dark cloud of tragedy enveloped him. Born out of wedlock, his mother was a foreigner to the tribe, an inferior woman and a harlot (Judges 11:1-2).

He was driven from his Gilead home by his "legitimate" brothers. He took up residence in Tob not far from Gilead. Here he became the successful captain of a band of free booters who went raiding with him.

Finally some one remembered Jephthah whose brave deeds had been told throughout the land. He was the leader to which Israel turned, asking that he rule over them in their peril and be the ninth judge of Israel. He who all the days of his life had been scorned and cast out as illegitimate was now sought out. Denied his father's house because of the scandal of his birth, he was skeptical. At last he consented after a solemn covenant was ratified on both sides at Mizpeh in Gilead.

A Promise To God

In his great eagerness for victory Jephthah made a foolish vow. He promised the Lord God, "If thou shalt without fail deliver the children of Ammon into mine hands, then shall it be that whatsoever cometh forth of the doors of my house to meet me, when I return in peace from the children of Ammon, shall surely be the Lord's and I will offer it for a burnt offering" (Judges 11:30, 31)

The vow of Hannah who pledged to lend her child to God as long as he lived is a contrast to Jephthah's rash vow. The simple and sublime trust of Deborah who went against a fearful enemy, strongly armed with faith in God, is the antithesis of Jephthah's attitude.

Victory was his. The Ammonites proved powerless; twenty of their cities were taken, and the Ammonites' strength was destroyed.

Every drop of his blood surging and singing with his triumph, Jephthah returned to his home in Mizpeh. News of the victory had reached home before he returned. Women and maidens had assembled to greet this victorious warrior with songs and dances. With shock and poignant distress he saw his beautiful daughter coming to meet him from his door. Perhaps she was a teen-ager, full of a young girl's energy and vivacity, a girl full of life, with extravagant love for her father. In the fervor and enthusiasm of youth, she came prancing and singing to celebrate her father's victory.

Innocent Victim

Her face glowed with joy as she beat a timbrel and sang. She sang praise to Jehovah's strength; she sang of the glory of her father whom the Lord had chosen. What a beautiful picture her approach presents. Then she saw horror in his eyes!

"Alas my daughter: thou hast brought me very low, and thou art one of them that trouble me: for I have opened my mouth unto the Lord and I can not go back."

With a noble submission Jephthah's daughter gave the answer:

"My father, if thou hast opened thy mouth unto the Lord, do to me according to that which proceedeth out of thy mouth, for as much as the Lord hath taken vengeance for thee of thine enemies, even of the children of Ammon."

We may think of Jephthah's daughter as no longer a girl yet not quite a woman—at the age at which such daughters are usually married. At first she did not grasp her father's distressing predicament.

At last the realization came to her that all of her beautiful dreams as a wife and a mother would never come true. The hope within her, that hope of every woman of Israel, was gone.

She did not weep or bemoan her fate. She accepted it and still believed in the goodness and mercy of God. But she needed spiritual strength to face such a crisis so she asked her father for two months that she might go to the mountains to bewail her virginity.

Some commentators insist that Jephthah put his own daughter to the sword. Had death really awaited her, why should she have cared to "bewail her virginity"? And, under these circumstances, could be the sense in the statement, "She knew no man."

So the great sacrifice seemed that he was never to allow her to marry. She was an only child. Jephthah would have no posterity. His name would be blotted from Israel's record.

The prophet Jeremiah cries out against human sacrifice (Jer. 19:3-5). The law of Moses strictly forbade it.

Not by choice but because of her father's vow, she was to live at the Tabernacle as one dedicated to the Lord, segregated from her friends and family until her death.

She today is the embodiment of courage, submission, meekness and patience.

The sad fate of Jephthah is not unique, although it seems to be so. Tragedies occur every day, suffering and separation and death falling on the innocent.

The cry comes often, "Why should this happen to me?" Jesus taught that the meek, those who can accept the storms of life and still say the Lord is good and gracious, shall inherit the earth.

STUDY SUGGESTIONS

What was meant by Jephthah's vow? If a clean beast, it was to be sacrificed, if a person devoted to the Lord's service. (Lev. 27)

Discuss the phrases: "Bewail my virginity." (Judges 11:37) and "She knew no man." (Judges 11:39)

Discuss Jeremiah 19:3-5.

What does the New Testament tell us of Jephthah? (Heb. 11:32)

How did she place victory of Israel over her welfare? (Judges 11:36)

To what extent are children to obey their parents? (Eph. 6:1)

Name some beautiful traits of character exhibited by this lovely maiden.

Manoah's Wife

Judges 13-16

"Then Manoah entreated the Lord, and said, O my Lord, let the man of God which thou didst send come again unto us, and teach us what we shall do unto the child that shall be born" (Judges 13:8).

THE INFLUENCE of Jephthah and his daughter lasted about twenty-five years. "And the children of Israel did evil again in the sight of the Lord; and the Lord delivered them into the hands of the Philistines forty years" (Judges 13:1). Perhaps the fathers and mothers never did set up the idols they had torn down, but when their sons and daughters grew to maturity they wished to have gods like their heathen neighbors. So they made idols like those their neighbors worshipped. They placed the idols in their cities, under the trees in their yards. They bowed down before them.

In those day the tribes of Israel were trying to be all things to all people, and to their gods. It was a dark period, with no clear vision or purity of faith. How clearly the Scriptures reveal when the days seem the most hopeless—there is a mother, a father or a family whose faith in God has not wavered. The Lord has used the family as a channel of blessing to the world. There was such a family in the days of the Judges. The mother bore no name of her own in the record. She was the wife of a certain man of Zorah, of the family of the Danites, whose name was Manoah. She seemed to have been a stronger character than her husband. Like the mothers of Isaac and Samuel, she lived for a time in a state of barrenness. The intense sorrow and disappointment of every childless woman were no doubt in the heart of this wife of Manoah.

AN ANGEL'S PROMISE

On a certain day the angel of the Lord appeared unto the woman and announced that she would bear a son. Her child was to be consecrated to the Lord God; he was to be brought up a Nazarite and his hair was never to be touched with a razor.

During her pregnancy she was to eat no unclean thing and to abstain from the fruit of the vine.

When the angel appeared before her, she was reverent, obedient, and filled with faith.

Manoah's wife regarded this messenger as a man of God, although she reported to her husband, "that his countenance was like an angel of God, very terrible."

She did not inquire from where he came, where he was going, or even his name.

Then Manoah entreated the Lord to let this man of God come unto them again, "and teach us what we shall do unto the child that shall be born" (Judges 13:8).

Would that all parents with humble sincerity pray this prayer! God answered the prayer. Manaoh's wife was in the field alone when the angel of God appeared to her again. Excitedly she ran to tell her husband, and together they both stood before the angel. After being questioned the angel assured Manoah that he was the man of God who had appeared before.

"How shall we order the child, and what shall be done with him?"

Both Manoah and his wife recognized this child as a gift from God. They seemed to know clearly that he had a divine mission, and as his parents they too would play an important part in this divine mission. Every child born into the world is from God. Every child is born to glorify God in his life upon this earth. The parents are the teachers; the home is the school to aid and assist God's purpose to be achieved. "How shall we order the child?"

The first message was repeated to both Manoah and his wife. They manifested the gracious spirit of hospitality as Manoah offered to prepare a kid for him. The angel refused and advised Manoah, "and if thou wilt offer a burnt offering, thou must offer it unto the Lord" (Judges 13:16). Manoah desired to know the angel's name, so that when the things he had promised them came to pass, they might honor him again. His request was denied. Manoah prepared a sacrifice; as the flames rose toward the heavens from off the altar, the angel of the Lord ascended in the flame.

They fell on their faces before him because they now knew that he was an angel of the Lord. Manoah became fearful and pessimistic, "We shall surely die because we have seen God" (Judges 13:22). But Manoah's wife remained unshaken in her faith. The vision passed, but the message of God remained clear and true to her. And in due time the child was born and she gave her people Samson. She taught her son that no intoxicating drink was to enter his lips, no razor should touch his head. His long hair was the outward sign of his sacred vow to God.

Manoah's wife is an example to wives today. A wife who had a simple, trusting confidence in God—she lived so close to God, that an angel of the Lord appeared twice to her. Each time she hurried and told her husband.

THE CHILD, SAMSON

Through the influence of his father and his mother, Samson felt very close to the Lord God, and believed he had a divine mission to his people.

Samson grew to be the strongest man that ever walked the earth. Often his parents worried about him. We find them protesting his marriage to a daughter of the Philistines, out of whose hands he was to deliver his people.

But Samson informed his mother and father, "Get her for me; for she pleaseth me well" (Judges 14:36). How often this happens!

The Lord through Moses forbade the Israelites to make marriage with other nations; "Thy daughter shalt thou not give unto his son, nor his daughter shalt thou take unto thy son. For they will turn away thy son from following me—that they may serve other gods; so will the anger of the Lord be kindled against you, and destroy thee suddenly" (Deut. 7:3b-4).

As a godly mother, Manoah's wife must have taught these Scriptures to her son. For of old the Lord through Moses had said, "Thou shalt teach them diligently unto thy children" (Deut. 6:7).

Every incident in the life of this family of Zorah indicates there was perfect agreement and harmony between the husband and wife. There was a perfect understanding about this son of theirs. And all of his days, even unto his marriage, they desired to do unto him according to God's will and purpose.

SAMSON'S CHOICE

So we hear them say: "Is there never a woman among the daughters of thy brethren or among all my people, that thou goest to take a wife of the uncircumcised Philistines?" (Judges 14:13).

They must have talked often and prayed fervently about this marriage. And with misgivings and sorrow they went to his wedding. No sooner was Samson married than his trouble began. His wife's friends displeased him; and he became angry with them, and returned to his father's house.

After his anger had cooled, he decided to visit his wife and take her a present. But her father would not allow him to see her. He learned she had become the wife of another man.

In his anger he wrought great destruction upon the Philistines. He prayed to God and his prayers were answered. He performed many marvelous feats. But he lacked self-control. He allowed his passions to master him. And his parents must have been horrified when he again married a Philistine. Her name was Delilah. She lived in the Valley of Sorek. Samson was the hero of God, but was like putty in the hands of Delilah.

A DAUGHTER-IN-LAW

Delilah loved money, the beautiful things that money can buy. She loved her own people; and she quickly consented to the rulers in their plans to capture Samson.

It is easy to visualize her in the deceitful play of treacherously feigned love: dressed in gay clothing, purple and gold, painted face, her ears, wrists, fingers and ankles adorned with brilliant jewels; a gorgeously adorned woman.

Her home was in all probability a perfect setting for her beauty—charming and restful. She bestowed every attention upon the mighty Samson. The air of the room was drowsy with perfume and burning incense. Musicians played softly. He was completely blind to the fact that she was a deceitful woman. After much persuasion and love-making, he pointed to his long hair and betrayed the honor of a Nazarite to an infamous woman. His weakness is more astonishing than his strength.

Poor, unhappy Samson! He realized when it was too late that the woman he loved was not his friend. What a sad mistake he had made when he disregarded his parents and kept company with a Philistine woman. Now he must suffer the remainder of his life.

The son of a faithful mother and father yielded to temptation.

Did his parents live to see their son blind, bound with fetters of brass, "as he did grind in the prison house"?

STUDY SUGGESTIONS

What did Manoah's wife have in common with Sarah and Rebekah? (Judges 13:3)

Name her wifely traits.

Discuss her as a mother.

Do you think she failed in training her son? Give reasons.

Discuss the women who attracted Samson. (Judges 14-16)

Was Samson justified in visiting these strange women?

What was the great sin of Delilah? (Judges 16:5)

How likely did she lose her life? (Judges 16:30)

Ruth

"Thy God shall be my God" (Ruth 1:16).

THE BOOK OF RUTH belongs to the period of the Judges, a period of much strife and bloodshed—God's people often were delivered to their enemies because of their disobedience. When life became hard, they turned again to God calling for deliverance. God raised up "Judges which delivered them out of the hands of them which spoiled them."

The beginning of this beautiful story is a family in want—Elimelech, Naomi, and there two sons, Mahlon and Chilion. Their home was in Bethlehem. There was a famine in the land. So this Ephrathite family went to sojourn in the country of Moab.

The Moabites, descendants of Lot, were not friendly to the Israelites. They did not serve and worship the God of Abraham, Isaac and Jacob. They served an idol named Chemosh. He was worshiped with fire. Children were even offered as sacrifice to this god. Ruth, the heroine of this beautiful narrative, was taught to fear and worship him.

Elimelech and his family came to live near Ruth's home—"And they came into the country of Moab and continued there." They had left their home for a short time until the rains should come again, but they continued in the heathen land.

THREE WIDOWS

Famine and death seems to have been the lot of Naomi, the pleasant, for this is the meaning of her name. She was widowed in this foreign land—Elimelech died; Naomi and her two sons continued there. The two sons married Moabite girls, Orpah and Ruth. Ten years after these marriages Mahlon and Chilion died, and the story is the story of three widows.

Both sorrow and joy caused Naomi's heart to turn homeward. She heard that the famine had ended in her homeland, and the loss of husband and sons created a longing for the familiar places and faces of home. No doubt there was much sadness in her heart as she left this strange country where her husband and sons lay buried.

Ruth and Orpah had lived with Naomi, possibly from the time of their marriages. And there these young women learned about the God of the Israelites. Instead of teaching her young husband to serve

Chemosh, the fire god, Ruth learned to serve the true God.

Orpah and Ruth started the journey with their mother-in-law. Naomi urged them both to turn back. She knew the journey would be long and tiresome. They had no friends awaiting them. They would be as strangers among the Israelites; so the unselfish Naomi made a generous gesture, "The Lord deal as kindly with you as you have dealt with the dead and me." And she advised them to seek husbands: "Find rest each of you in the house of her husband." Moreover it would be unlikely that they would find husbands in Bethlehem. And Naomi knew that to share her lot would be to share sorrow: "The hand of the Lord is gone out against me."

"Let Me Go With You"

Orpah, being thus warned, kissed her mother-in-law and turned back unto her people and unto her gods. Ruth cleaved unto her mother-in-law, who had taught her of the true God. She answered Naomi in one of the most beautiful sayings of the Bible, "Entreat me not to leave thee, or to return from following after thee; for whither thou goest, I will go; where thou lodgest, I will lodge; thy people shall be my people and thy God my God. Where thou diest, will I die, and there will I be buried, the Lord do so to me, and more also if aught but death part thee and me."

Ruth's confession is a confession of love. There are no more beautiful words to be found than this confession of a young woman's love for her mother-in-law. It is a confession of her faith in the God of Israel. It is a confession of love and loyalty through every vicissitude of life until death.

Naomi saw how truly Ruth loved her, and she did not talk to her any more about going back to her own mother. Together these two women walked on over the fields and hills; at last they came to the City of Bethlehem where Naomi had once lived so happily with her husband and two little boys.

All the people of the town came out to see and welcome Naomi home, but they noticed quickly the ravages of sorrow and trouble in Naomi's face, "Is this Naomi?," they asked.

"Do not call me Naomi, call me Mara, for the Lord hath dealt bitterly with me. I went out with a husband and two sons, I left them in graves in Moab. And the Lord hath brought me home again empty." Naomi the pleasant is now Mara, meaning bitterness. Yet Naomi is not embittered because of her trials. She acknowledges God's hand in all the affairs of her life; she confesses his nearness to her in whatever state she is in; "the Almighty hath afflicted me, the Lord hath testified against me."

Ruth Works

So they came to Bethlehem in the beginning of the barley harvest. Ruth not only chose to share Naomi's lot, but she was willing to support her mother-in-law. And she asked permission to go out into the fields to glean. It is easy to believe that Naomi had exerted a profound religious influence and created a deep impression in the mind of Ruth respecting the God of Israel. The law of Moses required some stalks of grain to be left in the field for the poor people to gather—Ruth seems to have been taught this by her mother-in-law.

There was no man to support Naomi: a childless widow bereft of domestic joys. She had no land that others might work for her. Ruth realized the situation and she goes to the fields to glean ears of corn.

Ruth, "the foreigner," commanded the respect of all who saw her by her bearing and kindness. Now it happened that Ruth began to glean in the fields of a very rich man named Boaz. This man lived in Bethlehem and his servants worked in the fields. Boaz, a mighty man of wealth of the family of Elimelech—he was related to Naomi by marriage—was owner of the field where Ruth gleaned. Ruth had hoped and prayed that she would find grace in the eyes of some kind-hearted man as she went to glean food for Naomi and herself.

The harvest was a great social event, and the girls who went out to glean arrayed themselves in bright holiday attire. The gleaners wore a variety of colors, red, yellow and blue, the headdress being the brightest and the most conspicuous part of their apparel.

While Ruth was busy at work, Boaz came to talk with his servants. His salutation, "The Lord be with you," and the servants' reply, "The Lord bless thee," indicated a very happy relationship between the man and his employees.

Boaz Is Attracted

Ruth's beauty and industry attracted his attention. Upon inquiry he was told, "This is the young Moabitess who came with Naomi from her own land." The servant that was set over the reapers had given his consent for her to glean after the reapers of Boaz. Perhaps Boaz had heard much talk in the market places, the streets, the fields, wherever people gather to discuss the things of common interest. They told how Ruth had forsaken her idol-worship and began to serve the true God. They found much to say and repeat, too, about how kind she was to her mother-in-law. He saw her toiling patiently among strange people to obtain food for herself and Naomi. As all who knew her, he admired the beautiful young woman. He told her to come back every morning and glean in his fields and to work with his maidens. The reapers are charged to treat her kindly. The young men are commanded to respect her. She was invited to eat with the servants, and to drink from their water pitchers. "And let fall also some of the handfuls on purpose for her, and leave them that she may glean them, and rebuke her not."

Ruth was thankful for his kindness. She bowed with her face to the ground, "Why have I found grace in thine eyes . . . seeing I am a stranger (or a foreigner)."

"I have heard about your kindness to my kinswoman, Naomi, I have heard how you left your own people and came unto a people that you had not known. The Lord recompense thy work, and a full reward be given thee of the Lord God of Israel, under whose wings thou art come to trust."

It is very doubtful that Ruth realized how fully the Lord would recompense her work. So she gleaned in the fields until even, and beat out that she had gleaned; and it was about a bushel of barley. It is said that she took home much more than barley—Ruth carried home the heart of Boaz.

Her mother-in-law asked in whose fields she had gleaned. "The man with whom I wrought today is Boaz." Naomi cried out in joy, "Blessed be he of the Lord, who hath not left off his kindness to the living and to the dead." Upon Naomi's advice, Ruth gleaned every day in the fields of Boaz unto the end of the barley harvest and wheat harvest.

NAOMI'S PLAN

Naomi knew the law concerning the rights and duties of a kinsman regarding a deceased relative. Not only did she know the law, but she was wise in the ways of a man toward a maid. She knew Boaz was attracted to the lovely Moabitess, and that Ruth herself was not averse to the attention of Boaz. So Naomi suggests the following of an old custom which was really a proposal of marriage.

The law was that if a man died leaving his wife childless, it was the duty of the nearest kinsman to marry her. Naomi's plan was very bold, but Ruth's love and confidence in her mother-in-law caused her to comply with her wishes. Ruth made herself attractive and went to the threshing floor. When Boaz had lain down at the end of the heap of corn, "she came softly and uncovered his feet and laid herself down."

At midnight he discovered Ruth at his feet. "I am Ruth, thine handmaid, spread therefore thy skirt over thine handmaid, for thou art a near kinsman."

This has often been considered a very unwomanly bit of advice that old Naomi gave to the lovely Ruth. But Naomi knew Ruth, and she knew Boaz, and she longed to see her daughter-in-law "at rest in the home of her husband."

What a wonderful example of a mother-in-law is Naomi—unselfish, generous and understanding, teaching and leading her daughter-in-law to accept the true religion of Jehovah. The beauty of her life caused Ruth to say, "Thy people shall be my people."

"Thou art a near kinsman," said Ruth to Boaz at midnight on the threshing floor. Boaz had seen how well Ruth behaved; he admired her industry and modesty. "I will do to thee all that thou requirest, for all the people of my city doth know that thou art a virtuous woman."

Boaz was very concerned about the reputation of Ruth and also his own good name. He told her there was a nearer kinsman, and if that man would not perform the part of a kinsman, that he would gladly make her his wife.

He was very careful that none of the reapers knew that a woman had been on the threshing floor that night. She lay quietly until the day began to dawn. While it was yet too dark to be recognized, Ruth hurried back to Naomi's house. In her veil was six measures of barley for Boaz had said, "Go not empty unto thy mother-in-law."

There is a bit of shrewd understanding of human nature in Naomi as she counsels Ruth to "sit still, for the man will not rest until he have finished the thing this day." Boaz, as Naomi had predicted, did not delay. He went to the nearer kinsman who surrendered his rights and even advises Boaz to redeem his right for himself.

The inheritance is redeemed according to law and with it, he also bought Ruth the Moabitess, the widow of Mahlon, "to raise up the name of the dead upon his inheritance." This was accomplished in the presence of witnesses. And so Ruth and Boaz were married; a godly home was established; a son was born.

The women rejoiced with Naomi. Her daughter-in-law was praised for her goodness and kindness toward Naomi. And the women, her neighbors, gave it a name saying, "There is a son born to Naomi; and they called his name Obed: he is the father of Jesse, the father of David."

What wonderful blessings came to Ruth when she took shelter "under the wings of the God of Israel."

Christ's Ancestors

The last chapter of this beautiful story reveals that the young Moabitish woman who left Moab for Canaan with her mother-in-law, whose heart had been pierced with many sorrows, was to be an ancestress of our Lord. David was her great grandson, and this was the family through whom the Christ was to come. It may be that in this life she never knew this. She knew that Boaz was of the tribe of the Messiah, but no one knew up to that time the family to be so exalted.

Ruth did not belong to the Hebrew race; the Moabites were descendants of Lot, and she was of the stock of Abraham. How God over-rules events and circumstance to His own glory is beautifully displayed in the lives of every character in this narrative. Naomi saw God's hand in her sorrow. God was very near and very real to

Naomi. Boaz too recognized God's providence in the good fortune that gave him Ruth for a wife.

From the very hour that Ruth declared "thy God shall be my God," we see the presence of God in all her affairs.

"And we know that all things work together for good to them that love God, to them who are called according to his purpose."

The power of choice and decision is dramatically illustrated in the Book of Ruth. Ruth's decision and choice never faltered. Never once did she look back on her home land. Never once did she look back with regret or sorrow.

Orpah had been under the influence of the wonderful Naomi. Orpah started. She seemed on first glimpse to have definitely decided to go. But when she arrived at the boundary line, she yielded to Naomi's entreaties and turned back to Moab.

So many start the journey. So many young women seem at first to have a desire to be a Christian. They never get beyond the boundary line. They never seem to be able to break with the world. There are too many girls who marry and bring children into the world with no real desire to establish a Christian home. What great things depended on Ruth's choice and decision!

STUDY SUGGESTIONS

Read the entire Book of Ruth.

Do we know the author of this Book?

With what family does this story deal? (Ruth 1:1-5)

Give the sad story of Naomi's life in Moab. (Ruth 1:3, 5)

Picture the plight of the three widows. Use your imagination. Relate their decision to go to Judah—or was it Naomi's decision alone? (Ruth 1:6)

Do you think that Naomi counselled Orpah and Ruth Wisely? (Ruth 1:8-14; Titus 2:4)

What is your opinion of Naomi as a mother-in-law?

If Christian mothers-in-law followed Naomi's example, would in-law problems be prevented?

Learn by heart and discuss all points of Ruth's choice and decision. (Ruth 1:16-17)

Could Ruth have made this wonderful choice without teaching and example?

Tell of their return to Bethlehem and the town's reaction. (Ruth 1:19)

Did Naomi's bitter affliction cause her to be embittered? (Ruth 1:20-21)

Discuss Ruth's beautiful character (Ruth 2:2, 10-13, 17, 18; 3:11)

Chapter two introduces Boaz. What of his character?

Would Naomi be called a matchmaker? Is that wrong for older women to teach the younger women how to select their life's companion?

Does the divorce rate and juvenile delinquency in our midst indicate that the older women have neglected to teach the things which become sound doctrine? (Titus 1:1-6)

Teaching young women to love their husbands is commanded. Should there be teaching along this line before marriage?

Would you think the home established by Boaz and Ruth followed God's plan? Give reasons for your statement.

What do you think of Naomi's position in this home?

Do you think her care of the little Obed to be more beneficial than the care of a hired servant?

Do grandparents in the home cause friction and spoil grandchildren, generally speaking?

Using Naomi as an example, discuss the ideal situation.

Isn't this possible if all parties are Christian?

Hannah

1 Sam. 1, 2

"For this child have I prayed . . . therefore, have I also lent him to the Lord" (1 Sam. 1:27-28).

HANNAH means "grace," and there is much in the character of this woman to indicate she was fittingly named. She was the wife of a man named Elkanah. Their home was not far from Shiloh where God's tabernacle was located. This man worshipped and feared God. Every year he went to Shiloh, taking his offering for sin to the tabernacle. He did not go alone, but took his family and they worshipped God together. This would suggest a happy family, but Hannah was not happy. This home was marred by polygamy. Not only was her husband's affection shared with another woman, but Hannah had no children. She was barren, and she considered herself under the displeasure of God. Peninnah, who was her rival, grieved and provoked Hannah. Peninnah had children. There was no happiness in this yearly pilgrimage for Hannah because of her barrenness and her rival's taunts.

Elkanah was a devoted husband. He loved Hannah very much. He gave her double portions to sacrifice. But she wept and did not eat.

"Why do you cry, Hannah; why are you so grieved? Am I not better to you than ten sons?" Still Hannah would not be comforted.

HER PRAYER

One year at Shiloh she was in bitterness of soul, and prayed unto the Lord and wept grievously. And she vowed a vow unto the Lord and said, "O Lord of Hosts, if thou will indeed look on the affliction of thine handmaid, and remember me, and not forget thine handmaid, but will give unto thy handmaid a man child, then I will give him unto the Lord all the days of his life . . . ."

How fervently, how desperately did she cry unto the Lord! So ardently did she pray that Eli, the priest in charge, thought she was drunk. When he admonished her, she earnestly protested, "I am a woman of sorrowful spirit . . . I have poured out my soul before the Lord. For out of the abundance of my complaint and grief have I spoken."

Eli Encourages

Eli's answer seems to be an assurance that the God of Israel will grant her the petition that she has asked. This was an effectual, persistent prayer of a woman who wanted to be a mother. She talked to God of her affliction. She regarded her barrenness as an affliction. Too, Peninnah was a source of affliction to Hannah. And as she continues in her supplication, a spirit of submission is manifested; three times she calls herself, "the Lord's handmaid." A handmaid is a personal attendant, a very personal servant of the Lord. The handmaid was property by right of purchase. She indicated her submission to the will of God as the servant to the Master. The intensity of the prayer reveals the deep faith of Hannah. She is convinced that she is asking according to God's will. She was beseeching a gift from God to be used in his service and to his name's honor and glory. Surely a prayer such as Hannah's is sweet incense unto the throne of God. In her distress, Hannah surrendered herself completely. If I may have a son, "I will give him unto the Lord all the days of his life."

The prayer finished, she arose from her knees, went her way, did eat and her countenance was no more sad. She fell to her knees in bitterness of soul; she arose comforted, assured and happy.

> At the blessed hour of prayer
> Trusting in Him, we believe
> That the blessings we're needing
> We will surely receive.
> In the fulness of this trust
> We shall lose every care,
> What a balm for the weary
> Oh how sweet to be there!
> —Fanny J. Crosby

In the fulness of Hannah's trust, she did lose every care. As Sarah prayed for Isaac and Rachel prayed for Joseph, so Hannah prayed.

And they rose up early in the morning, and worshipped before the Lord and returned to their Ramah.

Hannah Is a Mother

"And the Lord remembered Hannah." She had asked God not to forget, and to remember. So the child was born, an answer to a deeply sincere prayer. And she named him Samuel, because "I have asked him of the Lord."

Elkanah and all his family continued to go to Shiloh and offered unto the Lord the yearly sacrifice and his vow.

But Hannah did not go. She confided in Elkanah that she would stay at home with the boy until he was old enough to "appear before the Lord and there remain forever." And her husband joined her in her plans. She had his full cooperation and support.

Hannah loved the little Samuel as dearly as a child was ever loved, but she did not forget her promise to the Lord.

HANNAH LENDS HER BOY

When Samuel was still a little boy, she packed his clothes in a neat bundle and brought him to Shiloh. When they had made the consecration offering, they brought him to Eli, the high priest.

"I am the woman who prayed," she said to Eli. "For this child I prayed; the Lord hath given me my petition which I asked of Him: Therefore I have lent him to the Lord; as long as he liveth he shall be lent to the Lord."

Hannah typifies the ultimate in motherhood. Truly unselfish and self-sacrificing, she wanted a son. She had him for a few years and she fulfilled her vow.

She missed him at home. She spent long hours making little coats for him, stitched in love. She went every year to worship and to see the child. She never asked him to come home.

"The child did minister unto the Lord before Eli, the priest." He was a true son of this mother's vow.

BLESSING ON PARENTS

Eli pronounced a benediction upon these God-fearing parents, "The Lord give thee seed of this woman, for the loan that she hath lent to the Lord."

Hannah bore Elkanah three sons and two daughters.

There was never any regret in Hannah's life. Never was her countenance sad. She broke into a song and a shout of victory. This song is to the Old Testament what Mary's is to the New Testament. In her first prayer she cast her burdens and cares upon the Lord. After her vow was fulfilled, her prayer was a prayer of joy. The providence of a wise God is confessed and praised.

STUDY SUGGESTIONS

Read 1 Sam. 1-2:21.

Discuss Hannah's grief, giving two reasons why she was so sad. (1 Sam. 1:4-5)

Do you think her attitude was justified?

Would these be just causes for a godly woman to grieve today?

To whom did she turn in her bitterness of soul? (1 Sam. 1:10)

What was the burden of her prayer? (1 Sam. 1:11)

Would this prayer be suitable for a godly woman who has a similar problem today? Would a prayer like this be answered through the aid of a physician?

Discuss Hannah's change of countenance. (1 Sam. 1:18)

What should be the Christian woman's source of strength and peace?

How is faith obtained? (Rom. 10:17)

Can you picture Hannah's joy at the birth of Samuel? Discuss the significance of the name.

Discuss the child as a gift from God.

What care did Hannah give to this precious gift? (1 Sam. 1:22; 2:19)

Why did she not go with her husband for a few years?

What would be the result today if Christian mothers would sincerely "lend their child to the Lord as long as he liveth"?

What lessons may be learned on rearing children? (Prov. 22:6; 23:13, 14) Do you agree?

What lesson may be learned from unison of parents?

What instruction did Paul give to parents? (Eph. 6:4)

Read the Song of Hannah. (1 Sam. 2:1-10)

    a. The source of her strength.

    b. Her faith in the greatness of Jehovah God.

    c. God's hand recognized in every condition of life.

    d. Her complete and absolute trust in God.

Discuss her attitude toward God.

How can Christian women today maintain this attitude?

Do you think this would increase beauty of character?

The privilege of prayer is ours at any moment. The Psalmist said, "Call upon me in the day of trouble; I will deliver thee; and thou shalt glorify me."

Michal

"Therefore Michal the daughter of Saul had no child unto the day of her death" (2 Sam. 6:23).

1 Sam. 14:49; 18:20-28;
   19:11-17
2 Sam. 3:13, 14; 6:16-23; 21:8
1 Chron. 15:29

A S WE JOURNEY through the Bible, seeing God's woman in the language, one is impressed with the honor and dignity accorded to the godly wife and mother. Her life is often narrated in the history of her family. Ofttimes her name is not given, but she is described through her husband and her children.

Not every wife and mother recorded in the Scriptures brings glory to Jehovah. Every good woman who appears in the Bible holds a significant place as a worthy example to be imitated; the evil woman stands with grim warning against her.

Whatever her station in life, God's purpose and plan for her was ever to be a helpmeet unto her husband.

MICHAL'S MOTHER

Ahinoam is first a wife and mother. She was Israel's first queen, the wife of King Saul. No doubt she had to be both father and mother to her daughters and her sons. This is her story, rather than the glamorous story of a queen.

Saul was a military leader; there was neither palace nor capital. He was absent from home much of the time. She was helpless in the face of his insane jealousy of David. Caring for him during periods of insanity must have beset her life with many problems.

She was the mother of two daughters and three sons. A noble son, Jonathan must have been a great consolation to his mother. His lack of ambition for the throne, his unselfish love for David is the classical story of beautiful friendship. Merab was the oldest princess in this first royal family. She was promised to David for a wife, "if thou wilt be valiant for me and fight the Lord's battle" (1 Sam. 18:17). Thus King Saul schemed that David would lose his life at the hands of the Philistines. David felt his station in life too lowly to be the son-in-law to the King.

But the King soon forgot his promise and Merab missed being the wife and queen to Israel's King David, "But it came to pass at the time when Merab, Saul's daughter, should have been given to David, that she was given unto Adriel, the Meholathite to wife" (1 Sah. 18:19). She bare Adriel five sons, but the Scriptures indicate she did not live to rear them (2 Sam. 21:8; 1 Sam. 18:19).

Michal was the younger daughter of Ahinoam. She loved David and this pleased Saul very much. Surely this daughter would assist him in causing David's death. He demanded the foreskins of one hundred Philistines as David's dowry for Michal. David promptly delivered the foreskins and Michal became his wife.

MICHAL AIDS DAVID

Saul now feared David more than ever and tried to think of some other plan by which to destroy this one who he believed would some day take his throne. David came to play on his harp before Saul, but the troubled king did not care for his sweet music. He picked up his javelin and aimed it at David, but David was watchful. He stepped aside quickly and ran out of the room. Saul sent messengers to David's home to guard the house and capture David in the morning.

But Michal dared her father's wrath by letting him down out of her window.

She concealed an image in the bed and told the soldiers her husband was ill. Saul commanded the soldiers to carry David in the bed to the palace. But when they came with the bed, the king realized Michal's deception. "And Saul said unto Michal, why hast thou deceived me so, and sent away mine enemy that he has escaped?" (1 Sam. 19:17).

She evaded her father's question, telling him that David had said to her, "Let me go; why should I kill thee?" (1 Sam. 19:17).

These must have been dark troublesome days for the queen-mother. She must have been anxious for the clever and courageous Michal who would defy her father, the king.

David ran away to Ramah. He remained an outlaw in exile until King Saul's death. After some time had passed King Saul arranged for Michal to marry Phaltiel. Perhaps her love waned in the absence of her husband, perhaps she did not dare antagonize the madman king, her father, again. Before David ever saw Michal again, he too married another. He married Abigail, the widow of Nobal who shared his highest ideals.

Polygamy had been accepted for many years. When David became king, he demanded that his wife Michal be returned to him. Phaltiel yielded, but followed Michal with tears to Bahurim.

SHE DESPISES DAVID

On the great day when the ark of the covenant was brought back to Jerusalem accompanied by 30,000 chosen men of Israel, Michal looked from her window and saw David girded with a linen ephod leaping and dancing before the Lord; and she despised him in her heart (2 Sam. 6:16).

Michal came out to meet David as he returned to bless his household. She scornfully mocked him, "How glorious was the King of Israel today, who uncovered himself in the eyes of the handmaids of his servants, as one of the vain fellows shamelessly uncovereth himself" (2 Sam. 6:20). Perhaps she thought his exhilarated rejoicing was beneath the dignity of a king. She seemed to share none of David's faith in God's protecting power.

The ephod, a part of the priestly apparel might have been a cause for her chagrin. Should not the king have worn the royal garments?

Her queenly dignity had been reproached by his mingling with the common people. Perhaps the years she had spent with Phaltiel had been the happiest years of her life. Both marriages had been arranged by King Saul, her father. King David could command whomever he chose, and she did not forget her husband's grief when she was taken from him.

David answered curtly, "It was before the Lord, which chose me before thy father and before all his house, to appoint me ruler over the people of the Lord, over Israel. Therefore will I play before the Lord. I will yet be more vile than thus, and will be base in my own sight, of the maid servants which thou hast spoken, of them shall I be had in honor."

Then follows the statement that was a reproach to every Israelite woman whether a maid servant or a queen—"Therefore Michal the daughter of Saul had no child until the day of her death" (2 Sam. 6:23).

Though she bore no child, she reared five sons of Merab, her sister, who was married to Adriel. And the Scripture says they were sons of Michal.

The first royal family of Israel seemed destined to tragedy and unhappiness. The beautiful, courageous young princess became a disillusioned woman oppressed with many tragedies.

She had been cruelly torn from two husbands. How her sister died is not told. But Michal in all probability saw the five boys she had reared hanged in revenge for her father's wickedness. Her father died a suicide rejecting and rejected of God. Every indication is that she also rejected God in her life.

STUDY SUGGESTIONS

Name the many problems with which the first queen of Israel was beset.

Do you think being a queen added greater responsibilities to her duty as a wife and mother?

Would you say Jonathan inherited his noble qualities from his mother?

Do you think her children were fully devoted to God? (1 Sam. 19:13)

Can the wife fully devote her children to the Lord if the father is not cooperative? What should this suggest about marriage?

Did Merab and Michal encourage the treachery of their father?

Read: 2 Sam. 6:23; 2 Sam. 21:8; 1 Sam. 18:19. What is your conclusion?

Who was the wife of Adriel? (2 Sam. 21:8b) How many sons did she bear him?

Discuss children's submission to parents' wishes in marriage. (Gen. 29:21-26; Judges 14:1-2, 3)

Michal adopted her sister's children. Was this a good way to fulfill the natural desire for motherhood?

Abigail

1 Sam. 25:3-42

"Blessed be the God of Israel which sent thee this day to meet me: And blessed be thy advice" (1 Sam. 25: 32-33).

THESE ARE the words of David unto Abigail, the wife of Nabal. This is a lovely compliment, gracious words to a woman to whom the Scriptures accord high praise. "And she was a woman of good understanding, and of a beautiful countenance" (1 Sam. 25:3). An unusual combination of both outward and inner beauty is ascribed to Abigail.

At this period in the history of Israel the marriage relationship was deeply degraded. Polygamy was accepted. As a result of this arrangement, the marriage relationship was profaned and women had become the slaves of men. Abigail's marriage is an example of a woman being married to the wrong man. The same verse of Scripture that describes Abigail's charm and worth says of her husband, "but the man was churlish and evil in his doings; and he was of the house of Caleb" (1 Sam. 25:3b).

Nabal was a wealthy man in Maon whose possessions were in Carmel. He had three thousand sheep and a thousand goats. Sullen, morose, ill-tempered, he loved only his money. One might ask why a woman as discreet and as intelligent as Abigail married such an ill-tempered miser as Nabal.

Leah had not been asked if she wanted to marry Jacob. The right of personal choice was quite frequently denied the woman.

Abigail's relationship with her husband must have been very trying. Nabal's surly disposition must have made it difficult for her or his servants to get along well with him.

David and his six hundred followers were in exile near Maon. He was hiding from King Saul. David heard in the wilderness that Nabal was shearing his sheep in Carmel. He and his men had often protected the sheep of Nabal.

Shearing time was feasting time. It was a busy season of hospitality and good will. We can imagine Abigail dressed becomingly in the bright colors of that day, extending kindness and courtesy to every guest. David's provisions were running low, so he sent ten of his men up the hill to Carmel to ask for a little food during this time of feasting.

His request was polite. Nabal's young men knew full well that David and his men had befriended them many times, so David instructed his men to remind Nabal of this.

HER HUSBAND'S MISTAKE

"And Nabal answered David's servants, and said, 'Who is David? And who is the son of Jesse? There be many servants nowadays that break away every man from his master'" (1 Sam. 25:10). Likely he belonged to King Saul's party, and had no sympathy for David. So he greeted David's men rudely and abusively sent them away empty-handed.

Abigail's good judgment and innate dignity had won the loyalty of the workers of her household. Through them she heard of Nabal's insult to David and his men.

ABIGAIL ACTS

Quick of perception, she lost no time; for she knew David and his men would not let this deliberate insult go unpunished. She also knew how foolhardy was her husband when he was drunk. What a surprising sight for David to see an hour or so later—Abigail the wife of Nabal, alighting from an ass, followed by asses laden with baskets of fruit, dried meal and bread, dressed sheep and skins of good wine! (1 Sam. 25:18).

In all womanly modesty she began to intercede for her husband. She assured David that her husband, true to his name Nabal, which means "fool," was not worth the thing that David was about to do to him.

In humility she told David that he was providentially hindered from shedding the blood of churlish Nabal. She graciously presented the gifts of food and begged David to forgive her trespasses.

She praised David, telling him, "because he had fought the battles of the Lord evil hath not been found in thee all thy days" (1 Sam. 25:28b).

She was convinced that David was marked for a great destiny. She predicted his ascendancy and rule over Israel and that "his soul would be bound in the bundle of life with the Lord thy God" (1 Sam. 25:29b). Not once did she overstep the bounds of modesty and decorum. She took no honor to herself for this mission of peace, for her keen awareness of David's situation, or for holding him back from bloodshed. In every sentence she manifested an unwavering faith in God and assured David he was an object of God's love and care. David accepted her gift and expressed a deep appreciation for her advice. "Blessed be the Lord of Israel which sent thee this day to meet me, and blessed be thy advice" (1 Sam. 25:32-33).

He was deeply impressed with her beauty and intelligence. She possessed every quality a man could desire in a wife.

Abigail without any delay hurried to her home. Nabal was still feasting and drinking. "He was very drunken" (1 Sam. 26:36). She wisely refrained from talking to him until next morning. "But it came to pass in the morning, when the wine was gone out of Nabal, and his wife told him these things, that his heart died within him and he became as a stone" (1 Sam. 26:37).

Ten days later "the Lord smote Nabal and he died" (1 Sam. 25:38).

HER REWARD

David heard that Nabal was dead. It seemed to him God intended Abigail to be his wife. He sent for her. There was no indecision; Abigail took her five maid-servants, followed the messengers of David, and became his wife.

Abigail and David seemed to have been perfectly suited to each other. They both had a deep and abiding faith in the providence of God. She was as humble and gentle as David was quick and impulsive. She was no doubt a source of inspiration and encouragement to David. She bore David one son and named him Chileab.

Ziklag was captured and burned by the Amalekites. All the women were taken captive. Among these women was Abigail. Later David defeated the enemy and rescued her.

STUDY SUGGESTIONS

Would you think that Abigail married for money?

Does money help or hinder a marriage?

Do you think she became David's wife because she was convinced that some day he would be King?

Contrast the personalities of Abigail and Nabal. Would this lead to strife in the home?

Is it ever necessary for the wife to ignore the lead of the husband?

Discuss Abigail's intercession to David (25:23-31). Discuss some traits of character revealed in this intercessory plea.

Give David's benediction. (25:32-35)

What had become of David's first wife? (25:44)

After reading 2 Sam. 2:1-4, would you consider this the happiest occasion of her life?

Discuss a Christian marrying a sinner: Could this contribute to the high divorce rate? Is marrying for money a factor in divorce? Is marrying a man to reform him a factor in divorce? Did Abigail's first marriage enable her to make a wise choice in her second one?

The Woman Of Endor

1 Sam. 28:7-25

"Behold, thine h a n d m a i d hath obeyed thy voice, and I have put my life in my hand" (1 Sam. 28:21).

NECROMANCY, SORCERY and familiar spirits were mediums employed by the heathen of Canaan to spread the evils of idolatry. These practices and those who indulged in them were an abomination to God (Deut. 18:4-9). Among the laws that Moses gave unto the Israelites, with the ten commandments, was the law against witchcraft. "Thou shall not suffer a witch to live" (Ex. 22:9-4).

Early in King Saul's reign he had been very zealous for the purity of Jehovah's worship, and he "had put away those that had familiar spirits and the wizards out of the land" (1 Sam. 28:3).

Samuel was dead; the Philistines were drawn up in battle in Shunem. Saul's army was encamped at Gilboa. When the King saw the host of the Philistines, he was afraid and his heart trembled greatly (1 Sam. 28:4-5). Saul had learned at long last that he could not run his life and his kingdom without God. "When Saul inquired of Jehovah, Jehovah answered him not, neither by dreams, nor by Urim, nor by prophets" (1 Sam. 28:6). Saul's early career was brilliant. Modestly he sought the advice of Samuel. He relied upon God. He fought down all of his enemies, Philistines, Ammonites, Moabites, Amalekites. He started well, but popularity and power caused his downfall.

Now he needed God. He needed Samuel. He had called; there was no answer.

SAUL'S WISH

Old, afraid and alone, the king said to his servants, "Seek me a woman that hath a familiar spirit, that I may go to her and inquire of her. And his servants said to him, Behold there is a woman who hath a familiar spirit at Endor" (1 Sam. 28:7).

Once he had sought to destroy her and all of her kind. Now disguised and under the cover of darkness he went down the road to Endor, which lay between Little Hermon and Mt. Tabor. He and his two servants came to the woman by night.

Let us imagine this woman very much like the women of her profession today. A cheap fortune-teller, a spiritualist, a wizened old woman with a turban bound upon her head, claw-like hands, piercing black eyes, and dark coarse skin. Perhaps she was adorned with gypsy-like jewelry in her ears, around her neck, upon her arms and around her ankles.

Her abode was a gloomy cavern or some unlighted hovel. She dared not show herself in the light of day, for it had been commanded, "Regard not them that have familiar spirits, neither seek after wizards, to be defiled by them: I am the Lord your God" (Lev. 19:31).

The once proud King of Israel who had rejected the voice of God, now sought the voice of the witch of Endor. And he said, "Divine unto me, I pray thee, by the familiar spirit, and bring me up whomsoever I shall name unto thee."

This woman with cunning caution reminds Saul, "Behold, thou knowest what Saul hath done, how he hath cut off those that have familiar spirits, and the wizards out of the land; wherefore then layest thou a snare for my life, to cause me to die?" (1 Sam. 28:9).

When Saul had assured her there would be no punishment, then the woman asked him, "Whom shall I bring up unto thee?" And when the woman saw Samuel, she cried with a loud voice; and the woman spoke to Saul and said, "Why hast thou deceived me? for thou art Saul."

SURPRISE

It was evident that she was very surprised and alarmed when she saw the departed Samuel. This was not at all what she expected, nor was it due to any occult power of the woman.

Saul recognized Samuel. He felt sure that God would give him a message through Samuel as in days gone by. And Samuel said to Saul, "Why hast thou disquieted me to bring me up?"

The King with his face to the ground told him he was in distress, and God had departed from him.

The vision was no illusion. None but Samuel could have answered, "wherefore then dost thou ask of me, seeing the Lord is departed from thee, and is become thine enemy?" (1 Sam. 28:16). He reminded him of the things he had spoken to him in his lifetime. He pronounced the death sentence upon Saul and his sons on the morrow at the hand of the Philistines. Saul was so overwhelmed with fear and fatigue that he swooned away.

The woman of Endor seemed to know perfectly that this was something totally different from those things with which she was familiar.

She cast away all pretense. No longer was she the fortune-teller of Endor. She became very kind and hospitable to a weary old man. She had his servants lay him upon her bed. She prepared an abundant meal for him, giving to him assistance and comfort. The woman of Endor still possessed womanly and noble traits.

Who can say to what heights of spiritual achievement she might have risen had she yielded herself to God instead of Satan? How sad and tragic that her type is present today—God-given talents being wasted by women who should be in the service of the Lord Jesus.

STUDY SUGGESTIONS

Where did this woman live? (1 Sam. 28:7c)

What was her sinful profession? (Lev. 19:31)

Read and discuss Deut. 18:9-14.

Describe Saul's sin. (1 Sam. 15:23)

What had he done to those with familiar spirits? (1 Sam. 28:3)

Tell of Saul's visit to the witch. (28:8-11)

Did she really call up Samuel? (28:12-14)

Give the prophet's message to Saul. (28:15-19)

What happened to indicate that the woman still had some feminine virtues? (28:21-25)

Does one renounce God if he turns to fortune-tellers? (1 Sam. 15:23; Lev. 19:31)

Who in Hades wanted to help his brothers? (Luke 16:27-28)

The answer? (Luke 16:29)

What was the final answer? (Luke 16:30, 31)

Bathsheba

2 Sam. 11:3; 12:24
1 Kings 1:11-31; 2:13-19
1 Chron. 3:5

". . . Is not this Bathsheba, the daughter of Eliam, the wife of Uriah, the Hittite?" (2 Sam. 11:3).

B ATHSHEBA was the daughter of Eliam (2 Sam. 11:3), called Ammiel in 1 Chron. 3-5 which means the "People of my God." This is a good indication that Bathsheba came from a God-fearing family. She was a very beautiful woman. Her husband was Uriah, the Hittite. Uriah was a brave and faithful general in David's army.

The Scriptures tell us that it was the time of year "when Kings go forth to battle" (2 Sam. 11:1). David had sent Joab, his servants, and all Israel against the Ammonites. Uriah was with Joab at the siege of Rabbah.

In the evening-tide David walked upon the roof of the king's house. This is yet a custom on flat-roofed houses in the East. "And from the roof he saw a woman washing herself; and the woman was very beautiful to look upon" (2 Sam. 11:2).

Many questions might arise in our minds: was there design in this? Was it the custom that women bathed nudely exposed to the view of anyone upon the roof of an adjoining house? Would a woman of modesty and refinement thus expose herself?

Likely King David gratified his whims freely in matters of beautiful women.

DAVID'S SIN

The Savior said, "whosoever looketh on a woman to lust after her hath committed adultery with her in his heart" (Matt. 5:28). David looked upon Bathsheba and lusted after her. The Bible frankly tells that the King "sent messengers and took her; and she came unto him, and he lay with her, for she was purified from her uncleanness; and she returned unto her house" (2 Sam. 11:4).

She conceived and informed David, "I am with child." The Scriptures do not tell us if she were terrified with guilt, or if she were exultant at the hold she might have over the King of Israel.

The king frantically tried to conceal the crime he had committed. Not only their honor, but their very lives were at stake; for death by the Law of Moses was the penalty for adultery.

At his request Joab sent Uriah to King David. He came to Jerusalem, no doubt thinking the King wanted a report on the war, completely unaware of David's fear and guilt. He would send Uriah to Bathsheba, thus shield her honor and conceal his crime. Murder was not in David's heart, nor any design to take Uriah's wife from him. But Uriah remained on guard with all the servants, and did not go home at all. David must have been alarmed and inquired why he did not spend the short leave at home. Uriah's answer was that of a brave, generous and faithful general, "I will not indulge myself, while Joab and the servants are exposed to hardships in the fields and even the Ark of the Lord is in danger."

David was now panicky; he made Uriah drunk, supposing he would hasten down to his house, but he remained with David's servants that night and the King's second attempt to conceal the sin had failed.

The conscience-stricken David wrote a letter to Joab. Treacherously he instructed Joab to place "Uriah in the forefront of the hottest battle and retire ye from him, that he may be smitten and die" (2 Sam. 11:15). Uriah delivered the letter unto Joab which carried his own death sentence.

ANOTHER SIN

Now David was guilty of murder to conceal the sin of adultery.

When the wife of Uriah heard of her husband's death, "she mourned for her husband" (2 Sam. 11:26)—very careful to observe all the customs and maintain the appearance of respectability. Perhaps she was grief-stricken over the turn the events had taken.

When the days of mourning were over, probably seven days, Bathsheba married the King of Israel. No doubt they both sought to hide the shame of her pregnancy.

David and Bathsheba were soon to realize that God is not mocked. The Lord sent Nathan the prophet to reprove David. He charged him with guilt, "Thou are the man" (2 Sam. 12:7b). David was overwhelmed with horror and brought into the dust before the Lord God. He cries unto Him,

"Have mercy upon me, O God, according to thy lovingkindness; according to the multitude of thy tender mercies blot out my transgression.
Wash me thoroughly and cleanse me from my sin.
For I acknowledge my transgression: and my sin is ever before me.
Against thee, thee only have I sinned and done this evil in thy sight; that thou mightest be justified when thou speakest and be clear when thou judgest" (Ps. 51:1-4).

David confessed his sin to Nathan. The prophet gave him hope of God's mercy but told him the child conceived in adultery would die. David fasted and prayed during the illness of the child. On the seventh day the child died. David ceased to grieve and spoke his beautiful elegy that has been even until this day a source of comfort in the hour of the death of loved ones, "But now he is dead, wherefore should I fast? I cannot bring him back again. I shall go to him, but he shall not return to me" (2 Sam. 12:23).

Her Children

Bathsheba bore David four sons, Solomon, Shimea, Shobab and Nathan. Solomon succeeded to the throne of his father David, and it is through this famous and favorite son that Bathsheba takes her place among the renowned women of the Bible.

In the genealogy of our Lord we read, "And David the king begat Solomon of her that had been the wife of Uriah" (Matt. 1:7b).

The Bible gives us no record of Bathsheba during the years of Solomon's youth. But in the First Book of the Kings we are given another glimpse of the beautiful Bathsheba.

Later Years

David was old and stricken in years. No longer could the brave old warrior who had united twelve war-torn tribes into a peaceful nation, cross the threshold of his bed chamber. It was a time of waiting; priest, prophet and soldier wanted to know why Adonijah, the king's oldest son had not been called to the bedside of his father for the blessings of the first born.

It was a time of conspiracy and intrigue. Joab, the captain of David's army and Abiathar, the high priest, were plotting to take the throne and proclaim Adonijah the King. Haggith the mother of Adonijah waited fearfully. The stately and beautiful Bathsheba waited with confidence. Had not David promised her that Solomon would be his successor: had not old Nathan, the prophet of God told her that God had chosen Solomon to sit upon David's throne? So Nathan came to Bathsheba and told her of the plot outside the city hall. She must have been highly regarded and a woman of influence to have been sought by the prophet Nathan. She hurried to the bedside of King David, not only to plead the throne for her son, but also for their lives. Every pretender for the throne would be slain, when the king should be proclaimed.

Wisdom, dignity, courtesy are all mainfested in this mother who pleads for her son.

And the king swore and said, "As the Lord liveth, that hath redeemed my soul out of distress, even as I swore unto thee by the Lord God of Israel, saying, Assuredly Solomon thy son shall reign after me, he shall sit upon my throne in my stead; even so will I certainly do this day" (1 Kings 1:29-30). He told his servants to bring his own mule from the stable and place Solomon upon it, then go with him to Gihon, where the priest Zadok should anoint Solomon with oil. Soon there was the sound of trumpets, and the shout of the people, "God save King Solomon."

BATHSHEBA'S INFLUENCE

Bathsheba's influence at court continued after the death of David. Her son, the king, extended to her every courtesy and honor due to the queen mother.

Adonijah, King Solomon's brother, had been allowed to live, "as long as he shall show himself a worthy man." He went to Bathsheba, asking her to petition the king that he might have Abishag, his father's young concubine. There is much revealed in this incident about Bathsheba: her kindness and her forgiveness. She intervened in his behalf. Although Solomon did not grant this request, he gave his mother the right to be heard. The king answered and said, "Why dost thou ask Abishag the Shunammite for Adonijah, ask for him the kingdom also; for he is mine elder brother" (1 Kings 2:23a). Adonijah was put to death that day.

Many of the Proverbs are attributed to Solomon. It is worthy of note that the Proverbs are filled with warnings against the strange woman who was a loose woman or a harlot. Could these be a parallel to his mother's experience? The closing chapter pictures the trusted wife and devoted mother as the ideal woman.

Today we can search deeply into the character of this wife and mother who was an ancestress of the Christ.

STUDY SUGGESTIONS

Why is the David and Bathsheba affair referred to as "David's sin"?

Can Bathsheba's conduct be condoned or justified?

Do modest women carelessly expose themselves to the gaze of men?

Does the attire of women and girls today contribute to lust of the men who see them?

Would a young woman attired in a brief bathing suit presenting herself to the gaze of men have a design in such exposure?

Why are Christian women instructed to adorn themselves in modest apparel? (1 Tim. 2:9)

Should Hollywood be the Christian's standard of modest dress?

Can we lay the whole guilt of this sin upon David? Was Bathsheba an accomplice?

What is the purpose in recording this and many other sins of such horrible and repulsive character?

What evidence is this that the Scriptures are of Divine origin?

What do we learn of God's mercy?

How did the Lord regard the sin of David? (2 Sam. 11:27b)

Read Psalms 51:1-4; 7-13. Discuss David's penitence and confession.

What assurance was given him? (2 Sam. 12:13)

Can we find anything to indicate sorrow and penitence in Bathsheba?

Discuss her influence over the King. (1 Kings 1:17, 29, 30)

Discuss her influence over her son. (1 Kings 2:16, 17)

Name and discuss incidents in her life that indicate an intelligent, a kind and a righteous woman.

Wherein was her great influence, as a wife, a mother or as a queen?

Read Titus 2:5. Discuss: *discreet, chaste, keepers at home.*

What is your emphasis on dress for your daughter? Do you dress your little girl to attract attention?

Are you teaching your children that the body is not an end in itself, but it is a means to an end?

Do you teach your little girl (and boy too) that the body as designed by God is for a lofty purpose?

Rizpah

2 Sam. 3:7; 21:8, 10, 11

"And Rizpah, the daughter of Aiah, took sackcloth, and spread it for her upon a rock, from the beginning of harvest until the water dropped upon them out of heaven, and suffered neither the birds of the air to rest upon them by day, nor the beast of the field by night" (2 Sam. 21:10).

RIZPAH, was a concubine for King Saul. At Saul's death she had been taken by his commander-in-chief, Abner. He and Ishbosheth, the son of Saul, a successor to the throne, quarreled over Rizpah. To take the king's concubine was tantamount to taking the throne. After the quarrel, Abner turned against the house of Saul and aligned himself with the house of David. Later he was stabbed to death by Joab, David's right hand man. Rizpah and King Saul had two sons, Armoni and Mephibosheth.

In the days of David there was a three year famine. When David inquired the reason for the famine of the Lord, it was made known to him that King Saul had broken an oath that Joshua had made to the Gibeonites. These people had deceived Joshua with their mouldy bread and old shoes. He concluded that they were not Canaanites—he thoughtlessly made a treaty with them in the Lord's name. They were permitted to live in Canaan as slaves of the Israelites. Through the years this treaty had been very carefully regarded. The oath Joshua had taken in the Lord's name in their behalf was broken when Saul made war against them.

THE HANGING

"Wherewith shall I make the atonement?" David inquired of the Gibeonites. The heartbreaking news came to Rizpah that seven of Saul's sons were to be hanged in Gibeah, as the Gibeonites had requested.

The king took Armoni and Mephibosheth and the five sons of

Merah and Adriel that were brought up by Michal. The sons and grandsons of King Saul were delivered to the Gibeonites, "and they hanged them in the hill before the Lord: and they fell all seven together, and were put to death in the days of the harvest, in the first day, in the beginning of barley harvest" (2 Sam. 21:9).

The sorrow and grief of this mother were the consequences of King Saul's sin, a sin in which she had no part.

RIZPAH'S MOURNING

She came in sackcloth, she who had worn the magnificent raiment of a queen; she spread sackcloth on the rock underneath the gallows upon which her sons had been slain. Some authorities suggest that a tent was also fashioned out of sackcloth and draped over the gallows to cover the bodies of her sons.

The broken-hearted mother kept her watch for five months, from the barley harvest until the season of rain. For five months Rizpah protected the bodies from the hawks and vultures that would consume the decaying corpses on the gallows. Night and day she guarded her dead. How weary must have been her vigil in the heat of the day, the dark of the night, fighting weariness, sleep, and the beasts of prey.

David was told of this mother's long wake. He ordered the bodies to be taken down, and he buried them with those of Saul and Jonathan. Her duty had been fulfilled to her children. She had glorified her motherhood. Only a devoted mother could have endured such intense suffering as that of Rizpah.

How many women, wives, daughters and mothers have sat by the bedside of loved ones, tenderly caring for them or grieving at their death! Then they go on to take up the duties of life silently and bravely.

STUDY SUGGESTIONS

Whose daughter was Rizpah? (2 Sam. 3:7a)

Was she ever a wife in the true sense of the word? Was she Saul's wife? Was she Abner's wife?

Compare the polygamous condition that existed in the Jewish age with the divorce evil that exists in the Christian age.

Would you say that the woman's responsibility was less then than now?

Discuss Rizpah as an example of mother love and sacrifice.

Read and discuss 2 Sam. 21:10—Does this indicate five months or until rain fell as a result of the atonement? Or the removal of the famine?

Did God require the sacrifice of Saul's sons? Were they not innocent of the alleged crime of their father?

Was a respectable burial of her sons by the king a reward for her great ordeal?

Solomon's Wives

1 Kings 3:1; 7:8; 11:1-8

"He maketh the barren woman to keep house, and to be a joyful mother of children. Praise ye the Lord" (Psalms 113:9).

THE POET in this psalm renders praise unto the Lord that he has made the childless woman a joyful mother, and given her a house to keep.

The Bible says that a man should "leave his father and mother and cleave unto his wife and they two shall be one flesh" (Gen. 2:24). Jesus added to this statement, "what therefore God hath joined together let not man put asunder" (Matt. 19:6).

This relationship of man and woman is stressed throughout the Bible; and as we read of the wives and mothers in the Scriptures, we are more and more certain of how man and woman were made for each other.

God's woman is revealed to us in every role from prophet to poet. Yet it is as a homemaker, wife and mother in which she plays the most honorable role and fulfills her God-given destiny.

The influence of a mother is stressed throughout God's Book: "As is the mother, so is her daughter" (Ezk. 16:44); "Walked in the way of his mother" (1 Kings 22:52b).

The reign of Saul, David and Solomon is a period of power—the United Kingdom.

STRANGE WOMEN

Bathsheba gave to the Hebrew nation a great son and a great king in Solomon; yet during his brilliant rule began the decline. At his death the kingdom was about to crumble, filled with rebellion and discontent. Perhaps we can find the explanation of his sad failure in this statement, "But King Solomon loved many strange women" (1 Kings 11:1).

Solomon's first wife was the daughter of Pharoah. Egypt was the wealthiest and most powerful country in the world when Solomon's reign was first begun. Peaceful alliance with this powerful neighbor was greatly desired. Political prestige also was gained in his marriage to Pharoah's daughter. This was a great event and no doubt added to his reputation as a man of wisdom.

The beginning of his apostasy was when he allowed political consideration to predominate God's law. Through Moses God had commanded his people before their entry into the promised land, "Neither shalt thou make marriages with them; thy daughter thou shalt not give unto his son, nor his daughter shalt thou take unto thy son. For they will turn away thy son from following me, that they may serve other gods; so will the anger of the Lord be kindled against you, and destroy thee suddenly" (Deut. 7:3-4).

Solomon made also a house for Pharoah's daughter. It was to the rear of his splendid royal palace and in his palace court. It was of costly stones and cedars, the same materials used in the "house of the Lord" (1 Kings 7:8-12). And Solomon brought up Pharoah's daughter out of the city of David unto the house he had built for her.

Turned Away His Heart

Pharoah gave the Canaanitish city of Gezer to his daughter, Solomon's wife. This alliance was so satisfactory and profitable that Solomon made coalition with many nations through marriage, "And he had seven hundred wifes, princesses, (1 Kings 11:3a) women of the Moabites, Ammonites, Edomites, Zidonians and Hittites. And he had three hundred concubines (1 Kings 11:3b); these were wives of second rank." "And his wives turned away his heart" (1 Kings 3:11c). "For it came to pass when Solomon was old, that his wife turned away his heart after other gods: and his heart was not perfect with the Lord his God, as was the heart of David his father." For Solomon went after Ashtoreth, the goddess of the Zidonians, and after Milcom the abomination of the Ammonites, and Solomon did evil in the sight of the Lord" (1 Kings 11:4-6). There is nothing to indicate that Solomon loved any women, or converted even one of his heathen wives. They were evidently women who loved money and all the things money can buy.

And in 1 Kings 11:9-13, we read of God's final ultimatum to the King. The Lord was angry with Solomon. He had broken the Deuteronomic law (Deut. 17:17). And unto Solomon he said, "I will surely rend the covenant from thee and give it to thy servant."

STUDY SUGGESTIONS

Read Genesis 2:18, 24; Matt. 19:6. Discuss the husband and wife relationship outlined in these Scriptures.

Discuss the two attitudes: "What am I going to get out of this marriage? What am I willing to put into this marriage?"

Did the marriages of Solomon indicate the first rather than the second?

What did his wives want?

What did he want?

Why was Rehoboam, his son, a weakling? (1 Kings 11:6b; 1 Kings 22:52)

Read Amos 3:3. Apply this to the husband and wife relationship.

Do you think one prolific cause of broken homes is religious differences?

Does every broken home have a court record? Isn't the home broken to begin with where the husband and wife do not conform to God's plan?

Do you believe the "hand that rocks the cradle rules the world"?
Explain: "Parents wonder why the streams are bitter when they themselves have poisoned the fountain." (John Locke)

Jeroboam's Wife

1 Kings 14:1-18

*"Every wise woman buildeth her
house; but the foolish plucketh it
down with her hands"* (Prov. 14:
1).

B Y NO MEANS are all the women whose lives are portrayed in the
Bible there for the reason that they are models of *chastity*. The
foolish woman who destroys her house with her hands teaches us the
danger and folly of partly clinging to God (Matt. 6:24).

Every woman, whether wise or foolish, that we read about in the
Bible has an important place in the history of the human race.

King Jeroboam and his wife the Queen had a son they called Abijah
(1 Kings 14:1-20). But one day the child became sick, and Jeroboam
said to his wife that she must disguise herself and go to Shiloh where
Ahijah the prophet lived and inquire of him what should become
of the child (1 Kings 14:1-3).

Jeroboam was the king who led Israel to sin. He was the first king
of the Northern Kingdom. He knew he had not pleased God when
he had set up golden calves, one in Bethel and one in Dan. He made
altars at those places to offer sacrifice to heathen gods. He appointed
common men to be priests; he set feast days at the same time of year
the feasts were held in Jerusalem. This was a great sin.

He was afraid to have the Lord's prophet know whom he was send-
ing to him. So he told the Queen to pretend she was some poor woman
in trouble. Then she took ten loaves of bread, some cakes, and a bottle of honey as a gift to the prophet. Although Ahijah was blind, the
Queen did not deceive him. He was forewarned of God.

"Come in thou wife of Jeroboam; why feignest thouself to be another? for I am sent to thee with heavy tidings." He then told her to
return to her husband and tell him that because he had made idols of
gold and caused his people to serve them and cast the Lord behind
their backs, evil would be brought upon the house of Jeroboam (1
Kings 14:7-12). The sick child was to die, "and the people of Israel
shall mourn for him and bury him because in him there was some
good toward the Lord." But his other sons and daughters would be
killed and their dead bodies thrown out into the streets and the

fields for the wild dogs and birds to eat.

Just as she entered her home city, Abijah took his last breath, and when she came into the room he was lying dead upon the bed.

STUDY SUGGESTIONS

What was King Jeroboam's sin? (1 Kings 12:20-29)

Name their sons. (1 Kings 14:1, 20b)

How did the Queen show obedience to her husband? (1 Kings 14:1-6) Was this commendable?

To what extent should wives obey their husbands? (Eph. 5:22)

Relate the message of doom she bore to her husband. (1 Kings 14:7-16)

Who killed her son Nadab? (1 Kings 15:27)

In what way did this wife and mother contribute to the downfall of the house of Jeroboam?

Was woman's low position in society at this time due to her own sin?

Jezebel

1 Kings 16:31; 18:4-19; 21:5-25

"But there was none like unto Ahab, which did sell himself to work wickedness in the sight of the Lord, whom Jezebel his wife stirred up" (1 Kings 21:25).

TYRE AND SIDON were commercial cities on the coast of the Mediterranean Sea in Phenicia—two great and famous cities. In Christ's opinion they were very little superior to Sodom and Gomorrah.

This land is of particular interest in relation to the Bible period known as the Period of Decline because of Jezebel, a Phenician princess, who became the wife of Ahab, king of Israel. Ethbaal, king of Tyre and Sidon, was the father of Jezebel. He established the worship of Baal and Asthoreth and was a priest of Asthoreth, the female divinity of Phenicia. He came to the throne by slaying his brother.

Jezebel inherited her father's religion and ambition for power. She was very zealous and fanatic for Baalism. She established this sensual and revolting religion in Israel. She housed and fed 450 priests of the sun-god Baal. She built a grove near her palace where an annual festival was held which demanded the gift of virgins. Her complicated, sensual surroundings and attendants brought into Israel the impure worship of Baal which was degrading and destructive to manhood and womanhood.

Her Influence

Jezebel was the power behind the throne. Ahab was the weak and spineless son of the wicked king Omri. Like many queens of history her power over her husband was evil. In her fanaticism she became the enemy of Israel's God. A great conflict ensued between Jehovah and Baal, as it was fought between Elijah and Jezebel.

She is an example of every thing a woman ought not to be. She converted her husband to the heathen god, and brought up her children in its belief. She not only dominated her household, but she in turn ruled Israel with an iron hand.

"For it was so when Jezebel cut off the prophets of the Lord, that Obadiah took an hundred prophets and hid them by fifty in a cave, and fed them with bread and water" (1 Kings 18:4).

There had been three years when neither dew nor rain had fallen, according to the prophecy of Elijah the Tishbite. The Lord directed him to flee to the wilderness and there he was providentially cared for. At last it was time for him to show himself to Ahab and to fight the false religion that was fast claiming the people of Northern Israel. Mount Carmel was the scene of a great and dramatic contest between the God of Israel and Jezebel's god, Baal.

The fiery old prophet's cry rang out unto apostate Israel, "How long will you halt between two opinions? If the Lord be God, follow him; but if he be Baal, then follow him."

The sacrifice was slain and laid upon the altar, with no fire under it. The prophets of Baal would call upon him to answer by fire. Elijah would call on the name of the Lord, "and the God that answereth by fire, let him be God" (1 Kings 18:21-24).

All day the heathen prophets cried unto the dumb idol, "but there was no voice nor any that answered" (1 Kings 18:26b).

Elijah prayed to the omnipotent God, "and the fire of the Lord fell and consumed the burnt sacrifice, and the wood, and the stones, and the dust, and licked up the water that was in the trench" (1 Kings 18:38). The people fell on their faces and said, "the Lord he is the God" (18:39). The false prophets were brought to the brook Kishon and there they were slain.

Elijah told Ahab, "There is the sound of an abundance of rain" (1 Kings 48:41b). And he prayed again, and the heaven gave rain (Jas. 5:17a).

A Woman's Anger

Jezebel was infuriated when Ahab told her that Elijah had slain the prophets, and she vowed that she would do to Elijah as he had done to them. Again he fled for his life into the wilderness.

In the little city of Jezreel Omri, the father of Ahab had built an ivory palace. It was here that wicked Jezebel continued to dominate Israel. The palace was on a hill, commanded a view of the mountains and valleys surrounding the little city. Just across from the king's garden was the fine vineyard of Naboth. Ahab desired the vineyard for a herb garden, but Naboth did not care to sell the vineyard. Jezebel was indignant that a subject of the king would have the affront to refuse his king, "Dost thou now govern the kingdom of Israel?" (1 Kings 21:7). There was contempt and arrogance in her voice as she promised, "I will give thee the vineyard of Naboth, the Jezreelite" (1 Kings 21:27b).

With the king's signature and his seal she sent a letter to the elders and the nobles. These men did as Jezebel had instructed them. "And there came two men, children of Belial, and witnessed against him, even against Naboth, saying, Naboth did blaspheme God and the king." Then they carried him forth out of the city and stoned him with stones, that he died" (1 Kings 21:13).

When Jezebel heard that Naboth was dead, heartlessly she says to the king, "Arise, take possession of the vineyard of Naboth, the Jezreelite, which he refused to give thee for money: Naboth is not alive, but dead" (1 Kings 21:15).

The word of the Lord came to Elijah; he was told to meet Ahab in Naboth's vineyard and in the very place where Naboth died the Lord said the dogs would lick Ahab's blood. The house of Ahab would be completely destroyed, and "the dogs would eat Jezebel by the wall of Jezreel" (1 Kings 21:23).

The prophecy was literally fulfilled: Ahab was killed in battle, and the dogs licked up his blood.

Elisha anointed Jehu king, and he was commissioned to avenge the blood of the prophets and servants of the Lord.

Jezebel continued her wicked and evil influence over Israel about ten years after Ahab's death. Ahaziah, her eldest son did evil in the sight of the Lord, and walked in the way of his father and his mother. He reigned only two years and died when he fell from a window. Again God's word was sure and steadfast. The next son, Jehoram, ruled seven years. He was assassinated by Jehu and his body cast into the vineyard which had belonged to Naboth. Before taking Jehoram's life, he denounced the queen mother's whoredoms and witchcrafts.

She killed the prophets, drove Elijah into hiding and forced all but seven thousand men of Israel to bow to Baal. She continued to be an evil and wicked queen until the day of her death.

A heartless woman is more dangerous than a heartless man. A God-fearing woman does often excel men in goodness. The godly woman can bless lives more than man can ever attempt to do. Art, music and poetry eulogize the noble women of humanity.

"The ideal which the wife and mother makes for herself, the manner in which she understands duty and life, contain the fate of the community. Her faith becomes the star of the conjugal ship, and her love the animating principle that fashions the future of all belonging to her. Woman is the salvation or destruction of the family. She carries its destinies in the folds of her mantle."—Henri F. Amiel in *Light from Many Lamps*.

The woman who surrenders her innate dignity and goodness sinks deeper into sin and becomes more brutal than man.

She Tempts the King

When Jehu entered the city, Jezebel placed herself before the window, her face painted and her head adorned with a tiara. Even on that last day she sought to conquer and disarm Jehu.

As Jehu entered in at the gate, she said, "Had Zimri peace, who slew his masters?" Some interpret this as intended to conciliate; others to taunt and provoke.

He commands her to be thrown down. She is dashed to pieces by the fall, and the brutal Jehu trampled her mangled body under his horses' feet.

Jehu callously went in and ate and drank and ordered the cursed woman to be buried, "for she is a king's daughter" (2 Kings 9:34b). She was truly of a very high lineage. She was daughter of the King of Tyre; wife of Ahab, king of Israel; mother of Jehoram, king of Israel; mother-in-law of Joram, king of Judah; and grandmother of Ahaziah, king of Judah.

When they would have buried her, all that could be found was the skull, and the palms of her hands. How literal was the prediction, "and the dogs shall eat Jezebel by the wall of Jezreel" (1 Kings 21:23). She had not the honor of a tomb. The dogs had eaten the flesh of this woman who dared to live and rule without God.

What a gruesome lesson to apostate Israel. How deep are the counsels of God and how terrible are his judgments! Jezebel's evil did not die with her. Her daughter, Athaliah, walked in the footsteps of her mother. She was the wife of Jehoram, king of Judah. She promoted the worship of Baal in the Southern kingdom. Her son Ahaziah came to the throne after the death of his father; when he was slain by Jehu, Athaliah seized the throne. After six years she was supplanted by Jehoash and killed.

The name Jezebel carries with it reproach; it is a synonym for whoredom, witchcraft and seduction.

In Revelation 2:20 we read: "That woman Jezebel which calleth herself a prophetess, to teach and seduce my servants to commit fornication and to eat things sacrificed unto idols."

What a terrible thought, that someday this wicked woman will be judged before the seat of Christ!

As the Home Decays

The history of Israel recorded in the Old Testament shows that when the home decays, the nation heads toward destruction. This period

in Bible history called the Period of Decline is a historical drama of
the decay of the Hebrew Nation, but it is first the account of the
failure of the home.

The Lord through Moses gave the instruction that would make a
strong and mighty nation, "And these words I command thee this day
shall be in thine heart, and thou shalt teach them diligently unto thy
children" (Deut. 6:6-7b).

How miserably the mothers and fathers had forgotten this command.
Israel was drifting further and further into apostasy.

There is a story of how Henry W. Grady went to the Capitol of the
United States to collect material for an article he was writing.

"And this is the Capitol of the United States," he remarked as he
gazed at the imposing structure. On his way home, he spent the night
with friends, a poor family in a small house. In that home he was invited
to join them in Scripture reading and prayer which was their daily custom.
Afterwards he wrote, "I have been to the Capitol of the U. S.; but it is
not in Washington; it is in the American home where Christian father and
mother respect and read the Bible and where children are reared in the
teaching of Christ."

The Christian home should truly be the Capitol of America, but
actually so many of the "homes" can only be put in quotation marks.
They are not real homes. They are broken homes, broken by illness,
by desertion, by drink. Mothers have left the home to work for money.
There are so many things we want that *only money can buy.* Forgotten
are the things that money cannot buy. The woman's God-given sphere
is the home, but we have in a sense rebelled against this order—the
father as the bread-winner, and the mother the helpmeet.

A very sad picture on the Lord's Day is a father and the children
at worship—the mother not present, behind the counter in some drug
store or at a common drink stand. Granting there are some instances
when it is necessary for the mother to help supply material things
needed for a growing family, how very carefully should that mother
be not to make material values more important than spiritual values.

The influence of the home upon the child is the prime source of
moral and spiritual training. The child's character is fixed for good
or ill by the time he reaches school age. Neglected in these early
years, the most promising time in his life has been lost.

God told parents through Moses to talk to their children, "when
they sit in the house, when they walk by the way, when they lie down
and when they rise up." How much time does this leave the mother
for a job outside the home?

A woman answered the knock on her door; the man who knocked
asked one question, "Does Jesus live here?" She was so astonished,
she closed the door in his face. Later her husband said, "Why didn't

you tell him that we go to Bible school and worship and read the Bible occasionally?"

"I know that, but he asked, 'Does Jesus live here?' Frankly, I don't know." What about your home—does Jesus live in it?

It is later than we think, time is short, eternity is long. How earnestly should we pray, "Oh, Jehovah, make me a better parent."

Let the fine noble women of the Bible encourage and inspire us. Let the evil and wicked ones such as Jezebel be a warning against neglect and carelessness in doing God's will.

STUDY SUGGESTIONS

Define the Period of Decline.

With what event did it begin?

With what event did it end?

The length of time and the Scriptures studied. (388 years; 1 Kings 12-2 Kings 25)

What dispensation? (See any outline of Old Testament History, Roy H. Lanier, Bible History; Bible Women, Coleman Overby)

In what environment was Jezebel reared?

To what extent are homes the product of their environment? (The tenement, the slums.)

Discuss Jezebel's influence as a wife, as a mother. (1 Kings 21:25; 1 Kings 22:51-53; 2 Kings 11:1; 2 Chron. 24:7; 1 Kings 22:52; 2 Kings 3:2)

Did Jezebel's influence affect the later life of Israel?

Compare the nature of man and woman. (1 Cor. 11:7; Gen. 1:27; Ps. 8: 6-8; Gen. 1:26-28; 1 Tim. 2:15; 1 Cor. 11:9; 1 Cor. 11:8; Gen. 2:2-23; Gen. 2:18; 1 Pet. 3:7)

Does she not by nature have a finer sensibility, a deeper emotional nature?

If she surrenders this nature, does she become more brutal than man?

Widow of Zarephath

1 Kings 17: 8-24
Luke 4:25, 26

"But unto none of them was Elias sent save unto Sarepta, a city of Sidon, unto a woman that was a widow" (Luke 4:26).

I N CONTRAST to the Phoenician princess Jezebel, the avowed enemy of the prophet Elijah, is the unnamed widow of Phoenicia. Zarephath was eight miles south of Zidon (or Sidon) on the road to Tyre in Phoenicia.

Now God had told Elijah where to hide from Jezebel. Elijah had hurried away from the King's palace to a hiding place by the Brook Cherith. So he went and did according to the word of the Lord. "And the ravens brought him bread and flesh in the morning and bread and flesh in the evening; and he drank of the brook" (1 Kings 17:6).

The brook dried up; there had been no rain in the land for two and one half years, God having sent the drought as a testimony against the idolatry that Jezebel had brought to Israel.

"Take heed to yourselves, that your heart be not deceived, and ye turn aside, and serve other gods, and worship them. And the Lord's wrath be kindled against you, and he shut up the heaven, that there be no rain, and the land yield not her fruit; and lest ye perish quickly from off the good land which the Lord giveth you" (Deut. 11:16-17).

Then God spoke to Elijah again and told him to go to the heathen city, Zarephath. God told him he would be cared for by a widow in that city.

Christ said there were many widows in Israel, but Elijah was sent to none of them. He was sent to the widow whose name is unknown. Now the King's men were searching for Elijah, and he had to cross through the land of Israel, but he was not afraid to obey God's voice. He approached Zarephath with positive assurance that God would continue to supply all his needs.

Near the gates of the city Elijah saw a woman gathering sticks. He saw by her dress that she was a widow. Perhaps he thought, "This is the widow to whom the Lord hath sent me."

Let us focus our attention on this widow. Famine was in the land, famine because the idolatry of a wicked woman has supplanted the true worship of Jehovah. Christ implied there was not one widow in all Israel to whom a man of God could go for hospitality.

A POOR WOMAN

A woman and a little boy were hungry. Her husband was dead. The early rains failed and the harvest failed. Despair was in her heart. She would bake the last cake and then there was nothing left for her and her son, but death by starvation.

As she gathered sticks she saw Elijah, clad in coarse clothing and wearing the mantle of the prophet. He spoke to the woman and asked for a drink of water. As she was going in search of water, he called to her and said, "Bring me I pray thee a morsel of bread in thine hand" (1 Kings 17:11).

This was putting the widow's faith to an extraordinary trial: to take and give to a stranger the small pittance necessary to keep her child alive was almost too much to be expected.

Now the widow turned around to speak to the stranger who was asking for both food and water. She said, "I have no bread to give you. I have only a handful of meal in a barrel and a little oil in a cruse.

I am gathering two sticks that I may go in and dress it for me and my son that we may eat and die" (1 Kings 17:12).

In her despair the prophet of the Lord came to her with a message of hope, "Fear not, he said, go and do as thou hast said, but make me a little cake thereof first, and bring it unto me, and after make for thee and thy son" (1 Kings 17:13). A message of assurance but a trying request. "For thus saith the Lord God of Israel, the barrel of meal shall not waste, neither shall the cruse of oil fail, until the day that the Lord sendeth rain upon the earth" (1 Kings 17:14).

Great things are so simply stated in the Scriptures that we are apt to miss their significance.

FAITH AND OBEDIENCE

The faith, courage and self-denial of this woman are pictured in this brief statement, "And she went and did according to the saying of Elijah and she and he and her house did eat many days" (1 Kings 17:15).

She must have experienced great astonishment as she prepared the meal, the oil and water, frying the prophet's cake first—and the meal and oil were not exhausted.

This miracle continued one year according to the word of the Lord which he spoke through Elijah. She, her son and the Man of God were sustained and fed by the Almighty God.

The humility of a deep faith characterized this impoverished widow. She is like another in the days of our Lord of whom He said, ". . . but she of her want did cast in all that she had, even all her living" (Mk. 12:44). And as he beheld the rich who gave much, he declared unto his disciples, "This poor widow hath cast in more than all they which have cast into the treasury."

The Widow of Zarephath gave "even her living" with all faith and confidence that there would be more.

"Faith comes by hearing, and hearing by the word of God" (Rom. 10:17). This woman's cares far exceeded her ability to cope with them. There comes a time when God is all there is left. He is always present, but not always recognized. Despair and death for her son were in her future, so when Elijah brought her a knowledge of God, her ready acceptance is proved by her works. She provided shelter as well as food and drink to the prophet. "And God is able to make all grace abound toward you: that ye, always having all sufficiency in all things may abound unto every good work" (2 Cor. 9:8).

These words (spoken hundreds of years later) might have been spoken to this woman who was a widow indeed. She "had all sufficiency in all things." How different was Jezebel, the queen of Israel, who might have had the same faith based upon a knowledge of God.

She rejected Elijah's message and his warnings; she fought God until the day of her death.

On Trial

The widow demonstrated her faith in God's providence; now her faith was to be on trial. When her son died, her faith wavered and she upbraided Elijah bitterly. "What have I to do with thee, O Man of God? Art thou come unto me to call my sin to remembrance and to slay my son?" (1 Kings 17:18).

Elijah answered, "Give me your son." He picked up the lifeless body of the child and carried him upstairs to the loft. He placed the child upon his bed and prayed earnestly to God, stretching himself three times upon the child, "O Lord, My God, let this child's soul come into him again" (1 Kings 17:21). Then the Lord heard Elijah's prayer and restored life into the child. He brought the child to his mother saying, "See thy son liveth."

The widow confessed her faith anew, "Now by this I know that thou art a man of God, and the word of the Lord in thy mouth is true" (1 Kings 17:24).

God has great pity and concern for his creatures. He sent to this Phoenician woman the wonderful teacher, Elijah. He taught her that God sustains and controls and guides. "If God be with us, who can be against us?" (Romans 8:31).

Where faith is, there is courage, there is fortitude, there is steadfastness and strength . . . Faith bestows that sublime courage that rises superior to the troubles and disappointments of life, that acknowledges no defeat except as a step to victory; that is strong to endure, patient to wait, and energetic to struggle . . . Light up, then the lamp of faith in your heart . . . It will lead you safely through the mists of doubt and the black darkness of despair; along the narrow, thorny ways of sickness and sorrow, and over the treacherous places of temptation and uncertainty" (James Allen, *Light from Many Lamps*).

"I will lift up mine eyes unto the hills, from whence cometh my help,
My help cometh from the Lord which made Heaven and Earth."
—Psalms 121

STUDY SUGGESTIONS

Discuss the extent of the famine and the reason. (1 Kings 17:1; Deut. 16-17)
How must the innocent suffer because of the evil? (Num. 16:22)
Was the widow of Zarephath suffering because of the wicked Jezebel?
Picture the widow's dark despair. (1 Kings 17:22)
Discuss Elijah's trying request. (17:13)
What miracle was performed? (17:14-15)

What lesson did the woman learn by this miracle? (Deut 4:31; Deut. 7:21; 10:17; 2 Cor. 3:15; Acts 10:34; Matt. 19:26; Mk. 10:27)

Study the Prophet Elijah. (1 Kings 17:1-23; 1 Kings 18:2-46; 1 Kings 19: 1-20; 2 Kings 1-2; Matt. 17:3)

Discuss widows: God's care for them. (Ex. 22:22; Deut. 14:29; 16:11, 14; Deut. 26:12; Acts 6:1; Acts 9:39-41)

What is pure religion? (Jas. 1:27)

What reference did Jesus make to the widow of Zarephath? (Lk. 4:25-26)

The Shunammite Woman

2 Kings 4:8-37; 8:1-6

"And it fell on a day that Elisha passed to Shunem, where was a great woman, and she constrained him to eat bread" (2 Kings 4:8-37).

SHUNEM, a small village in the tribe of Issachar, was the home of one of the unnamed women of the Old Testament. She is called a great woman, and as her story unfolds we see a woman remarkably great in faith, contentment, hospitality and wisdom. In the Scriptures she is referred to as the Shunammite. It is thought that she was the sister of Abishag, another Shunammite well known in the history of David. The Song of Solomon is the story of a lovely maiden of Shunem.

The Shunammite was evidently a woman of wealth and prestige. Her house was located on a much traveled road that led from Nazareth to Jerusalem across the Esdraelon Plain. In his labors among the ten tribes, Elisha must have often passed in front of the great woman's house. It must have been common knowledge that Elisha had inherited the mantle of Elijah. Perhaps the miracles of these two mighty prophets were frequently subjects of conversation among the inhabitants of Shunem. This man of God, this Elisha, would be known for having multiplied the oil in the jars and vessels of a prophet's widow. Oppressed by a merciless creditor, she was enabled to pay her debt and live. These miracles must have produced faith in the heart of this woman of Shunem.

One translator says she was a woman fearing sin. She believed that Elisha was a prophet of the true God. This woman considered it an honor and a privilege to show her respect to such a great man by entertaining him and his servant. And so as oft as he passed by her house he turned in to eat bread. In Biblical days to offer food and shelter meant even more than that—it meant friendship and protection. It was the rankest treachery for a man to turn against one with whom he had eaten bread.

HOSPITALITY

When Elisha accepted the Shunammite's hospitality, it meant an everlasting friendship between them. Hospitality is more than a gracious gesture, it is a Christian virtue. "I was an hungred and you gave me meat" (Matt. 25:35). "Given to hospitality" (Romans 12:13) is listed as a Christian attribute. It is a requirement for a bishop (1 Tim. 3:2). Peter warns us that hospitality should not be given grudgingly (1 Peter 4:9). In Hebrews it is pointed out that we may be entertaining angels unaware (Heb. 13:2).

She had married an old man while she herself was comparatively a young woman. She had a good home, the confidence of her husband. They were respected in the village. In this marriage the wife seemed to be the active and responsible person in the home. She did not disregard the husband as her head, but asked his permission and approval in all that she did.

HER PLAN

Small deeds are often stepping stones to greater service and labors of love. One day this woman said to her husband, "I perceive that this is a holy man of God which passeth by us continually. Let us make a little chamber, I pray thee, on the wall: and let us set for him there a bed, and a table, and a stool, and a candlestick: and it shall be when he cometh to us, that he shall turn thither" (2 Kings 4:9-10). The upper room was reached by an outer stairway. Let us visualize the room as a cool and quiet retreat. Perhaps there was a rug of goat's hair on the floor, a bright coverlet on the bed and a jug of cool water on the table. Thus they built a special room for Elisha and his servant. God's prophets have ever put their stamp of approval upon the home and the family. How often God selected a certain home for a special work. And what could be a greater service than providing food and shelter for one whose life is devoted to the Lord God. The home is enriched by these contacts.

Elisha wanted to repay this woman for her kindness. He inquired what might be done for her, if she would desire a favor from the king or the captain of the host. And she answered, "I dwell among my own people." She was perfectly satisfied and content with her lot in life. She lived on the best terms with her neighbors. She had no desire to make a change. How few women there are who would not sacrifice every thing they possessed for honors, popularity and parade. Truly she was a great woman! Elisha and Gehazi, his servant, discussed the matter. Gehazi answered, "She hath no child and her husband is old." The childless woman in Israel was looked upon with pity. The deep longing in the heart of this woman was *not to be honored by the king.* And when Elisha said, "About this season, according to the time of life, shou shall embrace a son," (2 Kings 4: 16a), hope lights her face and voice. "Nay, my lord, do not lie to thy handmaid." That is, "May thy words be true!" These words were spoken in the long ago to Abraham by the Lord in the Plains of Mamre; and Sarah, listening, laughed. Like Sarah, she could scarcely believe this promise. But she did conceive and the next spring her son was born. It is certain that she recognized this child as a gift from God, and her faith and adoration were increased.

A Tragedy

A few years passed by and the child grew old enough to follow his father about. One day he went with his father to the harvest field. It was the hot season of the year. As he ran playing in the sunshine, suddenly he became ill. He called to his father, "My head, my head." The father told a servant to carry the child to his mother. Has it not ever been thus? "Carry him to his mother." Sad indeed when sickness and death come and there is no mother to whom the child can be carried.

When the servant came bringing the sick boy, she held him on her lap until noon. *Then he died.* Not one cry of anguish did the mother make; her trust in the God who gave this child was supreme. She carried the child to the prophet's room and laid him on the prophet's bed. She called at once for a servant and prepared to go at once and find Elisha. It was a long ride to Mount Carmel. Faith knows no distance and so she hurries, urging the servant, "Drive and go forward." Hers was a trust that did not for one moment falter or doubt.

Elisha saw the woman coming far down the road, and he sent Gehazi to meet her. He was instructed to ask if it were well with her, her husband and her child. The woman answered, "It is well." And when she came to the man of God, she caught him by the feet; but Gehazi came near to thrust her away. And he spoke, "Let her alone for her soul is vexed within her: and the Lord hath hid it from me, and hath not told me." Even now, she does not say her son is dead. Finally the woman cried, "Did I desire a son of my lord? Did I not say, Do not deceive me?"

So he told his servant to take his staff and hurry on to Shunem and place the staff on the face of the child. She implored, "As the Lord liveth, and as thy soul liveth, I will not leave thee." Elisha went with her. They met the servant returning; when he came to them he said, "I have obeyed your words, but the child is not awakened."

The Cure

The prophet now understood the mother's distress; *the child is dead.* He shut the door to the room and began to pray earnestly that God would cause life to come into the child again. He stretched himself upon the child until his body grew warm. And the child sneezed and opened his eyes. He called Gehazi, and said, "Call this Shunammite." And when she was come unto him, he said, "Take up thy son" (2 Kings 4:36).

No words could express the feelings of this noble woman. She fell down at his feet in voiceless gratitude. Her marvelous faith had been sustained. Yet there is every indication that had this son not been restored, this great woman, leaning strongly upon her faith, would have said, "It is well."

Christian mothers, too pass through rough and trying times. They should ever strive to glorify God in every experience of life. "We know that all things work together for good, to them that love God, and are called according to His purpose" (Romans 8:28).

SHE MOVES

From the day that this woman offered to Elisha the hospitality of her home, she lived in a spirit of victory. Her story continues: "Then spake Elisha unto the woman whose son he had restored to life, saying, Arise and go thou, and thine household and sojourn wheresoever thou canst sojourn: for the Lord hath called for a famine: and it shall come upon the land for seven years" (2 Kings 8:1).

She left Shunem and went into the land of the Philistines that she might escape the famine. After seven years she returned to find that her house and land had been confiscated. She was still resourceful and capable. When faced with difficulties, her courage never wavered; her decision was astute and she went to the proper source for the solution. She kept silence until she could go unto King Jehoram and cry unto him for her house and her land.

At that moment Gehazi at the king's request was telling him all the great things Elisha had done. As he was telling the king how Elisha had restored a dead body to life, the Shunammite walked in. Gehazi said, "My Lord, O king, this is the woman, and this is her son, whom Elisha restored to life." This was a very providential occurrence. "Restore all that was hers, all the fruits of the field since she left the land, even until now" (2 Kings 8:6b). Thus commanded the king.

AN EXAMPLE

This Shunammite's life is an inspiring example to women today. She had a receptive mind. She believed in God. She shared her food and home with the prophet of God. The fruits of her faith were manifested in her home. She was a happy and contented wife. In hours of trial she was quiet and serene. In anguish of spirit, even as her child lay dead, she hastened to the man of God, who she knew could restore her son. And when he asked about the child, she could answer,

"It is well." When she was forced to leave her home, there is not one word of complaint. The wealthy woman sojourned in a foreign land for seven long years. It seems very possible that during the drought her husband died; his name is not mentioned when they returned home. Land and house both gone, she calmly and energetically pleads for her son's inheritance before the king. Faith is indeed the victory that overcomes the world, as this woman even now does testify.

> Faith is a silvered brightness in the soul:
>   A shaft set there to point the way to heaven,
> And carved upon it is a lettered scroll,
>   Its words miraculously given
> To guide the traveler on his shining way
>   Upon the road today.
> God help me keep my faith undimmed by tears,
>   And uncorroded by the rust of years.

—GRACE NOLL CROWELL, *Songs of Faith*[1]

STUDY SUGGESTIONS

Do you think this woman "usurped authority over her husband"? State reasons for your answer.

Name some things that indicate strongly that she kept her proper place in the home.

Has God or society decreed that woman be a helpmeet for man? Give Scriptures to sustain your position.

Is hospitality enjoined upon the Christian today?

Do reputable hotels, motels and tourist cabins relieve Christians of this obligation?

Is the home enriched that extends hospitality to the visiting preacher?

Discuss the attitude of one's saying, "I had him last time. I do not have to take him again."

How can we foster hospitality in our children?

Should it ever be too much trouble to make our children's friends welcome in our homes?

Name the trials of this woman's faith and how she met them.

Name some things our faith should do for us. (Mark 5:36; Phil. 4:13; Matt. 6:33; Matt. 21:22; Rom. 8:37; Phil. 4:11; Titus 2:14.)

Give a word picture of a great woman. Would this not be the description of a Christian woman?

---

[1] Taken from *Songs of Faith* by Grace Noll Crowell. Copyright 1939, Harper & Brothers. Used by permission.

Athaliah

2 Kings 8:26; 11:1-20
2 Chron. 22:1-12

"He also walked in the ways of the house of Ahab: for his mother was his counsellor to do wickedly" (2 Chron. 22:3).

A THALIAH was the only queen ever to reign in the kingdom of Judah. She was the granddaughter of the politically ambitious Omri who obtained the throne by massacre. She was the evil daughter of Ahab, the successor to the throne of his slaughterous father. Her mother was Jezebel, who was the personification of evil.

Samaria was the capital of the Northern Kingdom of Israel. Samaria was built by Omri and here was located the royal palace, surrounded by groves, bubbling springs and Baal temples. It was in this atmosphere of immorality and godlessness that Athaliah was reared.

Her Influence Against God

The kingdom of Judah had remained apart from the lewd idolatries established in Israel by Jezebel. Athaliah was the wife of Jehoram of Judah, the son of the good king, Jehoshaphat. She went to Jerusalem, the capital of the Southern Kingdom. Jehoram ascended to the throne at the age of thirty-two, and the licentious Athaliah was the queen. Immediately she began to rule. The zeal with which she set about to fill Jerusalem with the doctrine of Baal was typical of her mother when she came to Samaria from Zidon. There was no crime to which she would not stoop to push Baal-worship to the fore in Judah.

"King Jehoram slew all his brethren with the sword and divers also of the princes of Israel" (2 Chron. 21:4b). "And he walked in the way of the kings of Israel, like as did the house of Ahab, for he had the daughter of Ahab to wife: and he wrought that which was evil in the eyes of the Lord" (2 Chron. 21:6). Not only was she zealous in spreading the doctrine of Baal, she also was determined to stamp out a knowledge of the true worship of the Lord God. So persevering was this shameful woman's designs, that she sought to plant in the mind of her son her deadly doctrine and motives. Thus he and his generations after him would keep alive in Jerusalem this lustful cult of Baal-worship.

Elijah, the prophet wrote Jehoram the King foretelling his death. "Thus saith the Lord God of David thy father, Because thou hast not walked in the ways of Jehoshaphat thy father, nor in the way of Asa, king of Judah, but hast walked in the way of the kings of Israel, and hast made Judah and the inhabitants of Jerusalem to go a whoring, like to the whoredoms of the house of Ahab, and also hast slain thy brethren of thy father's house, which were better than thyself" (2 Chron. 21: 12, 13). Because of this great sin the Philistines were permitted to capture his wives and his sons, except Ahaziah. In the eighth year of his reign, Jehoram died of an incurable disease. His youngest son, Ahaziah came to the throne completely dominated by his mother. The Scriptures tell us that Ahaziah, "walked in the ways of the house of Ahab: for his mother was his counsellor to do wickedly" (2 Chron. 22:3a).

Her Revenge

Within a year Ahaziah was slain by Jehu, whom the Lord had anointed to cut off the house of Ahab. When Athaliah saw that her son was dead, "she arose and destroyed all the seed royal of the house of Judah."

Now for six years she ruled with an iron hand, even to the destruction of the House of God; and also all the dedicated things of the House of the Lord did they bestow upon Baal (2 Chron. 24:7).

Athaliah's greedy ambition caused her to murder her own grandchildren. In this massacre she missed one baby, Joash, the son of Ahaziah. He was rescued by his aunt Jehosheba. "And he was hid in the house of God for six years" (2 Chron. 22:12a). In the seventh year Jehoida, the high priest, brought forth the young prince and proclaimed him king. The priest had the aid of the mighty men of Judah.

Her Final Appearance

When Athaliah heard the noise of the people praising the king, she came unto the house of the Lord. There at the Temple she saw and heard the coronation of the child Joash. She rent her clothes and said, "Treason, treason" (2 Chron. 23:13). The high priest gave orders to the captains to slay her with the sword and all that might follow her. They were commanded, "Slay her not in the house of the Lord." She was slain at the entrance of the horse gate by the king's house. How like her wicked mother in life and in death! The final Biblical epitaph of Athaliah is, "that wicked woman" (2 Chron. 24:7).

Two Pictures

How impartial is the Bible in its portrayal of character! In every age, woman in her God-given sphere is teacher of good things; a wife who does her husband good, not evil; the mother of children, who rise up to call her blessed. Her influence continues in her children and in her children's children.

The Jebebels and Athaliahs are also teachers. They and women of like character are teachers of evil things. They have tried to ignore God in their lives. She renders evil to her husband; a curse is pronounced upon her children. The influence of these evil teachers was felt in both the Northern and Southern kingdoms. Their history was changed. The fall of National Israel can be attributed to a certain degree to the teaching of wicked women. Israel was no stronger than the wives and mothers in Israel.

Today women are in open rebellion against the limitation of the sphere that God assigned to them from the beginning.

This is true of many Christian women. The home is in great jeopardy. Woman is the central figure in the home—the order, security, peace and affection in any home is, to a great extent, dependent upon the moral fiber of the woman.

The woman who is happy and content to abide where God placed her, is conscious of the sacredness of the family. The dignity of the woman in the home is not trying to compete with men in a man's world.

Women have fought battles at the polls, through magazines and newspapers, for equality with men. They have proved they can do a man's job in any field. But *what price glory!*

She has invaded man's domain and is frantically clinging to hers. She still wants to be a wife and mother at the expense of the home and child. The child is left to the care of a hired maid, until nursery school age, and then he is given to the public schools. Both parents labor and sacrifice to build a lovely home, and nearly all the family's waking hours are spent outside its sheltering walls.

There is a constant complaint of the drudgery and dreariness in homemaking and child rearing. There is tension and mental illness.

God's order is ignored and until every woman recognizes that she cannot run counter to God without disaster, her lot will be as miserable as Athaliah's. Let the older women be teachers of good things. Let the younger women teach the children. God is depending upon good women. No other can do the work planned for her.

STUDY SUGGESTIONS

Study First and Second Kings.

Discuss Athaliah's family background. (2 Kings 8:16a, 18b; 1 Kings 16:30a)

Should the young man considering marriage consider the family of the young woman? What values should be emphasized for both parties?

Who was Athaliah's husband? Discuss his parentage. (2 Chron. 21:1-5)

What is said of her influence over her husband? (2 Chron. 21:5, 6)

Read 2 Chron. 22:1-9; 2 Kings 8:25-27. Who was Ahaziah? Who influenced him to do wickedly? By whom was he slain and why?

What do you think of the fanatical zeal of this woman? What would have been the result had this zealous fervor been channeled in the right direction?

When Athaliah slew "all the seed royal," whom did this include?

Who was Joash? (2 Chron. 22:11) Contrast the influence of his grand-

mother and his Aunt Jehosheba?
Describe the occasion and the slaying of Athaliah. (2 Chron. 23:1-15)
In 2 Chron. 24:7 who is said to have desecrated the Temple?
Can the mother claim exemption from the sins of her children?
Can the entire responsibility for the failures of the home today be placed
upon the present generation?
Whose responsibility is it to teach for parenthood? Think.
Should the Christian mother cherish her role in God's plan?
Name some reasons why the young mother desires work outside the home.
Discuss the influential teaching of women, good or bad.

Huldah

2 Kings 22:14
2 Chron. 34:22

*"Hilkiah and they that the king had
appointed went to Huldah, the
prophetess and the wife of Shallum"* (2 Chron. 34:22).

JOSIAH WAS the sixteenth king of Judah. More than three hundred
years before he was born, a prophet had foretold his birth and
great work of reformation. Soon after Josiah became king, "while he
was yet young," he began to seek after the God of his father David.
He tore down the altars erected to idols; he destroyed the groves where
altars and images were dedicated as places of worship. Tombs of false
prophets were opened, their bones exhumed and burned on the altars
where they had sacrificed to idols (2 Kings 23:16).

Though many of the Hebrews were steeped in idolatry, there were
some as in the days of Elijah who had not bowed their knee to Baal.
Through some faithful women the light of God's word was still burning. Huldah, the prophetess, was one of those women.

As Josiah began to rid the land of the evils of idolatry, he began to restore the true worship. The temple was repaired, cleansed
and made beautiful. In the work of restoring the temple, Hilkiah
found the "book of the law" (2 Chron. 34:13). When the book of the
law was read to Josiah, he rent his clothes (2 Chron. 34:19). The
king selected five messengers and said, "Go, inquire of the Lord for
me and for them that are left in Israel and in Judah, concerning the
words of the book that is found . . . and Hilkiah and they that the
king had appointed went to the prophetess, the wife of Shallum . . .
And they spoke with her" (2 Chron. 34:22).

Her Reputation

Surely Huldah was well known in the kingdom of Judah. Perhaps Huldah was just an ordinary woman. She was married to Shallum. In spite of her humble background, or perhaps because of it, she was so highly reputed that the king sent the "book of the law" by his messengers to her.

The Scriptures tell us that Shallum's family was the keeper of the wardrobe. It isn't known whether this is the wardrobe of the priest or king. Very likely it was of the priest because she "dwelt in Jerusalem in the college." This was a section in front of the temple. She was probably well known in the temple and by the high priest and the men who came to her.

She answered the messengers with "Thus saith the Lord," and confirmed all the things that were written in the book which they had read before the King of Judah. Further God revealed unto her and she sent word to Josiah the king that he would not live to see the wrath of the Lord poured out upon Jerusalem because of his humility and tender heart (2 Chron. 34:38). Jehovah inspired Huldah to teach a king, a high priest, a scribe and a group of other men.

Why did King Josiah send this committee to consult a woman? It has been thought that there was no other to whom the king could appeal; there was no man to whom the high priest could go for instruction.

In Jerusalem where Huldah lived at the very time that the king sent the high priest and other men to her for instruction, the prophet Jeremiah was crying out against the sins of Judah. The word of the Lord came to Jeremiah in the thirteenth year of the reign of Josiah (Jeremiah 1:1-2). The prophet was commanded to go to Jerusalem to protest the backsliding of Judah (Jer. 2:1). The "book of the law" was found in the eighteenth year of the Josiah reign. So for five years there had been a prophet in Jerusalem with the same message that was in the "book of the law." Yet the king elected that Huldah instruct them regarding this new-found book.

Her Ability

We must infer that Huldah was a woman of intellectual attainment, a devout woman who had lived close to God. Her godly life and her knowledge inspired confidence. It was a time of spiritual darkness; a time of skepticism and ignorance of God's word. Jeremiah who had come from Anatoth had not been taken seriously in Jerusalem. A great and dramatic prophet, he was making no impression on the people. Previous to Jeremiah there had been no champion among the men. Huldah's ability was channeled in the right direction and God revealed his word through her.

So they brought the king word again and because of her testimony regarding the "book of the law" and her prophecy, Josiah was induced to renew the covenant with Jehovah. And so a woman inspired the reformation that was begun by Josiah.

The church of the Lord has been established in many places, because of the Huldahs of our day.

There are places where the church owes its very existence to the Huldahs of our day.

STUDY SUGGESTIONS

Who was Josiah? (2 Chron. 33:25)
How do you account for his fine character? He must have had a good mother, Jedidah. (2 Kings 22:2)
What meaningful sentence follows his name and his mother's name?
Discuss Josiah's work of reformation. (2 Chron. 34:3-8)
What did he do to restore the true worship of Jehovah? (2 Chron. 34:8-13)
Relate the finding of the "book of the law." (Deut. 31:26; 2 Chron. 34:15, 18) What was the book?
Who was Huldah?
Why was the delegation sent to Huldah instead of Jeremiah?
Did Huldah do wrong when she taught these men? Did she take upon herself any authority? Was she inspired? Would God have inspired her had she been out of her place?
Evaluate the character of Huldah.
In what was she an example to Christian women?
Discuss women as teachers. What can a woman teach and where may she teach? (Titus 2:3-5; Acts 2:8; 2 Kings 2:22)

Esther

Esther 1-10

"And who knowest whether thou art come to the kingdom for such a time as this" (Esther 4:14c).

THIS NARRATIVE brings us to a great crisis in the history of the chosen race. And God chose a woman through whom he saved the Israelites who were then called Jews. While the name of God is not in this book, the presence and rule of God are assuredly manifested.

The Book of Esther is a picture of the Jews in Persia. Esther is the central figure of the very dramatic story. It opens with the scene of a festivity of oriental splendor in the palace at Shushan.

The King, Ahasuerus was in possession of the entire Persian Empire.

He made a feast and invited all the nobles and princes of his Kingdom. For one hundred and eighty days he made a general exhibition of the riches and grandeur of his glorious kingdom.

At the end of this time the King made a feast for all the people of Shushan. The court of the garden was the place of this second feast. Very likely no apartment in all the palace could hold the people. The court was luxurious with white, green and blue curtains. These curtains were fastened with cords of fine linen and purple to silver rings and pillars of marble. The pavement was of red and blue and white and black marble.

The couches on which the guests reclined were covered with gold and silver cloth. The wine was served in vessels of gold (Esther 1: 6-7).

The Queen, Vashti

Vashti was the queen in the beginning of this narrative. She had made a feast for the women in the royal house. Women in the East never associate with men in public. Therefore the king and his guests were in the court of the garden, and the women were in the royal house.

After seven days of feasting and drinking, "the heart of the king was merry with wine."

The intoxicated king commanded that the eunuchs bring Queen Vashti that he might exhibit her beauty to the princes. (Some have said unclothed.) Social form in Persia dictated the Queen remain secluded. She was not seen publicly at banquets as are queens of Europe. The queen's sense of propriety, as well as her prudence and modesty, were offended. And in all of the Scriptures we do not find a more womanly woman than Vashti.

Vashti was neither proud nor immoral; she refused to surrender her honor. She refused to obey her king and husband. Not only was she modest, she was very brave. This would cost her her crown and perhaps her very life. Regardless of all this she refused to expose herself to the gaze of these men. The Persian King immediately resolved that her position be given to another.

Search for a New Queen

Upon the advice of his ministers, Ahasuerus began a careful search of the country from India to the Mediterranean Sea for fair young virgins (Esther 2:2).

Among these was the beautiful Hadassah, an orphan Jewess. When she came to the Persian Court, she was called Esther, which signifies a star.

When her parents died, Esther's cousin Mordecai took her for his own daughter. Mordecai was of the tribe of Benjamin, and an official gatekeeper at the palace.

When the royal decree was published, that beautiful young virgins would be gathered together for the king's harem in Shushan, and the maiden who pleased him would be queen instead of Vashti, Mordecai brought the beautiful Esther unto the king's house to the custody of Hegai, keeper of the women.

Her lineage was to be kept a secret. She was different from all other maidens. She did not come from an idolatrous family. Her education was in the home of Mordecai who was a devout Israelite, and it is very probable that she knew and worshipped Jehovah.

There has been much said about this Jew who would plan a marriage for one of Abraham's daughters to a heathen king. There seems to be only one explanation, that God intended to save the chosen race in this way.

Esther's Reception

Esther made a favorable impression upon all that saw her. She displayed her good judgment when she left the selection of her dress and ornaments to Hegai. When she was taken unto the king into his house royal, he loved her above all the women and she obtained grace and favor in his sight more than all the virgins; so he set the royal crown upon her head and she became queen instead of Vashti (Esther 2:16, 17).

Then King Ahasuerus made a feast unto all his princes and servants, even Esther's feast. Esther had not revealed her kindred nor her people. She was obedient to Mordecai who insisted that she not tell her husband she was a Jewess. Her beauty has been the subject of art, music and drama. There was nothing left undone by the seven maidens who attended her, that might enhance her natural loveliness. Her clothing and jewelry were the richest and most beautiful; they were chosen to set off to an advantage her dark hair, olive skin and radiant eyes. Did she know she had been placed in this high position for a purpose?

There was a feud between Mordecai and Haman, an Amalekite. The old hatred of Amalekite for Jew was fanned to life by Mordecai's refusal to pay reverence unto him.

Soon Esther learned that Haman's enmity included all the Jews in Persia. And he obtained the king's consent to kill all the foreigners on the thirteenth day of the Adar.

There were fasting and weeping and wailing among the Jews. Mordecai rent his clothes, put on sackcloth with ashes and stood before the king's gate, and cried with a loud, bitter cry.

Hatach, one of the king's chamberlains who attended Esther, was sent to her cousin. Mordecai sent her a copy of the writing of the decree that was given at Shushan to destroy the Jews, and charged her that she should go to the King, to make request before him for her people (Esther 4:1-9).

Esther reminded Mordecai that to go into the king's presence uninvited, meant death except to such to whom the king might extend
the golden sceptre. This was even more difficult because she had not
been called in unto the king for thirty days.

HER COURAGE

Her cousin's reply placed upon her a great responsibility. "Who
knoweth whether thou art come to the kingdom for such a time as
this?" (Esther 4:14). And her life was at stake with the Jews. She
commanded all the Jews in Shushan be gathered together and hold
a fast for her for three days and nights. She and her maidens would
join them in the fast. She expressed her determination to make an
appeal to the king, "And if I perish, I perish" (Esther 4:16). Faith,
courage and devotion to the cause of her people were embodied in
her brave speech.

Some have not given these virtues to Esther because it is said
she refrained from saving a whole nation until her own life was
threatened. Yet her action which followed her statement was very
courageous. She put on her royal apparel and approached the king
as he sat upon his throne. And when the king saw Esther standing
in the court, she obtained favor in his sight, "And the king held out
to Esther the golden sceptre that was in his hand. So Esther drew near
and touched the top of the sceptre" (Esther 5:1-2).

King Ahasuerus promised to give her her request even to one half
his kingdom. She proceeded slowly and cautiously. She was dealing
with a capricious and dangerous force. Let the King and Haman come
this day unto a banquet that she had prepared, and on the morrow she
would make her request known. Haman's joy knew no bounds until
he saw Mordecai at the king's gate. He refrained himself, rushed home
and boasted about the queen's invitation, his riches, his position, and
his children. But as long as he saw Mordecai at the gate, he felt
himself cheated. Zeresh and his friends suggested, "Let gallows be
made fifty cubits high on which to hang Mordecai." He was highly
pleased with this advice and he caused the gallows to be made.

After the banquet the king was unable to sleep. The Targum says,
"The king had a dream and a man warned him that Haman desired to
kill him and make himself king."

He ordered the Chronicles be read to him. And it was found written that Mordecai had saved his life when he had reported the treason
of two of his eunuchs.

GOD'S PROVIDENCE

It is true God's name is not mentioned here at all, but certainly
his Providence was with Esther the queen. Haman had arrived in
the court of the King's house to speak unto the king about hanging

Mordecai on the gallows he had prepared for him (Esther 6:4).

The King requested him to come in. Haman came in. "What shall be done unto the man whom the king delighteth to honor?" Foolish, conceited Haman thought himself the man and he requested the highest honor. He was chagrined and distressed when he learned that the king desired to pay honor to Mordecai.

With heavy heart and forebodings he went to the second banquet. His wise men and Zeresh had told him that he would surely fall before Mordecai of the seed of the Jews.

Ahasuerus again asked Esther her petition, assuring her it would be granted. Then Esther pleaded for her life and the life of her people, "We are sold, I and my people, to be destroyed, to be slain and to perish" (Esther 7:4).

"Who is he, and where is he that durst presume in his heart to do so?" And Esther answered, "The adversary and enemy is this wicked Haman."

Esther's Victory

No longer is he the proud and honored guest of the queen. He is a miserable suppliant pleading for his life. It was too late. The king ordered him to be hanged on the gallows he had prepared for Mordecai. The House of Haman was given to Mordecai, for Esther had revealed unto the king what he was to her (Esther 8:1).

Esther and Mordecai were now safe from the decree that had gone forth against the Jews. She faced the great obligation placed upon her by Jehovah and begged the King to reverse the law against her people.

No law of the Medes and Persians could be revoked. With fearlessness and intelligence she was instrumental in procuring a written edict signed with the royal signet that the Jews might defend themselves and slay their enemies.

The decree was given out at Shushan and published in every province. The Jews had great joy and gladness. Many became Jews for fear (Esther 8:17). Truly the heathen could see the hand of God in the affairs of Persia.

On the thirteenth of the month Adar the Jews destroyed their enemies. Five hundred were slain in Shushan, and Haman's ten sons were killed (Esther 9:6, 10). The king had great confidence in Esther and inquired what else she desired. She requested that the Jews might have one more day against their enemies and the ten sons of Haman be hanged on gallows. This has seemed to some to have indicated an expression of vengeance on the part of Esther. It is very probable that she had been informed that there were many enemies of the Jews who had escaped. She was not seeking security for herself. She was an instrument in the hand of God to preserve this people.

To this day the Festival of Purim is kept by the Jews wherever they are on the fourteenth and fifteenth days of March. Esther and Mordecai wrote with all authority and decreed for themselves and for their seed to confirm the days of Purim in their times appointed (Esther 9:27-32).

STUDY SUGGESTIONS

To what period of Bible History does the Book of Esther belong? (Period of Captivity).

When did this period begin and when did it end? Consult Bible Dictionary.

Why were the Jews in Persia? (2 Kings 25)

Discuss the splendor of the setting for this narrative as given in Chapter 1:1-9)

Tell of Vashti's refusal to the king's request. (10-12)

Relate her rejection and the law made for the subjection of women. (13-22)

What beautiful virtues can we attribute to this Persian queen? Did she not exhibit more modesty than the "Miss Americas" of today?

Are Christian women neglecting to teach modesty to their daughters?

"Because 'everybody else does it' makes shorts, brief swim suits, topless evening gowns, modest apparel." Evaluate this statement.

Read Isa. 3:16, 17 and compare Isaiah's description to the modern woman.

How does Peter describe a beautiful woman? (1 Pet. 3:1-4)

To what extent are women taught to obey their husbands? (Eph. 5:22)

Name two Old Testament books that are named for women.

Would the story of Esther be considered a "from rags to riches" story?

By whom was Esther reared? (2:7)

What about her beauty? (2:7b)

Describe her personality? (2:9)

Why did she hide her lineage? (2:10)

Why was a vigil kept over her? (2:11)

Tell how she became queen. (2:12-18)

Whom did she obey? (2:20)

How did Mordecai save the king? (2:21-23)

Who was Haman? Why did he hate the Jews? (3:6)

In Chapter 4, relate Mordecai's plan to save the Jews.

Discuss Mordecai's statement to Esther: "And who knows whether thou art come to the kingdom for such a time as this?"—as to the timelessness of service; woman's responsibility in crises.

Discuss Esther as the heroine of this narrative.

Name ways in which her name has been immortalized.

In what sphere are Christian women instruments of God? (1 Tim. 2:10 5:3-16; Titus 2:3-5; 1 Pet. 3:1-2; 1 Tim. 3:11)

The Virtuous Woman

Prov. 31:10-31

"Who can find a virtuous woman? For her price is far above rubies; the heart of her husband doth safely trust in her, so he shall have no need of spoil. She will do him good and not evil all the days of his life" (Prov. 31:10-12).

THE WOMAN whose price is "far above rubies" is depicted in the last chapter of the book of Proverbs. Nothing can add to the simple beauty of the Biblical picture.

These noble attributes realized in our own daughters will result in untold good in the welfare of the home, church and nation.

A mother is instructing her son as he reaches manhood. In the first verses of this wonderful chapter we realize her urgent sincerity as we hear the refrain, "My son, my son, the son of my vow." We recall Samuel, who was the son of Hannah's vow. How clearly and unmistakably the young man is advised and warned against giving his strength to women and wine.

Throughout the book of Proverbs are admonitions against the "strange woman," "fair woman without discretion," "the evil woman."

The closing and final admonition is the description of the ideal wife and mother. King Lemuel declares he was taught this by his mother.

FINDING THE RIGHT ONE

The Christian mother should be diligent to teach her son that a happy marriage depends upon his finding the right wife. "Who can find" indicates a search or a constant vigil for a virtuous woman.

A good and successful marriage is no accident. The joy and peace, the stability and contentment of the home depend upon the marriage relationship being according to God's arrangement. The young man who finds a worthy companion will have the reward of his trust.

Then as now, there were those who were unfaithful not only to the marriage vow but to the household trust. There are women who marry for what they can get, and spend all their married life seeing that they get it. This must have been true in the long ago. Husbands came home to dirty houses, ill-cooked meals and nagging wives.

MONEY PROBLEMS

"The heart of her husband trusteth in her, so shall he have no need of spoil."

Today the most difficult phase of marriage is perhaps in the economic area. The problem of making ends meet each month is the paramount issue. The young man prior to his marriage has had only himself to support, and too often he is not even experienced in his own self-support. Suddenly the responsibility of maintaining a home is upon him. Perhaps the wife earned more money before marriage than her husband. And there isn't enough money to go around. Each blames the other. This problem will never become a threat to the marriage if their relationship to each other and to God is understood before marriage.

Some kings went into battle for the spoil for their households; not king Lemuel, "he hath no need of spoil." She maintained his home within his income. "She doeth him good and not evil," she was constant. Her good was not mixed with evil. She had an unswerving attitude for his good. Not what am I getting out of this venture? But, what do I contribute toward the success of this undertaking?

"She seeketh wool and flax and worketh willingly with her hands,
     She is like the merchant ships; she bringeth her food from afar."

The ideal woman found adequate expression in home making. Marriage was her career. She was the center of the home. "Godliness with contentment is great gain," said the Apostle Paul (1 Tim. 6:6).

Today the housewife often has an inferiority complex because she underestimates the challenge of homemaking and character building. Too often she thinks her life is dull and drab. True there is a certain amount of drudgery in every field of accomplishment. Some things can be achieved only by dull routine work.

Our Savior said, "My Father worketh hitherto, and I work." By his work, and how wearisome and tiring it must have been, the world is filled with hope.

Perhaps the days which seemed to have the least accomplished are the ones in which the wife and mother has done her best work.

OUTSIDE THE HOME

An outside interest? This godly woman knew the value of real estate. She considered a field; she bought it; and she planted a vineyard.

Her husband had great confidence in her financial ability and good judgment.

Many of us can recall the days when our mother and grandmothers traded the eggs, the fryers, the butter, for sugar, flour or the bright piece of calico. Let us remember our great heritage.

PHYSICAL STRENGTH

"And maketh strong her arms," she was careful for her health. The writer of Proverbs implied that she made an effort to be strong physically.

The modern woman is confronted with every type of neurosis and illness. Psychiatrists tell us much illness is a means of escape from responsibilities. The tension of the routine of daily living, the deadline to be met, the dental appointment, the music lesson, the Scout meeting, P.T.A., and the seemingly inevitable telephone—all are at fault.

The wife and mother of today seems to be trying to cross a dozen bridges before she gets to them. What is the answer?

Today's woman needs the courage to live simply. The deciding factor is too often what the Joneses do. So she is tense; she is sick. She suffers, and so do her husband and children. Her spirit must be renewed each day. She must look up from the task. She must realize that she is building with God, and that His laws are ever on her side. A calm and quiet spirit is a great aid toward physical fitness.

INDUSTRIOUS

The woman of Proverbs was a careful worker. She manufactured the best articles; the materials and workmanship were the best. She worked even beyond daylight hours. Her industry enabled her to be charitable.

Not only did she care for her own, but she relieved the poor generally; with both hands she gave to the needy.

Her family's clothing and coverings for the winter were prepared in advance. "No sudden cold snap finds this woman unprepared."

PERSONAL APPEARANCE

She was well groomed. Her clothing was of fancy weaves and beautiful colors. She indulged in the luxury of silks and purples.

Her personal appearance was not neglected nor unimportant.

To maintain personal appearance after marriage is important. It is good to keep the admiration of one's husband. But the inward beauty, the expression of the face, shows kindness, sincerity and affection; the wife and mother will be beautiful to her family.

Again we look to this ideal woman. And her husband was well known. He was respected because of his wife and family. His home was so well ordered that he had time for business and civic affairs.

Dr. Herbert Ratner, an associate professor of preventive medicine at Loyola University charges that "women are trying to make second rate women out of men."

Much of a man's self respect and confidence is lost when the wife leaves home to take an outside job or when she is constantly complaining about her side of the partnership.

This woman reflects upon the worth of her husband. Throughout the chapter in Proverbs her industry is complimented, and the rewards of industry are surely seen.

She was happy and rejoiced in the time to come. Old age held no fear. And today whether Christian women can rejoice in the days to come depends upon how we have spent our earlier days.

She had no regrets. She used her husband's money wisely. The family was well-clothed and fed. She added to the family budget by her manufacturing skill. These products were superior in every detail. Nothing shoddy or second rate went into or resulted from her labors.

MATURE YEARS

When the family is gone from home, the busy mother is apt to find she must face a period of adjustment.

Now is a good time to begin teaching in the Bible school. Learn to do personal work. Much depends on how little regret we have for the past.

Now shall we consider the love and respect that she had. Her speech was "with grace seasoned with salt." She had not caused sorrow and heartaches by idle talk or unkind gossip. Kindness was the law of her tongue—her words were constantly courteous and gentle.

Her household disdained idleness. The children were taught the dignity and happiness of work well done. Idleness is the cause of much unhappiness in the home and church. Industry is a noble trait in either man or woman. It must be taught early in life. "Train up a child in the way he should go, and when he is old, he will not depart from it."

She was loved and respected by those who knew her best. Her children rise up and call her blessed. They gave to her the honor that Jehovah has required of the child to the parent. Her husband loved and appreciated her. He was satisfied with her conduct toward the household, the children and himself. She stood above all others.

"Favor is deceitful and beauty is vain, but a woman that loveth the Lord, she shall be praised." Favor is often withdrawn and beauty fades with time. Popularity and beauty are very transient. Too often these are the goal and aim of mothers for their daughters.

A "fear of the Lord" brings praise and admiration. Let what she has done be a memorial for her. Let her example be held forth in the most public places. Let her example be before the eyes of every woman. Other women have done worthily, but this one feared the Lord.

"Give her the fruit of her hands, and let her works praise her in the gates."

Whether this was a real woman or just an ideal one, she is still a source of inspiration to women today.

Every virtue should be studied and emulated.

STUDY SUGGESTIONS

Discuss the husband and wife relationship. (Prov. 31:10, 11, 12)
What was the reward of his trust? (31:11-12)
Show ways in which the husband's trust can be betrayed.
Show her efficiency in managing her household. (31 13-17)
What of her talents and skills? (31:18, 19)

What was her attitude toward work? (31:19-21)
Tell of her charity. (31:20)
What do you consider the source of her strength and dignity? (31:25)
What was the law of her tongue? (31:26b)
How did she guard her household? (31:27)
What was her reward? (31:28, 29)
What may be said of grace and beauty? (31:30a)

Elisabeth, the Mother of John the Baptist

"And behold thy cousin, Elisabeth, she hath also conceived a son in her old age; and this is the sixth month with her who was called barren" (Luke 1:36).

Luke 1:39-55; 1:57-80; 1:5-25; 1:36-37

E LISABETH, of the house of Aaron, was married to a priest named Zacharias. "They were both righteous before God, walking in all the commandments and ordinances of the Lord blameless." They had no children, because Elisabeth was barren, and now they were both old. She felt, as did all Jewish women, that her childless state was a reproach and disgrace.

They lived quietly in the hill country of Judea, possibly near Ain Karem, four miles north of Jerusalem. Even though they had been denied the joys of parenthood, they served God faithfully.

THE ANNOUNCEMENT OF THE FORERUNNER

Elisabeth's husband belonged to the priestly course of Abia, the eighth of the twenty four orders, or courses, into which David divided the priesthood. His lot was to burn incense in the Holy Place of the Jerusalem temple while the multitude prayed outside. This was a very distinguished part of the service. His marriage to this daughter of the Aaronic line evidenced a regard for the marriage law of the priests (Lev. 21:7-14). Their office and the honor and dignity of the religion of Jehovah required unblemished sanctity in their families as well as themselves.

One day while Zacharias was offering incense upon the golden altar he was surprised to see an angel standing on the right side of the altar watching him. The angel said, "Fear not, Zacharias, because thy supplication is heard and thy wife Elisabeth shall bear thee a son, and thou shalt call his name John."

The message from Gabriel was an answer to prayer, for even though they were both old, and Elisabeth was barren, they had not despaired. They believed that God could do all things. Perhaps Elisabeth was outside with the multitude praying, or in the quiet of her hill country home at the hour of incense, asking the Lord God to take away her reproach. What a joy must have been hers! She received the message in a reverent and humble Spirit, giving God praise for her happiness; recognizing this promised son as a gift from Him. "Thus hath the Lord done in the days wherein he looked upon me, to take away my reproach among men."

How pathetic that Zacharias could not tell his wife the wonderful message from Gabriel! He must write it, for his faith had not been sufficient to grasp the stupendous message of the angel, and he had asked for a sign. Consequently, he was to be mute until the child was born.

Barren Elisabeth was to bring forth a child in her old age, who "would be great in the sight of the Lord . . . he shall be filled with the Holy Spirit even from his mother's womb."

VISIT OF MARY TO ELISABETH

When Elisabeth was in the sixth month of her pregnancy, Gabriel again appeared to a woman who was to be a divine instrument in God's great promise to all the world. This visitation was to a virgin in Nazareth, whose name was Mary. He imparted to her the message that she would bear a son, whose name should be called Jesus. He strengthened Mary's faith, giving her an unsought sign, "And behold thy cousin Elisabeth; she hath also conceived a son in her old age, and this is the sixth month with her that was called barren. For with God nothing shall be impossible." In the long ago an angel had said unto Abraham, "Is anything too hard for Jehovah?" (Gen. 18:14).

Mary, transported with joy because of the announcement to herself, and the news made known to her of Elisabeth's condition, hurried to the home of Elisabeth, in a city of Judah.

These two highly-favored women, an old woman and her young cousin, had a common experience and bond that knew no age. Every step of the journey must have been in joyous anticipation of the confidences they would share with each other. "Is anything too hard for Jehovah?"

"And when Elisabeth heard the greeting of Mary, the babe leaped in her womb, and Elisabeth was filled with the Holy Spirit; and she exclaimed with a loud cry, 'Blessed are you among women, and blessed is the fruit of your womb. And why is this granted to me, that the mother of my Lord should come to me?'" Elisabeth lost sight of her own joy; the high honor conferred upon her as the mother of the forerunner of Christ was secondary, and no envy tinged the thoughts of this noble woman.

Even the extraordinary movement of the babe in her womb was of peculiar significance; a sympathetic emotion of the unconscious babe in the presence of the mother of the Lord. The Holy Spirit revealed unto this mother that her young cousin bore in her body the long-promised Messiah. A beautiful superiority to envy and jealousy was manifested by the mother of John the Baptist.

For three months Elisabeth's cousin was a guest in her home. "And why is this granted me, that the mother of my Lord should come to me?"

What an exquisite joy this visit must have held for both these highly-favored women. We can imagine how often they must have talked of the angel's visits—how they must have confided their fears, hopes, and aspirations. Perhaps Mary sought advice and counsel from the older woman. How humble and unselfish was Elisabeth; how readily she acceded that Mary's child would be greater than hers.

In the common bond of approaching motherhood, they planned for the births of their sons, as women have since the beginning of time.

As they made plans for the future how merciful it is that that future was hidden from these expectant mothers. They could not look across the years and see Mary's son hanging on Calvary's cross, nor the head of Elisabeth's son severed from its body at the command of King Herod.

BIRTH OF THE FORERUNNER

Soon after Mary returned to Galilee, Elisabeth's son was born. On the eighth day succeeding the event, friends and kinsmen gathered for the circumcision and naming of the child. They rejoiced with her, as had friends and neighbors rejoiced with Naomi when Ruth gave her a grandson. They naturally thought the son would be called Zacharias, for his father. But the mother said, "Not so; he shall be called John." Zacharias affirmed this in writing, saying, "His name is John." Immediately his speech was restored and he spoke, blessing God. He spoke his famous Benedictus, acknowledging his son to be the harbinger of the Christ.

What happiness must have been Elisabeth's. Her husband's speech had been restored; her son was in her arms. "Thus the Lord hath done to me in the days when he looked on me, to take away my reproach among men."

"And the child grew and became strong in spirit." How tenderly she must have watched over this child. If her life was spared long enough for her to witness the multitudes turning to repentance, how she must have rejoiced in her son's ministry.

The mother's story is always the story of her children. Elisabeth's unselfish spirit permeated her son when he said of Jesus, "He must increase, but I must decrease" (John 3:30).

A great tribute to the mother of John the Baptist were the words of Jesus when he said, "Verily I say unto you, among them that are born of women, there hath not risen a greater than John the Baptist" (Matt. 11:11).

STUDY SUGGESTIONS

Discuss these mutually happy companions. (Luke 1:6)

Of what family were they descended? (Luke 1:5d)

Discuss the marriage law of the priests. (Lev. 21:7-14)

Would the principle apply to Christians today?

For what had Zacharias been praying? (Luke 1:13) Was Elisabeth a partner in this prayer, either in the quiet of her home, or with the multitude outside?

Give the announcement of the angel. (Luke 1:11-13)

Describe the character of the promised child. (Luke 1:14-17)

How was the announcement confirmed to Zacharias? (Luke 1:18-22)

What did Elisabeth do and say? (Luke 1:24-25)

Who told Mary of her cousin's pregnancy? (Luke 1:26) Why?

Discuss the visit in the city of Judea.

   (a) The home of Elisabeth. (Luke 1:39-40)

   (b) Her unselfishness. (Luke 1:43)

   (c) Her confession of Christ. (Luke 1:43-43)

   (d) Her son's unselfishness. (Jno. 3:30)

   (e) How did her son compare with Jesus? (Jno. 4:12)

   (f) How did Jesus compliment her son? (Matt. 11:11)

Who rejoiced with Elisabeth? (Luke 1:57-58)

Discuss Romans 12:15.

Relate the experience in naming the child. (Luke 1:56-59)

Why was he called John? (Luke 1:13, 60-63) 'John' means 'grace' or 'mercy of God.'

Give the substance of the Benedictus. (Luke 1:67-68)

Discuss the child's growth. (Luke 1:80)

Would this suggest that Elisabeth was a careful and ideal mother?

Do you think Elisabeth was familiar with Proverbs 22:6?

Mary, the Mother of Our Lord

"Behold the handmaid of the Lord, be it unto me according to thy word" (Luke 1:38).

Luke 1:32-69
Luke 1:48-55
John 2:1-10
Rom. 1:3
Deut. 22:23, 24
Luke 8:2-21
2 Tim. 2:8
Matt. 1:20-22
John 19:26-27
Luke 11:28
Luke 2:5-52
Luke 23:29-49
Luke 1:32-38
Acts 1:14

MARY WAS A JEWESS. She lived in Nazareth centuries ago, and was betrothed to Joseph, a man of the house of David. The Biblical record indicates that she too was from the tribe of Judah and the family of David.

During the betrothal of Joseph and Mary, which by custom was to precede marriage by a year, the angel Gabriel announced to Mary that she was to be the mother of the Messiah.

This lowly peasant girl of Nazareth was greeted by the heavenly Messenger, "Hail, oh favored one, the Lord is with you." Truly, Mary was favored of God in a unique sense, and as the mother of our Lord, "she was most blessed among women." Yet we read that Christ himself said, "Blessed are those who hear the word of God and keep it."

The purity of Mary's character is revealed in her first words in the Scriptures, "How shall this be, seeing I know not a man?" This was her answer to the angel who said, "Fear not Mary; for thou hast found favor with God, thou shalt conceive in thy womb, and bring forth a son, and shalt call his name Jesus." Gabriel told her that "The Holy Ghost shall come upon thee, and the power of the Highest shall overshadow thee, therefore also that holy thing which shall be born of thee shall be called the Son of God." Her reply bespeaks her humble submissiveness, "Behold the handmaid of the Lord, be it unto me according to thy word." Thus she gave expression to her faith. And Elisabeth affirmed Mary's faith when she declared, "Blessed is she that believed; for there shall be a performance of things that were told her from the Lord."

Mary arose and went in haste to visit her cousin Elisabeth. The angel had told her that the older woman was to bear a son, and this was her sixth month. "For with God nothing will be impossible." She knew the older woman had longed to have a child for many years. The distance from Nazareth to a city of Judea was great, the journey presented many problems. Yet she would not be deterred, so great was her desire to visit her cousin.

Elisabeth's words of greeting when Mary entered her house revealed that God had caused her to know the secret which the angel had told Mary in her own home. She knew her cousin would soon be the Mother of Jesus, the Savior of men.

MAGNIFICAT

Mary's faith reaches to the heights sublime as she sings this hymn of praise. She pours forth her joy of her inmost soul in adoration of God. Exalted from her low estate, she will be remembered through future years because of her God-given destiny. She praised God for his grace and mercy throughout all time as He exalted the humble and brought low the haughty; and now she is aware that God's promise to Abraham is near its fulfillment. This hymn is based on Hannah's song and contains allusions to the Old Testament, the Psalms, and the law.

Today every woman can read and see in this poem the expression of simple faith and hope, humble gratitude and submission in Mary, the mother of Jesus.

These two women spent many happy days together. The roof that sheltered these cousins ceased to exist long years ago, yet the progeny of these two women, the one a forerunner of the other, have made the world new. As they visited, could they have foreseen the tragic end of their sons' lives, their triumphant faith would have led them again to say, "Let it be unto me according to thy word."

RETURN TO NAZARETH

After Mary had visited three months in the home of Elisabeth, in Judea, she returned to her home in Nazareth. This must have been an ordeal for Mary—to return to Joseph and her home town to face the social implications of her pregnancy. Though confronted with serious problems of her approaching marriage, she was ever willing to submit her entire being to the disposal of God.

Matthew's account of Joseph's attitude, "when Mary was found to be with child," indicates that he was kindly and chivalrous. Betrothal was regarded as valid marriage in the Jewish law. Therefore, to give Mary up he had to take legal steps. He could have brought her before the magistrates and charged her with *unfaithfulness*. This sin carried with it the death penalty. Also, he could have put her away privately by giving to her the writing of divorcement (Deut. 24:1). Being a just man, this last was what he considered doing. Surely Joseph and Mary must have discussed this after her return from Elisabeth's. His decision does not necessarily imply disbelief on Joseph's part. Mary, too, must have agreed with Joseph.

While he thought on these things, possibly in the stillness of the night, he could see no prospect for domestic happiness. "Behold an angel of the Lord appeared to him in a dream saying, 'Joseph, son of David, do not fear to take Mary your wife, for that which is conceived of her is of the Holy Spirit; she will bear a son, and you shall call his name Jesus, for he will save the people from their sins.'" Joseph was glad. He took Mary into his home and waited for the angel's promise to come true. Mary needed Joseph's love and devotion in those days. We can be sure there was much slander and gossip in Nazareth. Human nature has not changed. But Joseph, the humble carpenter, was Mary's protector.

Trip to Bethlehem

"In those days, a decree went out from Caesar Augustus that all the world should be enrolled. . . . Joseph went up from Nazareth to Bethlehem . . . to be enrolled with Mary his espoused wife, who was with child."

Some have said that it was necessary for Mary to go to Bethlehem with Joseph. They were both of the family of David; Bethlehem was the city of David; their names must be written upon the list in that place. Others have thought he took Mary to Bethlehem for the census taking to save her from the curious eyes of inquisitive neighbors.

The road to the south led through the country of Samaria, then over the hills of Judah into Jerusalem. From Jerusalem Mary and Joseph traveled further south to Bethlehem. This must have been an arduous journey for Mary, ninety miles by donkey. There were many days of tedious and tiresome preparation. Food must be prepared, goatskins filled with water. The swaddling clothes for the child, whose birth was so near at hand, were packed along with other provisions. The nights were probably spent under the stars. The morning sun found the gentle Joseph and his beloved Mary well on their journey. Mary was not living in the right place for the Messiah's birth. With the unknowing intervention of Caesar Augustus, she was brought from Nazareth to Bethlehem in time for the child to be born as had been foretold by the prophets.

No Room at the Inn

When they reached Bethlehem, they found it was swarming with people who belonged, as they did, to the city where David was born. And Joseph found no place for them to stay except in the stable of the inn. "And there she gave birth to her firstborn son, wrapped him in swaddling clothes and laid him in the manger." Had she none to help her?

And so it was that God's greatest gift to man came into that neighborhood, and people did not receive it as a gift from God, for they did not expect the Savior to be born of such a lowly, obscure person as Mary.

"A shining golden crown for her, O Lord!
  Who tried so hard each day
To make your world a better place
  For those she loved to stay.
I wonder now? How at the end
  Her faith and courage grew
When all her golden dreams in life
  Had failed and not come true.
Oh! Give to her a starry crown,
  A harp with golden strings;
She in this life forever had
  Her share of common things."

                              —CELTA C. JOSEPH

THE RISEN STAR

Shepherds were watching their flocks that night in a field near Bethlehem. An angel of the Lord came upon them, and a glorious light broke through the darkness. Then he spoke and said, "Fear not, for I bring you good tidings of great joy, which shall be to all people. For unto you is born this day in the city of David, a Savior which is Christ the Lord." The shepherds hastened to Bethlehem, and there they found Mary and Joseph in the stable, and the babe lying in the manger. They told Mary of the angel's heavenly message and "Mary kept all these things and pondered them in her heart."

JOSEPH AND MARY KEEP THE LAW

Mary's wisdom and spiritual discernment were evidenced in her strict respect and obedience to the Old Testament law. Her son was circumcised on the eighth day, and called by the name the angels had chosen. When he was forty days old, the time came for their purification. According to the law of Moses, they brought him to Jerusalem to present him to the Lord. An offering was made to the Lord for the first boy child born in the family. Among the rich, this offering was usually a lamb. If the parents were poor, two young pigeons would please God just as well (Lev. 12:2-8).

SIMEON'S PROPHECY

Now there was a righteous and devout old man in the Temple when Joseph and Mary came to bring their offering. Simeon had served God many years and longed to see the promised Savior.

When Mary brought the child Jesus to the Temple, the Holy Spirit revealed to Simeon that this child was the long-promised Messiah. He came to Mary and took her babe in his arms. She must have wondered at what Simeon said about her child: "Behold, this child is set for the fall and rising of many in Israel; and for a sign which shall be spoken against." Did she fully comprehend his prophetic words—"that the thoughts of many hearts may be revealed"? She never faltered nor manifested fear. (Yes, a sword shall pierce through thine own soul also.)

Another faithful servant of the Lord was in the Temple that day, the aged Anna, who spoke words of prophecy to the people, who "spoke of Him to all them that looked for redemption in Jerusalem." Mary's fate was further manifested.

"And when they had performed all things according to the law of the Lord. . . ." What a wonderful tribute to Mary! And how naturally it follows, "And the child grew, and waxed strong in spirit, filled with wisdom; and the grace of God was upon Him."

FLIGHT INTO EGYPT

How soon the sword began to pierce through the virgin's soul! Matthew tells that after the visit of the wise men bringing rich gifts, an angel of the Lord appeared to Joseph warning him to take the young child and his mother and to flee into Egypt. Joseph rose up at once, while it was yet dark, and took Mary and the child and hurried out of Bethlehem. They travelled to the southwest, the way descending to the lowlands. They slowly passed through the land of the Philistines, down to Gaza and through miles of desert.

How carefully must Mary have watched over this marvelous child as they journeyed to Egypt. There they lived until the death of Herod. An angel came again to speak to Joseph, telling him to take the mother and child and return to their own land. They began the long, arduous journey across the rough desert land and uphill climb once more, until at last they came and dwelt in the city of Nazareth.

The years following Mary's return to Nazareth must have been busy years filled with the many tasks of any mother. Mary's other children were born in Nazareth; Jesus' sisters, and his brothers, James, Joses, Judah, and Simeon.

JESUS IN THE TEMPLE

In the humble home of Joseph the carpenter, Mary nurtured the boy Jesus, feeding him, clothing him, teaching and guiding him. The Scriptures record the wonderful results of his home life: "And Jesus increased in wisdom and stature, and in favor with God and man."

Family duties did not prevent the devout Mary from going up to Jerusalem to the annual festivals. Every year after Joseph's and Mary's return from Egypt, they had attended the Feast of the Passover.

When Jesus was twelve years old, he was taken up for the first time to Jerusalem at the Passover season. After the Feast had ended, the company started on its homeward journey. On these sacred journeys whole villages travelled in groups for protection and for company. Mary did not see her young son, but she supposed he was among kinfolk and friends. She did not feel uneasy. However, when at evening he did not come, she and Joseph began to search for him. After three sorrowing days, they found him in Jerusalem in the Temple sitting in the midst of the doctors.

Mary's greeting carried not only a mother's solicitude, but her discipline, "Son, why hast thou thus dealt with us? Behold, thy father and I have sought thee sorrowing." Jesus' answer indicated a higher sonship. "How is it that ye sought me? Wist ye not that I must be about my Father's business?"

"And they understood not the saying; but his Mother kept all these sayings in her heart."

From this time on we have no more mention of Joseph. Somewhere between this and our Lord's public ministry, it is inferred that Joseph dies. The years pass, and the Biblical narrative is of the Son, and the mother is not mentioned. She appears again at the marriage feast in Cana of Galilee.

Elisabeth's son, John the Baptist, had baptized Jesus in the Jordan. He had left the carpenter's shop in Nazareth—this was the beginning of his public ministry. What a glorious experience for Mary to witness her son's first miracle! Yet Mary, still the mother, seemed to expect some display of His glory. She told him, "They have no wine." Jesus answered, "Woman, what have I to do with thee? Mine hour is not yet come." This was a gentle rebuke to Mary; this was a business in which personal relationship was excluded. Mary's faith was tested, and she was ready to give her son back to God. From now on Mary is completely in the background. Every brief glimpse that we have of her has to do with Jesus. How she must have exulted in his ministry! How fearful must she have been when he was rejected!

Matthew, Mark, and Luke all record a visit that Mary and his brethren made him, and they could not reach him for the crowd. He was told, "Your mother and your brothers are standing desiring to see you."

"But he said to them, 'My mother and my brethren are those who hear the word of God and do it.'" His disciples composed a family transcending and surviving this earth's ties. No doubt Mary was beginning to know that this, her son, was also her Savior. The spiritual life was to surpass the bonds of a human family. Her knowledge of God and His promise would sustain her in the great ordeal ahead. She could accept the anguish, the loneliness and the heartache. What a beautiful example she has been through the centuries!

She went with him to the cross and as he was lifted up, He saw his mother and the disciple he loved standing together, and he said, "Woman, behold thy son." To the disciple, "Behold thy mother! And from that hour that disciple took her unto his own home." He did not forget his bereaved mother.

Mary was among the women at the tomb after the resurrection but it was not to her that Christ first appeared, but to Mary Magdalene. It was not his mother who was told to tell "My brethren" of his resurrection, but Mary Magdalene.

The Scriptures refer to Mary the mother of Jesus as blessed among women. She shared with Joseph the parental responsibility of the rearing of Jesus. She followed his life's work with solicitude. And the cross of Simeon's prophecy was experienced—"And a sword will pierce through your own soul also."

The last we hear of Mary, she is with the apostles, the women and His brothers in the upper room in Jerusalem. No special honor is ascribed to her here. Neither in Acts or the Epistles is any kind of homage given to Mary. How inferior in the Scriptures is her position to that in which the Roman Catholic Church has exalted her! As a wife and as a mother, Mary typifies the noblest qualities of womanhood.

STUDY SUGGESTIONS

Where did Mary live, and to whom was she betrothed? (Luke 1:26-27)
How was Mary "blessed among women"?
Relate the Annunciation. (Luke 1:28-38)
Why was Mary granted this privilege?
Where did Mary go after this message? (Luke 1:3) Why?
Sketch the meeting of these two women. (Luke 1:40-45)
How did Elisabeth know Mary's babe was the Messiah? (Luke 1:41)
In your own words, narrate Mary's song. (Luke 1:46-55)
Discuss the complications when the virgin was found with child. (Matt. 1:18)
Breach of marriage contract carried what penalty? (Deut. 22:23-24)
What did Joseph decide to do, and why? (Matt. 1:24)
Discuss the journey from Nazareth to Bethlehem. Why did they go? (Luke 2:1-5)
Why did Mary go? (Micah 5:2)
What were the things Mary kept pondering in her heart? (Luke 2:8-18)
How old was the child when he was circumcised? Why was he named Jesus? (Luke 2:21)
Discuss Mary's wisdom and spiritual discernment. (Luke 2:22-39)

Did Mary's faith falter at Simeon's prophetic words? (Luke 2:35)

How did the aged Anna confirm Mary's destiny? (Luke 2:38)

What was the outcome of the visit of the wise men? (Matt. 2:11)

Sketch the flight into Egypt and return. (Matt. 2:14-20) Use your imagination to visualize Mary's courage and faith in this sojourn.

Does Luke 2:52 describe the mother as well as the child?

Does the family journey to the Passover Feast in Jerusalem when Jesus was twelve give us an insight into Mary's qualities as a mother? (Luke 2:41-49)

Discuss Mary's and the boy Jesus' relationship as revealed in Luke 2:49-51.

At the feast in Cana of Galilee, how did Jesus show his authority over Mary? (Jno. 2:1-5) (Catholics say Mary commanded and Jesus obeyed)

Did Jesus elevate Mary above any woman who hears and obeys the Word of God? (Luke 11:27)

How may one become related to Christ? (Matt. 12:48-50)

Discuss family relationship versus divine relationship. (Matt. 12:48-50)

Did she falter at the cross? How did Jesus show his love for his Mother even in death? (Jno. 19:25-27)

Did Mary have other children? (Matt. 13:55-56) Name them. (Mark 6:3)

What is the last record we have of Mary? (Acts 1:13-14) Were her sons present on this occasion?

Do the Scriptures teach that Mary went to heaven without dying?

Was Mary sinless? (1 Jno. 1:8-10)

Should prayers be made through Mary? (1 Tim. 2:5)

Evaluate Mary's noble qualities of womanhood.

Anna

Luke 2:36-38
Phil. 2:14

"And she, coming in that instant, gave thanks likewise unto the Lord, and spoke of Him to all them that looked for redemption in Jerusalem" (Luke 2:38).

"W HERE ye shine as lights in a dark world; holding forth the Word of Life." These words of the apostle describe the prophetess Anna. She lived in one of the dark periods of the history of Israel. They were subjects of the Roman Emperor. For many years the Jews had been a subjected people, and they longed for the restoration of David's throne. However, Rome was opposed to any such idea as the coming of a Messiah, and Herod the Great would have killed any who might have aspired to becoming king of the Jews. A revolutionary spirit was in many of the Israelites, but there were a few devout ones, "waiting for the Consolation of Israel." The gentle Anna of Luke's Gospel was one of these who knew that the prophecies long foretold would not fail. In spite of her environment she was the very embodiment of hope and expectation. To this lonely widow belongs the distinction of being the first to identify the child Jesus; "and spake of him to all them that looked for redemption in Jerusalem."

Anna was the daughter of Phanuel of the tribe of Asher, which was among the dispersed tribes of Israel. Ten of the tribes under Jeroboam had severed themselves from David's house. Through the centuries they remained apart and in apostasy.

It seemed, as Anna stood beside Simeon in the temple, that she called to all Israel, "This babe is the hope of your expectation"— that this rebellious people might again be gathered into one kingdom.

A DOORKEEPER IN THE HOUSE OF THE LORD

Anna was truly one of God's luminaries, though not much is told us about her. The brief picture is so like "stars in a dark world" (Moffat), shining brightly and then fading from sight.

In years, Anna was old. She had lived with her husband seven years from her virginity; and she was a widow of about fourscore and four years. Some commentators say she was eighty-four years old, while others say she had been a widow for eighty-four years. However, her age is of little importance. "You are as young as your faith, as old as your fears, as young as your hope, as old as your despairs. So long as your heart receives messages of beauty, cheer, courage, grandeur and power from the earth, from man, and from the Infinite, so long you are young."

We visualize Anna with a radiant face, walking firmly and erect in the Temple of Jerusalem. "She served God with fastings and prayers day and night." She lived spiritually aloof from the things of the world.

Hers was the last voice of prophecy. This coming had been foretold, and now this "widow indeed" confirmed that this babe was he of whom the Prophets spoke.

EXPECTANCY

Anna did not allow her grief and loss to separate her from God. She had drawn closer to Him and had scarcely been absent from the temple since her early widowhood. The hope and expectancy of this woman was not just a rare gift from above—a natural happy disposition, but something more, something Anna had learned through long fellowship with God. She had listened to the reading of the law and the prophets; she had been present at every hour of prayer; she had become a doorkeeper in the House of the Lord. And how gloriously was her waiting rewarded!

"The Lord is my portion,
Sayeth my soul;
Therefore will I hope
in him.
The Lord is good unto them
that wait for him,
To the soul that seeketh him.
It is good that a man
Should both hope
and quietly wait for
The Salvation of the Lord."
—Lam. 3:24-26

She was granted the high honor of seeing the Messiah with her own eyes. Forty days after his birth, Mary and Joseph brought the Holy Child to the temple and presented him to the Lord according to the law of Moses. She clearly understood Simeon's prophetic words, and she joined him in declaring to the parents and bystanders that this was the "Hope of Israel."

No doubt her words were whispered about the temple, that the fulness of time had come, but Anna's task had been fulfilled. In all probability she did not live to witness his divine teachings and his glorious resurrection, but she saw him and at the hour of prayer she spoke of him to all the people who had looked for the salvation he was to bring.

STUDY SUGGESTIONS

Discuss God's care for widows. (Ex. 22:2; Ex. 14:29; 16:11-14; 26:12; 1 Tim. 5:4-9; Acts 6:1; 1 Tim. 5:3; Jas. 1:27)

Would Anna fit the description? (1 Tim. 2:3)

Who was Anna's father? What tribe? (Luke 2:36)

What of her age and married life? (Luke 2:36b)

How long had she been a widow? (2:37a)

What of her constant devotion? (2:37b)

What was her great privilege? (2:39)

As a prophetess what other eminent figures did she join? (Ex. 15:20a; Judges 4:4; 2 Kings 12:14)

What command of Titus did she fulfill? (Titus 2:3-5)

Explain her radiant old age.

Why did Simeon and Anna recognize the Child? *Think.* Did God reveal it to them because they were looking for Him? What was Anna's concern? Things spiritual or just "things"?

Should old age be a season of cynicism and malice?

Discuss her service in the temple.

Two Women of Bethany

"And Martha served" (John 12:2).
"Mary, which also sat at Jesus' feet" (Luke 10:39).

Luke 10:38-42
John 11:1-46

AMONG THE most notable and lovable women in the Bible are two sisters, Mary and Martha, whose stories are told by Luke and John. They were close personal friends of Jesus, each loving and serving him in her own way.

The first scene, as pictured by Luke, takes place in the house of Martha in the village of Bethany. It is a simple home-like scene, showing the sisters at supper with our Lord. He was always sure of a warm welcome in this home; a safe retreat from his enemies, a haven of rest at the end of a weary day. Often he trudged from Jerusalem to Bethany, a distance of about three miles on the Jericho Road.

"A certain woman received him into her house," say the Scriptures. Martha seems to have been the head of the house; and with her lived her sister, Mary, and their brother, Lazarus.

We can picture an attractive, comfortable house, with an outside stairway leading to an upper room from a cool and well-shaded court. Martha would have the garden and house clean and inviting, for she was a good housekeeper.

How the friendship between this family and Jesus came to be we do not know. Some have suggested that Martha was a widow and had gone to Jesus for comfort. Or perhaps this family had heard Him say, "The birds have nests, and foxes have holes, but the Son of Man hath not where to lay his head," and had offered to share their home with him.

In this the last week of His life, he sought rest and refuge; and in this home he found these things. It reminds us of another home that was a place of rest for Elisha. The Shunammite woman, who built and furnished a room for the man of God, like Mary and Martha, was using her material possessions to the glory of God.

"Here Christ shall come; and here he shall abide;
Our table shall be set for our Great Guest;
Our lamp be lit; our hearth be warm and wide;
And here he shall find shelter, food, and rest.
And he will walk with us beside our fire,

And he will walk with us through every task.
We can confide each hope and each desire,
  No question be too great or too small to ask.
Because he lives with us, is one of us
  We shall take care no evil things be heard;
Because his ways are kind and courteous,
  We shall watch our ways, our every spoken word.
This is our new house, Lord, be thou its Head.
We gladly share its simple fare with Thee.
Sit at our table, break and bless our bread.
  And make us worthy of Thy company."
                              —GRACE NOLL CROWELL[1]

THE SUPPER

As Jesus and his disciples were going from Jerusalem to Bethany,
he related the story of the good Samaritan who showed kindness to a
man beaten and robbed on that very road.

Perhaps Martha was expecting him, and his disciples too. There
was a bustle of plans and preparation, for the writer tells us, "Martha
was cumbered with much serving."

Jesus arrived, and was no doubt welcomed with a holy kiss; water
was surely brought to wash his feet. He sat down to rest in the cool
shade of the courtyard, and was joined there by Mary while Martha
hurried off to complete the evening meal.

Martha strove for perfection; there was nothing too good for this
adored guest. She wanted everything to be just right, and in her
hurry and anxiety perhaps thought, "Where is Mary and why isn't she
helping me?"

Mary was sitting quietly at Jesus' feet, lost in His spiritual dis-
courses. She was not aware of Martha's irritation. Perhaps Martha
began to feel self-pity and a little self-righteousness as she said to
Jesus, "Lord, dost thou not care that my sister has left me to serve
alone? Bid her, therefore that she help me."

Martha should have been the happiest woman in all the world,
but instead she was worried. She was critical of her sister and her
guest, and we can be sure that no sooner had the words left her lips,
she became more miserable and ashamed.

Jesus, with kindness and tenderness, rebuked the rude intrusion
and interruption, "Martha, Martha, thou art careful and troubled
about many things; but one thing is needful and Mary hath chosen the
better part, which shall not be taken from her."

Notice carefully that Jesus did not rebuke Martha for her industry. Somebody had to prepare supper; if Martha had spent all

---

[1] Taken from *Songs of Faith* by Grace Noll Crowell. Copyright 1939, Harper &
Brothers. Used by permission.

her time at Jesus' feet, he and his disciples would have gone hungry. Jesus did not rebuke Martha for any lack of love or loyalty to Him; her love for the Savior was just as deep and tender as Mary's.

Jesus is teaching Martha that worry and anxiety are sinful. The meal was more elaborate than necessary, and could probably have been served more simply. True, Martha was worried and anxious about her service to her Lord; nevertheless, Jesus said, "Martha, you are anxious and troubled about many things."

Jesus said, "Man shall not live by bread alone, but by every word that proceedeth out of the mouth of God." Too much emphasis on "food for the body" to the neglect of food for the soul is improper perspective. So Martha, in her worrying about the supper, rebuked her sister, and criticized the Savior. He had come because he was sure he was welcome; now perhaps he felt he was a hindrance and a burden. Have you as a guest felt unwelcome and unwanted because of so much extra work? Worry wrecks the disposition, hurts loved ones, grieves and disappoints our Lord.

Many will ask how one can help but worry. We are living under the threat of war, threat of the atomic bomb, disease, and the pressures of trying to accumulate possessions. There are so many things that can waste our lives and break our hearts. Mary was living above worry as she sat at the feet of Jesus. "But one thing is needful. Mary hath chosen that good part, which shall not be taken away from her." Mary put Christ first. "Seek ye first the kingdom of heaven. Set your affections on things above and not on things of the earth" (Col. 3:2). "That Christ may dwell in your heart by faith; that we be rooted and grounded in love" (Eph. 3:17). Our relationship to Christ and the service we render to Him is that which abides forever. "In nothing be anxious, but in everything by prayer and supplication with thanksgiving let your requests be made known unto God. And the peace of God which passeth all understanding shall keep your hearts and minds through Christ Jesus (Phil. 4:6).

A FUNERAL

John tells of the death and funeral of Lazarus, in Bethany. The sisters sent word to Jesus, who was across the Jordan, saying, "Lord, he whom you love is ill." They waited for Jesus, but the days passed and he did not come. Finally death came to their brother, as it will come to all.

The clean house in Bethany was filled with many Jews who had come to console these sisters. Word came that Jesus had arrived. Martha ran to meet him, while Mary sat in the house. "Lord, if you had been here my brother would not have died. And even now I know that whatever you ask from God, God will give you." With these words, Martha met the Master.

THE RESURRECTION

Jesus said unto her, "I am the resurrection and the life; he who believes in me, though he die, yet shall he live; and whosoever lives and believes in me shall never die. Do you believe this?" Martha's reply is a magnificent confession of faith, "Yea, Lord, I believe that thou art the Christ, the Son of God, which should come into the world."

Martha returned to the house and told Mary that the Teacher had come and was calling for her. Mary hurried to meet Him, fell down at his feet, saying just what Martha had said, "Lord, if you had been here, my brother would not have died."

When He saw the grief and the sadness at the grave, "Jesus wept." Not only did he grieve for those he loved, but also because of the unbelief and hardness of heart of some of the people who stood by. Martha and Mary were so opposite in temperaments, yet one in spirit, but Jesus understood and loved them both.

Then followed the great scene at the sepulchre, when Lazarus came forth bound hand and foot with grave clothes. Jesus said, "Loose him, and let him go." What a happy reunion that night in Bethany!

There were mutterings and threatenings against the Lord, but Martha and Mary stood firm in their loyalty to Him. This loyalty meant much to Jesus in the dark and lonely hours ahead.

THE BANQUET

This is the last we hear of Mary and Martha, when they prepare for Jesus and Lazarus. Matthew says the feast was in the house of Simon the Leper. John said, "there they made him a supper and Martha served." The same capable Martha doing what she could do best, doing what she loved to do, serving those who meant so much to her. On this occasion she was not hurried, nervous, or anxious, but displayed calmness and poise born of a deep faith.

Mary was not helping Martha serve, but Martha was not upset, for she was expressing her love and thankfulness to Jesus.

Mary's heart, too, was flooded with gratitude and love. Something more than food was due the Lord. She had a pound of ointment, very costly, the most expensive she could buy. With it she anointed the feet of Jesus, wiped his feet with her hair, and the house was filled with the sweet odor of the perfume.

Mary understood that Jesus' hour was near. He would go up to Jerusalem, and eventually to Calvary. Her faith would not cry out against this. She understood, as none other, what Jesus was suffering. Martha stood by in approval of the gift of ointment.

Some of the disciples, led by Judas, complained about this waste. No doubt they thought Mary emotionally unbalanced, or perhaps their criticism had an uglier motive, when they said, "Think how many poor people right here in Bethany could have been fed and clothed." Possibly Mary was hurt by this criticism.

Though others found fault, Jesus praised her for her gift. "Let her alone, against the day of my burial hath she kept this . . . Verily I say unto you, wheresoever this gospel shall be preached throughout the whole world, this also that she hath done shall be spoken of for a memorial of her" (Matt. 26:13).

Mary gave the best she had, and was motivated by love and deep understanding of her Savior. Martha, too, loved Jesus devotedly, and manifested her love in service. Christ said, "But one thing is needful, Mary hath chosen that good part which shall not be taken away."

"This also that she hath done shall be spoken of for a memorial of her"—wherever the gospel of Jesus is preached the story of Mary will be told.

STUDY SUGGESTIONS

Contrast the traits of these sisters.
Does everyone possess like talents?
Should devotion neglect the home?
Should the home neglect devotion?
Discuss the confession Martha made at the deah of Lazarus.
What of Mary's deep spiritual discernment?
Did Mary love Jesus better than Martha because she knew Him better?
Did Christ condemn Martha for serving?
What was the point of his criticism? (Luke 10:41)
Discuss the criticism of the disciples and Judas.
Give Jesus' immortal defense of Mary. (Mark 14:6-9)
Would you say Martha and Mary were hospitable? (Matt. 25:35; Rom. 12:13)
How did Mary immortalize her name? (Mark 14:3b, 9)
How did Martha? (Luke 10:38; Jno. 12:2)
With the variety of gifts and talents, we cannot all give the same, but can we not all give our best?

Peter's Wife and Mother-in-Law

"When Jesus came into Peter's house, he saw his wife's mother laid sick of a fever" (Matt. 8:14).

Matt. 8:14, 15
Mark 1:30, 31
Luke 4:38, 39

PETER'S MOTHER-IN-LAW made her home with her daughter and her son-in-law. Their home was in Capernaum, the city Jesus had selected to be the center of his Galilean ministry. Perhaps Peter's house was headquarters for the Lord and his disciples. Jesus had enlisted the full time support of these fishermen, Peter, Andrew, James and John.

A native of Bethsaida, Peter likely had moved his household from there to Capernaum to be near the Savior. We hear of no objection or complaint from his wife and her mother, although they had to leave friends and familiar surroundings. They placed the affairs of the Christ above their personal wishes. It is plain to be seen that as the head of his household, Peter had full cooperation. He gave up his native home to follow the Master to Capernaum. Every indication is that the desire of their hearts was to serve the Lord. Their motive and purpose were to assist in the establishment of the kingdom.

A HOME DEDICATED

The Scriptures do not tell us the names of these two women in Peter's household. They are pictured to us as a wife and a mother. Here is abundant proof that Peter was married, yet Christ called him to be an apostle. His approval of this marriage was evidenced by his very presence in the home and by the great blessing which he bestowed that day.

Though the Biblical account of this household is very brief, we can envision a home as God would have it. Peter provided for his family. He owned a house; being so blessed, he was better off than his Lord. In this same chapter (Matt. 8:20) Jesus said, "Foxes have holes, and the birds of the air have nests; but the Son of man hath not where to lay his head." In this home there was room and affection for the mother-in-law. They showed concern and anxiety because she was sick of "a great fever." No doubt this woman was old, yet she was respected and taken care of, as old people ought to be, with all possible tenderness.

KEEPERS AT HOME

Peter's wife and her mother were keepers at home in the true sense of the word. We can be sure that this house, though modest, was neat and orderly. It was dedicated to the Lord's ministry, and the aged mother-in-law was in the habit of serving her son-in-law and the other disciples who came there. Food and rest were offered with gracious hospitality.

But now she was lying in bed, sick of a fever. She was unable to offer assistance in this labor of love unto Christ and his disciples.

Jesus came from the synagogue, weary from the hours of teaching. James and John accompanied him. "And he arose out of the synagogue and entered into Simon's house. And Simon's wife's mother was taken with a great fever; and they besought him for her." Surely this was a serious illness. The members of the family were deeply concerned for her welfare. They were fond of her, and they wanted her to get well. Therefore they besought Christ in her behalf. He came and took her by the hand and lifted her up. Immediately the fever left her tired body.

A MINISTERING SERVANT

Matthew, Mark and Luke all relate this same story, and each writer tells that after she was healed, she "ministered unto them." Inasmuch as she had been healed by Jesus and again felt in good health, with deep gratitude she ministered unto him. Those friends who had mentioned her to Jesus, who had besought him to do something for her, also were objects of her service.

CHRIST A WELCOME GUEST

How blest is the home where Christ is a welcome guest! How happy is the family where each member is devoted to the advancement of the kingdom!

In every home that honors Christ, there is regard for the personality of each one. The aged ones are respected and regarded with affection, and the sick are sustained and comforted. God has ordained that the Christian must provide for those of his own house.

STUDY SUGGESTIONS

Where did this woman live? With whom? (Mark 1:29)
What was her illness? (Luke 4:38)
Who told Jesus about her condition?
Did Christ heal her entirely? (Mark 1:31)
How did she express her love and appreciation?
What must have been the relation between Peter and his mother-in-law?
Should mothers-in-law rule their daughters' or sons' homes?
What doctrine of the Catholic church is here repudiated?

The Woman with an Issue of Blood

Mark 5:25-34
Luke 8:43
Luke 1:29
Luke 13:12-16

"For she said, If I may touch but his clothes, I shall be whole" (Mark 5:28).

THE HOLY SPIRIT has given unto us a picture of woman as she is in life. Sick women are included in this gallery of sacred pictures. Their names are not revealed; the old mother-in-law with a high fever, another with an issue of blood for twelve long years. One had a spirit of infirmity for eighteen years, crooked and bent so that she could not fully straighten herself. Their sufferings, their healing, and their joyous faith are on the pages of God's Holy Book for all time.

Mark tells us of a woman "who had suffered many things of many physicians and had spent all that she had, was nothing better, but rather grew worse." Even Luke, the physician, says she could not be healed by anyone.

For twelve years she had suffered from a flow of blood, and we can imagine how pale, wan, and haggard she was. She had gone to the doctors (notice the word is plural), and none had helped her. All of her money had been spent in this unrewarding round of doctors.

But she had not despaired of all hope. According to the law of Moses she was unclean and was forbidden contact with others, but she had not surrendered herself to her fate. She heard reports of Jesus.

THE PRAYER OF A SICK WOMAN

"For she said, if I may touch but his clothes, I shall be whole." She dared not expect Jesus to touch one unclean. She did not send a friend to tell Jesus about her condition. Nor did she send for him. Weakened by her malady, but strengthened by a great faith, she made her way to the Great Physician through a multitude of people. Timidly she reached out and touched the hem of his garment. "And straightway the fountain of her blood was dried up and she felt in her body she was healed of that plague." Jesus too, sensed the power gone out from him, and turned about in this crowd, saying, "Who touched me?"

"But the woman, fearing, and trembling, knowing what had been done to her, came and fell down before him and told him all the truth"—poured out the story of twelve years of suffering, discouragement, and poverty. And he said, "Daughter, thy faith hath made thee whole; go in peace, and be whole of thy plague."

This took place on a street in Capernaum, when Jesus was on his way to the bedside of Jairus' daughter. Even though all physicians had failed to cure this sick woman, she never lost confidence in the compassion and mercy of God. The greatest of all physicians sent her forth in peace again. Lovingly and tenderly he spoke these words of triumph, "Daughter, thy faith hath made thee whole."

WHOM SATAN HATH BOUND

Then there was the woman of long standing infirmity; for eighteen years her body was crooked, making it impossible for her to straighten herself. Perhaps she was the victim of something like arthritis. Often humiliated, bent and broken in body, but not altogether broken in spirit, she does not seclude herself in her home in self pity.

We see her first on the Sabbath day in one of the synagogues, where she had gone to worship. Her faith in God remained through the years. Did she know Jesus was there that day? Had the fame of his healing kindled a new hope within her heart? Luke tells us that Jesus was teaching in the synagogue on the Sabbath day, and that this poor twisted woman was there, though she could not even lift herself to see the face of Jesus. When He saw her, he called her to him and said unto her, "Woman, thou art loosed from thine infirmity." He laid his hands on her and immediately she was made straight.

The woman could once more walk like other women. She could look in the face of Jesus, so full of tender compassion. We read that she glorified God, from whence came this wonderful miracle. She did not accept her healing as something that should have come to her. Her praise and adoration was unto the Giver of all good. Probably many others who knew her joined her in glorifying God. This glory was also to the name of Him who was the cause of her cure.

Jesus said she was a daughter of Abraham. She was of the seed of the patriarch to whom a great promise was made many years before; "And in thee shall all families of the earth be blessed" (Ex. 12:3b). She was of the faith of Abraham.

Jesus further said of the woman, "Whom Satan hath bound, lo, these eighteen years." Perhaps her sickness had its seat first in her spirit. Today we are told that many of the aches and pains which people suffer are the sign and the consequence of emotional and mental disturbances.

STUDY SUGGESTIONS

Read Matthew 9:20-22; Mark 5:25-34; Luke 8:43-48.

What was the condition of a certain woman in this multitude who followed Jesus? (Mark 5:25)

What was her experience with doctors? (Mark 5:26)

How did she manifest her faith? (Mark 5:27)

Her faith became the channel of what great blessing? (Mark 5:29)

Did she attempt to keep her healing a secret? (Mark 5:30c)

Why did Jesus "ask who touched me"?

Was it needful that she tell of her need, her help and healing from Him?

Do you think she was the only one in that crowd of people who was sick? Were they so lacking in faith that they crowded around Him, but did not touch him? (Luke 13:10-17)

On what day was this miracle performed? (Luke 13:10)

Discuss these two statements: "A spirit of infirmity"; "whom Satan hath bound."

How long had this woman been sick? (13:11) Describe her pitiful condition. (13:11b)

Tell of Jesus' compassion for her. (13:12, 13)

Why was the ruler so provoked? (13:14)

What did Jesus call him? Why? (13:15)

Was he jealous for the *Sabbath*, or of *Christ?*

What was the ruler's judgment of values? (13:15)

Besides the common claim of humanity, what other claim did the woman have (13:16a)

How did his adversaries react? (13:17a)

What was the multitude's reaction? (13:17b)

The Sinful Woman

Luke 7:36-50

> "Thy faith hath saved thee, go in peace" (Luke 7:50).

JESUS HAD BEEN invited to dine with Simon, a Pharisee of the village of Nain. The invitation seemed to have been extended from a desire to find fault. Simon planned to watch his Guest closely, on the chance that he could find something wrong. Jesus accepted the invitation and entered Simon's house.

Others were also present; both invited and uninvited guests. The uninvited persons stood back looking, as was the accepted custom of the day. Those who had been bidden by the host reclined around a long table, leaning upon their elbows, with their feet stretched out behind. There were slaves to wash their dusty feet as they entered; there was oil for their parched skin and warm kisses of welcome.

PENITENT TEARS

Among the uninvited guests was a woman who was commonly called "the sinner" by the townsmen. While the feasting was going on this woman came into the dining hall and hurried to kneel at Jesus' feet. Her tears washed his feet as she bent to kiss them. Deeming them fouled, rather than washed, she hastened to wipe his feet with her hair, as she had no towel. She bestowed many kisses and tears upon the feet of the Savior, and broke an alabaster cruse of costly ointment that she might anoint them.

Simon, the Pharisee, knew this woman and her notorious sin, and wondered that Jesus did not spurn her. He thought to himself, "If he were a prophet he would have perceived who and what manner of woman this is, that toucheth him; that she is a sinner."

Jesus knew well about this woman, and he also knew Simon's thoughts. He looked at the proud Pharisee and told him the parable of the two debtors, one of whom owed five hundred pence, and the other fifty. Neither of them could pay. The creditor forgave them both, and Jesus asked, "Which of them will love him more?"

"I suppose," answered Simon, "that he to whom he forgave the most."

"You have answered rightly," said Jesus. Then he turned to the woman, saying to Simon, "I entered into thine house, thou gavest me no water for my feet; but she hath washed my feet with tears, and wiped them with the hairs of her head. Thou gavest me no kiss; but this woman since the time I came in hath not ceased to kiss my feet. My head with oil thou didst not anoint; but this woman hath anointed my feet with ointment."

He then made the application to Simon. "Her sins, which are many, are forgiven; for she loved much; but to whom little is forgiven, the same loveth little."

Jesus told the woman, "Thy sins are forgiven . . . Thy faith hath saved thee; go in peace."

THOUGH THY SINS BE AS SCARLET

Where had this sinful woman met Christ before? What had he said that resulted in such sincere penitence? Perhaps she had been among the publicans and sinners who came to Christ. She was scorned and avoided in the town where she lived; she had rejected her virtue and was living in the lowest sin into which a woman can fall. Jesus' gracious words had wrought a great change in this woman's heart. She had been induced to stop and take thought. The Lord's tender pity for all "that labor and are heavy laden" aroused shame and sorrow in her over her sinful life. Warm love and fervent gratitude were expressed in tears and kisses. Her remorse was genuine and her penitence was sincere.

Every woman in the world should rejoice in this story of the woman who was a sinner.

> "Beauty for ashes, God hath decreed!
> Help He provideth for every need;
> What is unlovely he will restore;
> Grace all sufficient; what need we more?"
> —GRANT COLFAX TULLAR

Christian mothers should be wholly concerned with the rearing and training of Christian daughters. True, Christ stands ready to forgive and restore, but how true the old saying, "The bird with a broken pinion never soars so high again." There was a time when the concern was the "prodigal son." Today the delinquent girls in the early teens are as numerous as the boys. This condition exists all over the nation and has come to be problem number one. Christians should be alert and aggressive in the face of the great responsibility confronting them with reference to these young souls.

With Bibles opened day by day, and prayers ascending to the throne of God, let every woman accept the responsibility of Christian motherhood. Let her set herself to the task of bringing to every girl and boy in the community the power and influence of the church in an effort to save our youth from ruin.

This woman who was a sinner was also some woman's daughter. To avoid a tragedy like this is the responsibility of the home and church.

STUDY SUGGESTIONS

Who invited Jesus into his house? (Luke 7:36)
Who was among the uninvited guests? (Luke 7:37b)
Name three things that indicated her penitence. (Luke 7:38)
How did she use her glory for the Savior? (1 Cor. 11:15)
What was Simon's attitude toward his guest? (Luke 7:39)
What was Christ's answer to the critical thoughts of this Pharisee? (Luke 7:40-42)
Why did Jesus forgive this sinful woman? (Luke 7:47)
Was she saved by faith only? (Jas. 2:20)
Name another sinful woman saved by faith and works. (Jas. 2:25)
Discuss the boundless love of God. (John 3:16)
Discuss the mission of Christ to the world. (Luke 19:10)

Herodias

Matt. 2:13
Mark 6:14-28; 27:28

"And she went forth and said unto her mother, 'What shall I ask?' And she said the head of John the Baptist" (Mark 6:24).

HERODIAS might well be called the Jezebel of the New Testament. Her story is a striking example of the evil influence of a heartless woman possessed of a wicked ambition. She hated John the Baptist as Jezebel hated Elijah. Not only was she guilty of the death of the forerunner of Christ, but it may be that she had something to do with the contempt heaped upon Christ by her husband Herod Antipas.

This evil woman was descended from a line of wicked people. She was the granddaughter of Herod the Great, who sought to destroy the child Jesus. Historians record that he had ten wives and killed his first wife, Marianone, who was the mother of Herodias' father, Aristobulus, and of Philip and Antipas.

Her first marriage was to Herod Philip, her half-uncle. He was exiled because his mother had plotted against her husband, Herod the Great. They were living in Rome. To this marriage was born one daughter, whom the Bible does not name. Some historians call her Salome. This daughter was a Herod on both her mother's and father's side. Her earliest training must have been in an evil environment. Her only accomplishment was sensuous dancing.

A HEART OF STONE

Once when Herod Antipas had visited Rome, he stayed in the home of Herodias and Philip. No doubt her husband's disinheritance was a bitter disappointment to this very ambitious woman. Thus she was ready and willing to indulge in an illegitimate love affair with her husband's brother. She would certainly never be close to the throne married to Philip, so she deserted her own husband and persuaded her brother-in-law to divorce his wife, a princess of Arabia, that she might reign as queen.

So through treachery, deceit, and intrigue, her daughter became a princess at the capitol, Tiberias. The immoral life at court was deceptively glamorous.

John the Baptist, who had the courage to reveal the sinfulness which prevailed, said to Herod, "It is not lawful for thee to have thy brother's wife" (Mark 6:18). Therefore, Herodias had a grudge against him, and would have killed him, but she could not. However, Herod had him bound and cast into prison. This sinful king was dominated by an equally sinful woman, and so often the Bible has revealed by example that a woman whose life is devoted to the bad and vicious is far more vile than a man.

So Herodias must have been chagrined that she could not immediately have this prophet of God killed. She never gave up within her heart, however; she waited and planned that some day he would die for the denunciation of her immoral life.

Her husband feared John the Baptist. He knew he was a just and holy man, and he heard him gladly, keeping him from the wicked designs of Herodias. How great was her power over Herod, that he should agree to what his conscience had kept him from executing!

REVENGEFUL

At last the opportunity came for her to accomplish her foul purpose. "Herod on his birthday made a supper to his lords, high captains, and chief estates of Galilee."

Herodias knew Herod. She knew his sensuous disposition. This woman used her own daughter to excite the passions of her husband. And when the daughter of Herodias danced before these men, Herod and those who sat with him were pleased. Passion and luxury destroyed self-control, and he said, "Whatsoever thou shalt ask of me, I will give it to thee, unto half of my kingdom."

Instructed by her mother, she requested, "The head of John the Baptist!"

How deadly was the hate of Herodias against this messenger of God!

It must have been very galling to Herod to find himself ensnared by his own rash folly. "Yet for his oath's sake, and for their sakes which sat with him, he would not reject her."

"And immediately he sent an executioner and commanded his head to be brought and he went and beheaded him in the prison. And he brought his head in on a charger, and gave it to the damsel; and she gave it to her mother." Though Herodias did not kill John the Baptist, she had it done. Her husband and her daughter were her tools. The Bible tells us no more of Herodias.

Her story closed as she received the head of John the Baptist. Did she live long with a guilty conscience? Did she ever realize how different her life and the history of this period might have been had she stood on the side of God?

STUDY SUGGESTIONS

Who was Herodias? (See Bible dictionary)
To whom was she first married? (Matt. 14:3)
To whom was she now married? (Mark 6:17)

Give John the Baptist's reproof for this unlawful marriage. (Luke 3:19)
Who was responsible for Herod's casting John into prison? (Mark 6:17)
Does the fact that he did it for Herodias' sake lessen his guilt?
Did Herod attempt to favor John? (Mark 6:20)
Was it that John's preaching disturbed the conscience of this king? (Mark 6:20)
Because of John's rebuke what did Herodias do? (Mark 6:19)
What kind of daughter would a mother like Herodias be likely to have? (Ezek. 16:44)
Tell of Herod's birthday party. (Mark 6:21-22)
What is revealed of this girl's shamelessness? (Mark 6:22)

A Woman of Canaan

Matt. 15:21-28
Mark 7:24-30
Luke 18:1-8
John 12:20
Rom. 1:17

"O, woman, great is thy faith; be it unto thee even as thou wilt" (Luke 6:28b).

MATTHEW tells that this woman of great faith was a woman of Canaan. The Canaanites were the founders of Sidon, and the Phoenicians were their descendants. Mark has it that she was a Greek, a Syrophoenician. After Alexander's conquest, when all the world was in subjection to the Greeks, the Jews divided the world politically into Jews and Greeks. The footnote uses the word Gentile. This woman was a Gentile, indicating her religion; she was not Jewish, but heathen. She was of the stock that God had said must be destroyed, root and branch (Deut. 7:2). But this excision had not been complete. She and her people were not included in the Savior's personal ministry.

A MOTHER'S PRAYER

She lived within the boundaries of Tyre and Sidon—their reputation was like that of Sodom and Gomorrah. Jesus and his disciples were in the region; and they entered into a house, not desiring that any man know they were there. This indicates they had not gone into this Gentile region to teach and perform miracles yet. But the fame of the Lord could not be hidden; his fame had spread from Galilee to this region. Everything was against this woman; race, religion, and position. But it did not prevent her from seeking and obtaining the favor that her soul longed for. She had a great favor to ask for her little daughter, who was possessed by an unclean spirit. Her child's deep misery was her misery. Worn and wearied in the constant care of this afflicted daughter, she came to the Savior of Israel. Her heart was broken as she helplessly watched the paroxysms of her child.

She believed that Jesus could save her daughter. Her faith was based on the many wonderful miracles he had performed; the deaf were made to hear, the blind to see, and those with evil spirits were healed. She had heard these marvelous things from her own people. Among those who went up to worship at the feasts were numerous Greeks. They requested of Philip that they might see Jesus. Like the woman of Samaria they carried wonderful reports of his miracles.

This Canaanitish woman came out from those borders crying, "Have mercy on me, O Lord, thou son of David; My daughter is grievously vexed with a demon." Her prayer was not her own burden, but she was lamenting the physical and spiritual agony of her daughter.

These words on the lips of a Gentile woman on Gentile soil are notable. She too had a knowledge of the Jewish idea of the Messiah. She had probably never been to Galilee. Jesus had never been in this vicinity, but his fame had spread through all Syria, of which Phoenicia was a part. She had doubtless longed for the opportunity to bring his great power to bear on her tormented child.

OUT OF THE DEPTHS

She did not find him the gracious helper and healer that he was reported to be. He answered her not a word. Jesus appeared to be oblivious to the woman's entreaties, until the disciples, annoyed by her cries, besought Him to send her away; "for she crieth after us." They desired that He grant her request so that she would go away and leave them alone.

But he answered, "I was not sent but unto the lost sheep of the house of Israel." Jesus said this to his disciples, not to the woman. His ministry was limited to the Jews. The wisdom of God imposed this limitation. It was only when Christ was crucified that the "wall of partition between Jew and Gentile" was broken down. The woman was not disheartened by the repulse which His disciples received. She had been crying after the Lord, but now she came and worshipped Him, saying, "Lord, help me." We can almost hear her saying, "True, Lord, you have not sought me. I have sought you." She had reached her lowest depth, her darkest hour; and from the depths of a despairing heart she cried, "Lord, help me."

The woman's faith was put to a still sterner test, as he looked down on the pleading face and said, "It is not meet to take the children's bread and cast it to the dogs." The Jews are the "children," the "children of the kingdom." He was comparing the Jews to the children of God's family, and the heathen to the dogs without; this was the customary language of a Jew. The gospel was first to the Jew, and also to the Greek. He would test her faith to the fullest.

There are very few to whom this would not have been enough. Many a woman would have been angry and would have departed in despair. Not so this heathen woman. Hers was a mighty faith. A ready wit and deep humility are manifested in her answer, "Truth, Lord; yet the dogs eat of the crumbs that fall from the master's table." I am not one of the "children of the kingdom"; one of the "dogs" it is true. I accept the title and the position. But the dogs have a portion too; the dogs under the tables are allowed to eat of the children's crumbs that fall. "Give me a crumb and I am content," was her reply. One crumb of thy power and grace and the child shall be healed.

As Thou Wilt

She was rewarded. She who before heard words of hopelessness, now heard him say, "O woman, great is thy faith." He who would have denied her the smallest request now opened to her the riches of His grace; "Be it unto thee even as thou wilt." Her daughter was made whole from that very hour, "And she went away unto her house, and found the child laid upon the bed, and the demon gone out."

Her mother's heart was made to rejoice. Great love for her child, great faith in Jesus, brought a great reward. Her love and faith were manifested in her complete lack of pride. The Lord Jesus looked deep into the heart of this humble woman, who was not of "the lost sheep of the house of Israel," and He saw a faith which would stand the test, and what is more, would emerge mightier and purer than if she had received her request, merely for the asking. This woman is another illustration of the Savior's admonition, "that men ought always to pray, and not to faint."

The Canaanite woman is a beautiful picture of noble motherhood; she was a channel of blessing to her child. With one hand, she laid hold on Christ, through her faith. With the other hand she laid hold on her suffering daughter. She was a living and vital length connecting Him to the one she loved. What a tragedy today that so few mothers see themselves as living conductors through whom the Christ-like personality might flow to their children.

STUDY SUGGESTIONS

What was the race and religion of this woman? (Mark 7:26)

Who were the Canaanites? (Gen. 12:6; 13:7; Ex. 3:8-17; Deut. 7:1; Joshua 3:10)

Did the personal ministry of Christ extend beyond the borders of the Holy Land? (Matt. 15:24)

Explain why He was in the borders of Tyre and Sidon. (Mark 7:24b)
What boon did this woman desire from Christ? (Matt. 15:22)
Discuss the seeming indifference of Christ to her plea. (Matt. 15:23a)
What did the disciples urge and what was their motive? (Matt. 15:23)
Give His reply (Matt. 15:24). (He was telling them that he had not brought
    his miracles to any other but the people of the covenant.)
What of John 1:16 and Gal. 3:14?
Repeat her entreaty. (Matt. 15:25)
How did he further test her faith? (Matt. 15:25; Mark 7:27)
Was she angry? Was she discouraged? Did she accept the title and place?
As a Gentile "dog," for what did she ask?
What was the Savior's gracious commendation? (Matt. 15:28a; Mark 7:29a)
How great was "as thou wilt"? (Mark 7:29b, 30)

Salome

Matt. 20:20-23; 27:56
Mark 4:19; 16:1-8
Luke 5:10; 14:11
Rev. 1:9

"*Then came to him the mother of
Zebedee's children worshipping
him, and desiring a certain thing of
him*" (Matt. 20:20).

SALOME was one of the notable mothers of the New Testament.
She lived in Capernaum, or Bethsaida, near the Sea of Galilee.
Matthew designated her on two occasions as the mother of Zebedee's
children. She was the mother of James and John, two of the most
zealous and beloved apostles of Jesus. As the mother of these two
men, she is considered a blessed woman. These two sons, James and
John, were chosen, along with Peter, to be nearest to the Lord.

A WELL SPENT LIFE

Salome's life had been well employed. She handed down to her
sons a rich spiritual inheritance. John was known as the disciple Jesus loved, and he was leaning on the Lord's breast at the Last Supper.
Jesus gave his mother into John's care before he died. He is the
author of five books of the New Testament, and was the only witness
on Patmos. James was the first apostle to die for Christ; he was put
to death by Herod Agrippa.

Salome was the wife of a fisherman, Zebedee, who operated boats
and nets, assisted by his sons and hired servants. They were about the
business of mending these nets when Jesus called them to become fish-
ers of men. The young men immediately left their nets with their
father and the servants, and followed Jesus. This involved the break-

ing up of a family industry; they sacrificed a material inheritance. Salome was especially honored. The most she could have left to her sons would have been a few boats and nets, but now they had become disciples of the Nazarene, who was proclaiming, "The Kingdom of Heaven is at hand."

She, with many others in Israel, was expecting an earthly king to sit upon David's throne. Her expectations and ambitions were exaggerated.

This family had gone out with the multitudes to listen to John the Baptist at the Jordan. They had been baptized and were ready to follow Jesus when he began his ministry. Salome gave up her sons gladly, and she was among the faithful women who followed and ministered unto Jesus. She was present at the crucifixion, and prepared linens and spices for His burial.

A SELFISH REQUEST

There is only one blot against this mother's character. She allowed her human ambition for her sons to blind her to the nature of the kingdom. Near the end of his ministry, she came to him worshipping him, and desiring a certain thing of him: "Grant that these my two sons may sit the one on the right hand, and the other on the left in thy kingdom." Maternal pride and perhaps a little jealousy prompted this request.

"But Jesus answered and said, 'Ye know not what ye ask. Are ye able to drink of the cup that I shall drink of, and be baptized with the baptism that I am baptized with?' "

Jesus answered the mother of these Apostles very gently and patiently. Mark, in his version of this incident, credits James and John with the request, indicating that théy too shared in their mother's worldly ambition. The reply to the Lord's question is worded, "*They* say unto him, *we* are able."

No one can doubt the sincerity of these two. They professed their willingness to endure any suffering that their Master might endure. However, Jesus answered them, "Ye shall drink indeed of my cup, and shall be baptized with the baptism I am baptized with, but to sit on my right hand and my left is not mine to give, but it shall be given to them for whom it is prepared of my Father."

Here is a brief foresight of what Salome's sons would have to pass through. James was baptized with his Master's baptism of blood. John was persecuted and shared in the sufferings and struggles of the infant church.

Christ continued his gentle rebuke to Salome and her boys, "For whosoever exalteth himself shall be abased; he that humbleth himself shall be exalted." The places of honor in the coming kingdom were not places of favoritism, but would be designated by the Father in a very different way.

The Lord did not say James and John would not occupy the place in the kingdom that Salome wanted them to have.

Her complete lack of understanding of the kingdom brought forth the Lord's disapproval. The very manner of her seeking would lose them the place of honor. Salome is typical of many mothers, and in this one instance she allowed her own desires for her children's advancement to come before their spiritual preparation.

We cannot be to critical of her, however, for she never faltered in her service to Him. Perhaps she realized that spiritual greatness was not a gift to be bestowed, but it was to be earned. "Let him that would be great become your servant." She was one of the faithful women who gave herself in service to Him until the end, and we can be assured that she was among the women assembled with the apostles after the ascension of Christ, which is recorded by Luke in Acts 1:14.

Too, her sons followed their Lord and Savior, drinking of the cup of persecution and being baptized with suffering. Herod the king killed James with the sword as he sought to harm the Lord's church. John was exiled for the "word of God and the testimony of Jesus Christ." What a glorious contribution did this mother make to Christianity!

STUDY SUGGESTIONS

Discuss the family of Salome; the husband, the sons, and their occupation. (Matt. 4:21)

What was the temperament of Salome's sons? (Mark 3:17)

How did Jesus honor these two men? (Matt. 4:21; Luke 6:13, 14) (Two thousand years later, they are still honored.)

Tell of Salome's ambition for her James and John. (Matt. 20:21)

Did James and John share these hopes and dreams? (Mark 10:35)

Discuss the reply of Jesus. (Mark 10:36-40)

Did she desire preeminence over the other apostles? (Mark 10:41)

What is the principle of greatness? (Matt. 20:26-27)

Consider the great potential of this fisherman's family.

Consider the potential of every Christian family.

Think about the honor of noble motherhood; the honor of giving sons to the service of the Lord Jesus and His church.

The Woman at the Well

John 4:1-42

"If thou knewest the gift of God, and who it is that saith to thee; Give me to drink, thou wouldst have asked of Him; and he would have given thee living waters" (John 4:10).

JOHN GIVES much space in his gospel to the story of the woman of Samaria, an incident which occurred early in our Lord's ministry. It is a beautiful and inspiring story for all time, and all women. Racial, religious and social differences were ignored by the Savior as he brought to this sinful woman the promise of living waters.

Samaria is located between Judea and Galilee, and was at one time the kingdom of Israel, but the Israelites were captured and carried away by the Assyrians about seven centuries before Christ. Colonists from other lands were brought into Samaria, resulting in a mixed race of people known as Samaritans. They learned about the God of the Israelites from the few Jews left in the land, but they never worshipped at the temple in Jerusalem. They built a temple on Mount Gerizim and worshipped there, a dual worship of idolatry and of the true God. They became bitter enemies of the Jews, an animosity still existing in Jesus' day.

The Lord and his disciples had left Judea to go to Galilee. John said, "They must needs go through Samaria." Because of the ancient feud between the Samaritans and Jews, no Jew would pass through the land when it could be avoided. Jesus did not show this bitter feeling.

They journeyed as far as Sychar, ancient Shechem, where Abraham had dwelt. Near the little city was a wayside well, known as Jacob's well. They arrived about noon, tired and footsore. Jesus sat down on the well-curb to rest while the disciples went into the city to buy food.

DRAWING WATER

As he looked toward the village, he saw an approaching woman, with a water pitcher on her shoulder. Drawing water was a common occupation of women in Biblical times. Rebecca, Rachel, the daughters of Jethro, all were renowned women whose duties led them to the wells. So there was nothing unusual in seeing a woman coming to the well for water; but the time of her approach was unusual— noontime was not the accustomed hour. Early morning or late afternoon seems to have been the time, "when the daughters of men came to the wells to draw water."

Perhaps she came in the heat of the day to avoid her neighbors, who knew her present and her past reputation. From bitter experience she had learned that the sneers and slights were less painful when the witnesses were fewer.

And so she came at noon. The cobblestones around the well were hot and dusty; the heat shimmered in the air. The leaves were still, and the birds had taken refuge in the shade. The woman came slowly, her footsteps heavy and listless. Every movement indicated a weariness. Her appearance was one of dejection. The dress she wore so carelessly was faded, and perhaps a little soiled. At one time she might have been beautiful; surely she never intended to become what she was. No doubt she had longed to be better; but now, a social outcast, she had given up hope of ever being accepted and respected. Now she had accepted the bread and bed of the man who had offered it, without the formality of marriage.

She glanced at the stranger and recognized him as a Jew. Knowing the Jews paid no attention to the Samaritans, she passed by and hurriedly lowered her water-jug into the well. Drawing up the jug full of cool, sweet water, she was amazed to hear this Jew ask her for water to drink.

"How is it that you, being a Jew, will ask a drink of me, a woman of Samaria? For the Jews have no dealings with the Samaritans." (Not altogether refusing, yet too surprised to grant this very unusual request.)

The Master Teacher

To this woman of a despised race, a sinful one whose sordid, shabby life was common knowledge, the Christ revealed some of the most sacred and profound truths.

"If you knew the gift of God, and who it is saying to you 'give me a drink,' you would have asked Him and He would have given you living waters." This answer must have aroused her deepest curiosity. Who could this Jew be, and who does he imply that he is?

"Sir, you have nothing to draw with, and the well is deep; where do you get that living water? Are you greater than our father Jacob, who gave us the well?"

Her voice no longer carried a note of unfriendliness. There seems to be a hopeful tone to the question. She was willing to claim even a common ancestor with her enemies. There is a knowledge of the Old Testament in her answer as she talks of the well. "Where do you get that living water?" There was a deep longing in the soul of this woman, that she could not put into words.

Jesus said, "Everyone who drinks of this water will thirst again, but whoever that drinks of the water that I shall give him will never thirst; the water that I shall give him will become in him a spring of water welling up to eternal life." What wonderful prospects this reply opened to this shunned and despondent woman! Never to be thirsty again! Never to walk from Sychar to Jacob's well to draw water! The long, toilsome task complete once and for all.

"Sir, give me this water, that I may not thirst, nor come here to draw." (Her attitude changed. No longer did she feel despaired of self-improvement.)

Jesus, knowing all about her life, said to her, "Go, call your husband, and come here." Perfectly honest, perhaps calloused by her manner of life, she said, "I have no husband."

"You are right," Jesus tells her, "for you have had five husbands, and he whom you now have is not your husband; this you said truly."

There is no resentment in her reply; no denial; no admittance of sin. Simply, "Sir, I perceive you are a prophet. . . . Our fathers worshipped on this mountain, and you say that in Jerusalem is the place where men ought to worship?"

Jesus revealed marvelous and wonderful secrets to this woman so coarsened by sin.

"God is a Spirit; they that worship him must worship him in spirit and truth."

The light of the knowledge of God's word began to dawn upon her. Rejoiced and revived she said to Him, "I know that Messiah is coming (he who is called Christ); when he comes he will show us all things."

Then Christ revealed unto her the promise of God so long awaited. "I, who speak to you, am he."

The Neglected Water Pot

The disciples returned with food for the noon meal. They did not voice their astonishment that he talked with this woman. They urged him to eat, but he was no longer hungry. "My food is to do the will of Him that sent me and to accomplish His work."

So the woman left her water-pot. She hurried to the city and said to the people. "Come see a man who told me all that I ever did. Can this be the Christ?"

> Samaria, and noon above the land—.
> A flushed-cheeked woman hurrying to tell,
> With strange, excited voice and lifted hand,
> Of one who waited by an ancient well.
> "Come, see a man who told me everything—
> Surely this is our long awaited King."

—GRACE NOLL CROWELL[1]

---

[1] Taken from *Songs of Faith* by Grace Noll Crowell. Copyright 1939, Harper & Brothers. Used by permission.

The people saw in the face of this careworn woman a new light. They saw a change that convinced them that she had received a spiritual message, and they longed for the same gift. Many of the Samaritans believed on him because of the woman's testimony.

When the Samaritans came to him, they asked him to stay with them; and he stayed there two days. "And many more believed because of His word. And they said to the woman, 'It is no longer because of your words that we believe, we have heard for ourselves. And we know indeed that this is the Savior of the world.'"

Even in despised Samaria, souls were to be won for the kingdom of God. Now the disciples understood what he had meant when he said, "Lift up your eyes and see how the fields are already white for harvest."

SATISFIED THIRST

This woman's story reveals that she, too, recognized her opportunity. She forgot her water pot in her enthusiasm and eagerness to share her good fortune with others in the city. She is a wonderful example for women today.

The Scriptures clearly state that God is no respector of persons. Doubtless many today would be inclined to avoid such a woman. Christ so enlightened and taught this woman of the world that she understood what it meant to partake of the waters of life freely. Only Christ can satisfy the thirst of an immortal soul. How many have searched for the springs of eternal youth, and how often they have failed.

How wonderful that there is a fountain free to refresh and renew; a spring of water welling up to eternal life.

There were many pious and gentle women in Israel, yet Jesus chose this woman with the tarnished reputation to receive deep spiritual truths; "God is a spirit and they that worship must worship in spirit and truth." Importance placed on the house of worship, such as the temple's significance, would cease.

In the light of John's story of the woman of Samaria, can we ever safely conclude when one's condition is hopeless?

STUDY SUGGESTIONS

Who came to draw water? (John 4:7a)

What humble petition did Jesus make? (Jno. 4:7b)

Why did she seem resentful? (Jno. 4:9)

Who were the Samaritans? Why the feud between them and the Jews. (See Bible Dictionary)

What did Jesus offer her? (Jno. 4:10)

Who was their common ancestor, and did she place him above Jesus? (Jno. 4:11-12)

Show how Jesus contrasted the waters. (Jno. 4:13-14)

What is this living water? (Jno. 7:37-39)
How did Jesus reveal her character? (Jno. 4:16)
Discuss this woman and her prototype.
What does this teach us about social relationships?
She contends for what place of worship? (4:20) Was this to avoid her own
personal problem?
What did Jesus teach about places of worship? (4:21)
How were the Samaritans worshipping; who had the true worship? (4:22)
What is acceptable worship? (4:23) Discuss the "must" of real worship.
(4:24)
When Christ revealed himself to her, what did she do? (4:28)

Mary Magdalene

Luke 7:36-50; 8:1-3
Matt. 28:1-15
Jno. 20:2-18

"Mary Magdalene came and told to the disciples that she had seen the Lord, and that he had spoken these things to her" (Jno. 20:18).

M ARY MAGDALENE was the first to report the glorious resurrection
message. Mary was among the group of women to witness
the death of the Redeemer and note the burial place. She went to the
tomb at dawn to anoint him with sweet spices, in the company of
Mary, the mother of James, and Salome, according to Mark. As they
walked they discussed someone rolling away the stone from the door
of the sepulchre for them.

When they drew near, they saw the stone already rolled away.
Mary hastened to tell Peter and the other disciple whom Jesus loved,
"They have taken away the Lord out of the sepulchre, and we know
not where they have laid him."

Peter and John, closely followed by Mary, hastened to see with
their own eyes. John, reaching the tomb first, stooped to gaze in,
but did not enter. Peter boldly went in and saw the evidence of what
had happened. The other disciple, which came first, went in, saw,
and believed.

A GLORIOUS HONOR

Mary stood outside the tomb weeping, and as she wept she stooped
to look into the tomb. Then it was she saw two angels in white sitting
where the body of Jesus had lain, one at the head and one at the foot.

Mary Magdalene's tears seem to have blinded her to the vision in
the empty grave. So absorbed in her grief was she that she spoke
without fear to the angels inquiry as to why she was weeping. "Be-

cause they have taken away my Lord, and I do not know where they have laid him."

She turned and saw Jesus standing, but she did not know it was Jesus. Nor did his voice and his words reveal himself to her. "Woman, why weepest thou? Whom do you seek?"

Jesus seemed to have tried her before revealing himself with the one word, "Mary." No doubt she was overwhelmed with a rush of memories and associations as she heard her name spoken. Then she turned to him with a glad cry of recognition, "Rabboni!" She would have clasped his feet, but Jesus said to her, "Do not hold me, for I have not yet ascended to the Father, but go to my brethren and say to them, 'I am ascending to my Father and your Father, to my God and your God.'"

Mary Madgalene went and said to the disciples, "I have seen the Lord," and she told them that he said these things to her.

To this loving Mary was given the honor of being the first to see the risen Redeemer.

DEMON POSSESSION

Mary Magdalene, or Mary of Magdala, derived her name from the little hamlet of Magdala, a town of Galilee at the edge of the plain of Gennesaret. There has been much conjecture and misunderstanding about Mary Magdalene. Early scholars have tried to identify her with the sinful woman recorded by Luke. This is not at all accurate. Luke first pictures this woman, Mary Magdalene, with evil spirits and infirmities; "Mary, called Magdalene, out of whom went seven devils," but there is nothing to suggest that she was a harlot.

Demon possession did not indicate a sinful and depraved character. There is a legend that says she was a dancer—young, and very beautiful of face and form, with flaming red hair. Her demon possession was in the form of epilepsy. She suffered attacks when she danced. More reliable sources say that that she was a highly neurotic person. Seven devils used her maladjusted personality. Today psychologists might describe her as a dual personality; two natures striving for expression and dominance in the soul of one woman, the sensual and the sacred.

But she was healed of this terrible mental disturbance. Jesus understood her, and cast seven devils out of her.

A BEAUTIFUL DEVOTION

The Biblical narratives picture her in the company of other women who lived and ministered to Jesus as he walked and taught upon this earth. She must have been a comparatively rich woman. She and the other Mary, as well as Salome, ministered unto the Lord and his disciples. They needed money for food, shelter, and clothing, and we can be sure that these women provided these things.

Mary Magdala's love and attachment never faltered, even when Jesus went up to Jerusalem "to suffer many things and be put to death." Peter, and those to whom Mary Magdalene delivered the glorious message of the risen Lord, were those who had fled from Him in his suffering. But Mary went to Golgotha and there witnessed the agony of her Lord and Savior.

She was characterized by zeal and fervor. The early dawn found her in company with those who loved Jesus at the grave. She hastened with the message of the empty tomb to Peter and John. After seeing the Lord, she at once understood and accepted joyfully the change from the material to the spiritual conception of life. Something beyond the flesh and its fires, a spiritual illumination, was Mary's, who witnessed Christ's victory over death.

STUDY SUGGESTIONS

Name things to indicate Mary Magdalene was of an aggressive disposition. What about her financial condition? (Luke 8:2-5; Matt. 27:55)

Contrast her faith with that of the disciples. (Jno. 18:25-27; 19:25; 20:1)

Discuss Mary Magdalene's courage, devotion and fortitude. (Jno. 19:25; 20: 1; 20:11-18)

What are rewards of a great faith which she received? (Jno. 20:18)

Is there a scripture that says Mary Magdalene was a harlot? (Mark 16:9)

Is there a distinction between a sinful woman and a demon-possessed woman? (The former could help it, the latter could not help her plight.)

Is a Christian woman busy in the Lord's service as subject to neurosis as her worldly sister?

Why should the Christian woman be careful about her health? (1 Cor. 6:19)

Does patience contribute to mental, physical and spiritual health? (James 1:3-4; 2 Pet. 1:6)

The Wife of Pontius Pilate

Matt. 27:15-31

"—Have thou nothing to do with that just man; for I have suffered many things this day in a dream because of him" (Matt. 27:19).

THE WIFE OF Pontius Pilate makes a brief but very revealing appearance in the Bible. She was the wife of the fifth Roman procurator. He governed Judea, Samaria, and Idiemea. His headquarters were at Caesarea, but he came to Jerusalem during the Passover Feast. So many visitors to the city during this season gave rise to disorders, and he came with his soldiers to keep order.

He was accompanied by his wife. Tradition gives her the name Claudia Procula. Perhaps she had been to Jerusalem during the major festivals many times. Possibly she had seen and heard of the ministry of Jesus. During these Jerusalem visits she probably lived in the Herodian Palace. Archaeological excavations as late as 1950 reveal this structure as having been a luxurious and commodious abode. It was richly decorated with costly objects, and its many wings could accommodate a hundred guests. Tile, ivory and marble contributed a dazzling and rich beauty to the palace; fountains and gardens were in abundance. Perhaps from this palace she looked out on the streets with their tumultuous milling and confusion. She knew that Jesus was the center of this ugly mob.

A WOMAN'S DREAM

The few words that are recorded in Matthew 27:19 picture her to us as a woman of strong conviction, a woman whose courage and bravery caused her to intercede for Christ in his hour of trial. However, the plea of the governor's wife was not strong enough to overcome the envy of the wicked priest and elders who had taken counsel against Jesus to crucify Him.

Perhaps Pilate had told her of the trial as it progressed. She was uneasy lest her husband commit an offense against this innocent man. Filled with uneasy premonitions, she fell asleep. She must have been filled with an intense anxiety for she says she "suffered many things this day in a dream because of Him." She was convinced that Jesus was an innocent man. She was fearful lest her husband should unjustly condemn Him.

"When he was set down on the judgment seat, his wife sent unto him saying, 'Have thou nothing to do with that just man, for I have suffered many things in a dream this day because of Him.'"

The praetorium where Pilate tried Jesus, and where he received his wife's warning, is said to have been a part of the Tower of Antonia, erected by the Maccabeans on high ground northwest of the Temple area. It was repaired by Herod the Great. The dream gave Claudia Procula courage to send a message of warning to her tyrannical husband, imploring him to release Jesus. Pilate's wife is an example of a worthy wife. She displayed feminine gentleness and concern as she tried to save her husband from committing a just man to death. She sensed her responsibility to her husband, a harsh and austere man. Pilate made a half-hearted effort when his wife's message was delivered to release Jesus instead of Barabbas, for whom the multitude clamored. Her intervention added immeasurably to Pilate's guilt, for he refused to profit from her wise warning. Time-serving politician that he was, he gave heed to the shouting mob, closed his ears to his wife's entreaty, "Have nothing to do with that just man."

As a wife she took interest in what her husband was doing. She tried to soften and temper her husband's violent disposition.

HER PLEA REJECTED

The Christian wife should realize the responsibility she owes to her husband. The great influence she can exert upon him by the gentleness of her emotional life is limitless. The man who hardens himself to the influence of his wife adds to the evil in his heart.

"Likewise ye wives, be in subjection to your own husbands; that if any obey not the word, they also may without the word be won by the conversation of the wives; while they behold your chaste conversation coupled with fear" (1 Pet. 3:1, 2).

Tradition has it that Claudia Procula became a Christian; that grief and remorse because of her husband's cowardice brought on an illness from which she never recovered. However, the Scriptures tell us nothing more about her after her intercession for the Savior.

STUDY SUGGESTIONS

How does Pilate's wife rebuke Christian wives who fail to admonish their husbands?

How did Pilate add to his guilt by not listening to his wife?

What of Pilate's tyrannical spirit? (Jno. 18:1-10)

What of his weakness to yield to the voice of the people? (Matt. 27:24)

What was the significance of Pilate's washing his hands? (Matt. 27:24)

Did Pilate's wife know his weakness? (Matt. 27:19)

How should wives use their gentle spirit to influence their husbands?

Was she interested in her husband's dealing justly?

Would you say that she was courageous in warning him?

Three Marys of the New Testament

"But standing by the cross of Jesus were his Mother and his mother's sister, Mary the wife of Cleophas and Mary Magdalene" (Jno. 19: 25).

"He went to the house of Mary, the mother of John, whose other name was Mark . . ." (Acts 12: 12a).

"Greet Mary, who bestowed much labor on us" (Rom. 16:16).

MARY, THE MOTHER OF THE APOSTLE

SOMETIMES called the "other Mary," this woman was the wife of Cleophas, also called Alphaeus. They had two sons, James and Joses. Jesus chose James to be one of his disciples, and he was found among the twelve Apostles. His mother, too, was a faithful follower of Jesus, and was among that group of generous, brave and true women who ministered unto him with her goods.

She served Jesus in every hour of his need; at the cross, at the burial; and she was among those women who heard that Christ was risen from the grave.

Mary, the mother of the apostle, first gave herself to the service of Christ. She reared a child to be an apostle of our Lord and Savior.

She gave her material possessions to the Lord. As a mother and companion we would consider this "other Mary" the highest type of motherhood. Certainly James and Joses were worthy sons of a worthy mother. Her choice of friends and companions are an indication of her character, for they were all friends of the Lord. Their mutual interests were to glorify the God who had created them and redeemed them by the blood of Christ. Her labors were richly rewarded; she was privileged to behold the risen Lord, and her apostle son, James the Less, served faithfully in the Lord's church.

MARY OF JERUSALEM

This Mary lived in Jerusalem, and was the mother of a famous son, John Mark, who wrote the gospel according to Mark. She owned a house in Jerusalem, which was in her name, indicating her widowhood.

Luke tells of the time when many were gathered together and were praying in her house for the welfare of Peter. Upon Peter's rescue from prison by an angel of the Lord, he hastened to Mary's house where this prayer meeting was in progress. The nature of the prayers offered up by these devout Christians tells us much about the nature of this Mary.

Like Mary Magdalene she was a woman of financial means. Her house was commodious enough to accommodate many of the early church. When Peter was released from prison, he knocked at the door of Mary's house, and a maid came to answer. She owned a house and engaged a maid, both of which facts establish her economic position somewhat.

The influence of the home which she maintained was manifest in the life of her son and the uses to which she put her abode. Mary's work in the church was very significant in making the church a candlestick (Rev. 1:20). As a faithful Christian woman, she did a great service for the early church; her home was used for a place of assembly. The home is woman's God-given sphere, and if we had more Marys, we would have more John Marks.

MARY OF ROME

Mary was a Christian woman in Rome. Paul sent his greetings to her: "Greet Mary, who has worked hard among you." The American Standard Version says, "Greet Mary, who bestowed much labor upon us."

Perhaps she had been a helper of the great apostle. He certainly indicated that she had been very active in the Lord's church in the city of Rome. She was worthy of Paul's commendation among those few women mentioned at Rome.

Jehovah has been exceedingly merciful to woman, who was deceived. She has been lifted from her fallen state and restored to her original place by man's side. The consecrated women of New Testament days gave their time and money to the Lord, and through the ages women have played a large part in the growth and spread of Christianity.

"Take my life, and let it be
    Consecrated, Lord, to Thee.
Take my hands, and let them move,
    At the impulse of thy love.

Take my silver and my gold,
    Not a mite would I withhold.
Take my moments and my days,
    Let them flow in endless praise."

These three Marys gave their lives, their all. One gave her son; another gave her time and the labor of her hands. The other gave her house to the use of the church for God's glory.

Our homes should be devoted to the Lord. They should be a center of devotion and family worship, and should be shared with others.

Christian womanhood has been instructed not to be anxious about her raiment. She is urged to consider the lilies of the field, how they grow, toiling not nor spinning. "Yet I say unto you, that Solomon in all his glory was not arrayed like one of these" (Luke 12:27 or Matt. 6:29).

"Where your treasure is, there will your heart be also" (Luke 12:34). The Lord has given us time to be put to good use, and we must someday give an account of our moments and our days.

STUDY SUGGESTIONS

Are women as devoted today as in the early church?
Discuss a woman's work in the church. (Eph. 2:10; 2 Cor. 5:10; 1 Tim. 2:10; 5:13-16; Titus 2:3-5)
In acts of love and devotion, what is said of women? (Acts 21:3-9)
Read Matt. 6:19-34.
Why is anxiety about food and clothes sinful?
What should be the supreme goal of every Christian woman? (Matt. 6:33)
What is the sign of "little faith"?
What does God require? (1 Cor. 4:2)
Do you consider these women faithful stewardesses?
How has God promised food, raiment, and shelter? (Matt. 6:33)
How should a woman's life be ordered?

Sapphira

Acts 5:1-14
Acts 2:41-45
Acts 4:32-35
1 Tim. 6:10
Rom. 12:9
Matt. 16:24

"How is it that ye have agreed together to tempt the Spirit of the Lord?" (Acts 5:9).

S APPHIRA is one of the immortals of the early church in Jerusalem. However, she was not among the gracious women such as Mary, mother of John Mark, whose homes were a shelter for the church.

Sapphira's name will live forever as a warning to women who love money. She is brought before us with her husband, Ananias. There seems to be nothing about either this woman or her husband that one would consider extraordinarily wicked. One might even be quick to include them among the faithful who had sold land and houses and shared all they had with one another to meet the common needs of all.

The name Sapphira means "beautiful." There are some complimentary things to be said of this Christian woman, who along with her husband had come under the influence of the apostles.

The apostles had been baptized with the Holy Spirit on the day of Pentecost in fulfillment of the promise of the Savior. Peter and the other apostles with this marvelous power were filling all Jerusalem with the gospel of Christ. "They that gladly received the word were baptized; and the same day there were added unto them about three thousand souls."

"Howbeit many of them which heard the word believed; and the number of them was about five thousand" (Acts 4:4). Among this last multitude of baptized believers were Ananias and Sapphira. No doubt they were among those who "continued steadfastly in the apostles' doctrine and fellowship, and in breaking of bread and prayers." And they were of the multitude "of them that believed were of one heart and one soul; neither said any of them that any of the things which he possessed was his own but they had all things common."

"Neither was there any among them that lacked; for as many as were possessors of lands or houses sold them, and brought the price of the things that were sold, and laid them down at the apostles' feet."

MUTUAL AGREEMENT

Sapphira and her husband were not compelled to sell their property. Peter clearly stated that it was not commanded of them that they give up all their property. Even after they had sold it, it was still theirs to share voluntarily with those in need.

The Bible tells us, "A certain man named Ananias, with Sapphira his wife, sold a possession, and kept back part of the price, his wife also being privy to it; and brought a certain part, and laid it at the apostles' feet." These were very commendable activities and would certainly put Sapphira in a most favorable light.

They mutually agreed to sell the land; but they also agreed together to keep back part of the money and say they were giving all that they had received for the land.

The congregation would think of them as generous people who had given their all to the church, yet at the same time they would have a nice little "nest egg" at home.

THE WAGES OF SIN

Sapphira was as guilty as her husband. Ananias made all these transactions, "and with his wife's knowledge." What a sad commentary on Sapphira. It can be well imagined that they spent many days and nights, discussing and considering their plot. Nowhere is it mentioned that she tried to persuade her husband that this was a dishonorable procedure. The evil was committed entirely with her knowledge and support, and possibly it was at her suggestion. They agreed together to deceive themselves, the church, and to lie to God. They were punished with death for this hypocrisy.

Sapphira and her husband cast the first trace of a shadow upon the young church when they agreed to tempt the "Spirit of the Lord." How clearly this tragic and gloomy incident teaches that we can deceive men, but we can never hope to deceive God.

For the love of money is the root of all kinds of evil; it is through this craving that some have wandered away from the faith and pierced their hearts with many pangs. Sapphira, like many Christian women of today and days gone by, could not stand a stern test where money was concerned.

God had been gracious to this man and his wife. They were privileged with possessions; they were members of the Lord's church; they had lived in the miraculous age of early Christianity. Great grace was upon all the people. Great sermons were being preached, and notable miracles confirmed the sermons. These early disciples were welded together in a great fellowship of heart and soul. Sapphira was committed to this good cause, but she did not love the church enough to be willing to give too much of her possessions. "Let love be without hypocrisy." She desired the reward of the righteous, but she could not quite bring herself to pay the price. "Ye cannot serve God and mammon."

GOD IS NOT MOCKED

She and her husband are the counterpart of many Christians in every period of the church. Sapphira was not spiritually motivated; she was more interested in what she had, than in what she was. Her sin was not that she withheld the portion of money, but that she was dishonest in her relationship with God. Satan had filled the hearts of Sapphira and Ananias with a willingness to lie to the Holy Ghost. In the eyes of the people she had done a very noble and generous deed, but in the eyes of God she was a hypocrite.

Thus was a great lesson taught to all the followers of that age, as well as those down to the present. When their deceit was revealed and they fell down dead, "the young men came in, and found her dead, and carrying her forth buried her by her husband. And great fear came upon all the church, and upon as many as heard these things . . . And believers were the more added to the Lord, multitudes both of men and women."

STUDY SUGGESTIONS

How did Sapphira immortalize her name? (Acts 5:2)
Who was her husband? (Acts 5:1)

Were they people of means? (Acts 5:1-2)
Discuss their decision to sell their land and withhold part of it.
What did Peter say about this? (Acts 5:3-4)
To whom were they lying? (Acts 5:3)
Who induced such deception? (Acts 5:3)
Before and after the land was sold, in whose power was it? (Acts 5:4a)
Wherein was the lie and deceit? (5:4b)
How was Ananias punished? (5:5a)
How were others affected by this punishment? (Acts 6:5b)
What did Peter ask Sapphira? (Acts 5:8)
What was her answer? (Acts 5:8b)
Was this a confession of guilt, or was she trapped by her own deceit?
    (Acts 5:9)
What doom was pronounced? (Acts 5:9)
Who buried her and where? (5:10b)
To what extent should a husband and wife cooperate?
How do many today commit the sin of Sapphira?
THINK!—What of Christian women today with commodious homes, well-
    clothed families who have been provided with every comfort, who give
    pitifully meager contributions to the Lord, then piously claim they have
    given all they can.
What if God were to exercise such discipline today?
What is to be the destiny of all who are dishonest with God? (Rev. 21:8)
Do you think Sapphira could have influenced her husband for good, had
    she let her better nature prevail?

Dorcas

Acts 9:36-41

"This woman was full of good works and alms deeds which she did" (Acts 9:36b).

THERE WAS living in the ancient city of Joppa a certain disciple named Tabitha. Her many friends called her Dorcas, which is the Greek word for Gazelle, meaning graceful.

The Holy Spirit has given us a revealing description of this devout Christian woman. "She was full of good works and alms deeds which she did." Like the ideal woman of Proverbs, "She seeketh wool and flax, and worketh willingly with her hands. She stretcheth out her hands to the poor; yea, she reacheth forth her hands to the needy" (Prov. 31:13-20).

CITY OF JOPPA

Dorcas lived thirty-four miles northwest of Jerusalem. The gospel had spread to her hometown of Joppa, a port on the Mediterranean Sea. A picturesque harbor situated on a "whaleback" ridge, this was the only high ground on a sandy stretch between Caesarea and Gaza, at the juncture of the Plain of Sharon. This harbor lacked safe break water for large ships, so for centuries cargoes were brought ashore in skiffs by boatmen. The people of Joppa were dependent upon the sea for their living. Many mariners lost their lives in the churning waters of the Great Sea.

Consequently, Joppa had many widows and needy people in want of alms. Dorcas sensed a special responsibility to the widows and their children. After almost 2,000 years Dorcas is an example and inspiration to women who love Christ and his Church.

GLADNESS FOR TEARS

The scriptures tell us that Dorcas fell sick, soon so severely that her death ensued. Her passing brought great sorrow to her friends, for they felt that they could not spare such a good woman as she. This woman was almost an indispensable boon to her community; not only had she made all her means available to relieve the widows and the fatherless, she had devoted all of her energies as well to the task.

Hers was a labor of love, and in turn she was loved. These widows wept because they felt such abiding affection for the generous and industrious Tabitha.

FAITH

The saints in Joppa were unwilling to have Dorcas taken from them, and as they had heard that the apostle Peter was only about ten miles from Joppa in Lydda, on the Plain of Sharon, they sent two messengers. He heeded their request, left his preaching and hastened on foot to Joppa with them.

Already Dorcas had been washed and prepared for burial, and was lying in an upstairs room; probably the very room where she had plied her needle for those in poverty. When Peter was brought into the room, many of Dorcas' friends stood about him weeping bitterly.

The widowed mothers brought the garments which Dorcas had made for them and their children, to show them to the apostle. Peter then commanded everyone to leave the room, and kneeling down, he began to pray. Presently he turned toward the body and said, "Tabitha, arise." She opened her eyes and seeing Peter, sat up. He gave her his hand and lifted her up, calling the saints and widows thither, and presenting her alive.

What fervent prayers and thanksgiving must have ascended unto the throne of grace that memorable day in Joppa. Jesus had said "I was naked and ye clothed me. . . ," and now he placed his divine stamp of approval upon the work of caring for the widow and the orphan, by restoring life to Dorcas through Peter.

How vast and extensive the influence of the "certain disciple in Joppa." News of the miracle became known throughout all Joppa, and many believed on the Lord.

Nothing is recorded of Dorcas after her healing, but we may be sure she will be among that number when "The King shall say unto them on his right hand, 'Come, ye blessed of my Father, inherit the kingdom prepared for you from the foundation of the world.' "

STUDY SUGGESTIONS

Would Dorcas be an example of pure religion? (Jas. 1:27)
Does her life suggest Paul's lesson to Timothy? (1 Tim. 2:9-10)
Read Matt. 24:35-36. Discuss Dorcas' reward.
How would you characterize Dorcas?
How did she adorn the doctrine of Christ?
Discuss opportunities in our own homes and community.
What can be said of the fame of Dorcas?
Give her story. (Acts 9:36)
What did loving hands do with her body? (Acts 9:37)
What prompted friends to send for Peter? (THINK)
Name the two-fold effects of the miracle. (Acts 9:42)
Discuss: Can a busy housewife and mother be "full of good works and alms-deeds"?
Can the home be the center of benevolence?

Lydia and Her Household

Acts 16:11-15; 16:40

"If you have judged me to be faithful to the Lord, come to my house and abide there" (Acts 16:15).

LYDIA WAS THE first Christian convert in Europe. She had lived in Thyatira, a town of Lydda, which was a city noted for the art of dyeing. When Lydia settled in Philippi, she sold the dyed garments of that region and was a very successful business woman, no doubt well known and highly respected in Macedonian Philippi. But more important, she was a pious woman, a true worshipper of God.

When she heard Paul, she accepted the gospel. It was here the gospel was first preached in Europe.

A PROFESSIONAL WOMAN

Lydia kept a shop from which she sold purple. The dye was obtained from shellfish, and the securing of it was a very costly process. It was pure white until exposed to sunlight, when it became a rich red-blue color, and was used to dye garments and textiles which only the rich could afford. Royalty arrayed themselves in purple. The hangings of the Tabernacle in the wilderness included purple, also the priestly garments.

Thyatira, Lydia's native city, was famous for its guilds of weavers and dyers, and it is from there that Lydia probably brought her merchandise. Her home must have been spacious, for she invited Paul and his companions to remain in her house as long as they were in Philippi.

But it is not as a successful business woman that Lydia's name is yet revered by Christians. She takes her place among the immortal women of the Bible because she and her household were the first to hear the gospel proclaimed in Europe, and the first to confess Christ and be baptized. They were the nucleus of the church of Christ in this Roman colony.

A WOMAN OF PRAYER

This was Paul's second missionary journey. He had come to Macedonia in response to a vision, in which a man of Macedonia beseeched him, saying, "Come over into Macedonia and help us." Straightway, he concluded that God had called him to preach the gospel there. And so came the band of apostles to Philippi, to tarry certain days.

In this city were only a few Jews, and they had no synagogue. However, Paul and his companions found a place outside the city where people met together by the riverside on the Sabbath days to pray. Luke later recorded the incident and said, "And we sat down and spake unto the women that were come together."

It is further recorded how "Lydia, the seller of purple, one that worshipped God, heard us, whose heart the Lord opened to give heed unto the things which were spoken by Paul." A woman of foresight and indomitable courage, she heard, believed, and was baptized. Her entire household became obedient to the faith. Lydia did not stop to consider any effect this might have upon her business. She put Christ first.

A WOMAN OF HOSPITALITY

"And she besought us, saying, if ye have judged me to be faithful to the Lord, come into my house and abide there." She did not offer this as a service, but begged it as a favor. Perhaps she wanted to know more of the gospel of Christ. Certainly she wanted to be active in the spread of the new truth of Christ. Her invitation was accepted by the apostles Paul, Silas, Luke, and Timothy. What a haven this must have been for these faithful gospel preachers. Possibly many of Lydia's friends were invited into her house to hear these men teach God's word.

Again we find this business woman placing Christian responsibilities above all other considerations. How inspiring to think that a woman as busy and successful as Lydia would take the time to open her home to this group of missionaries.

Apparently Lydia was an unmarried woman, or perhaps a widow, but the Bible doesn't tell us. She had time to devote to a lucrative business, but after Paul came to Philippi she had a new interest, a new objective. She desired to learn about spiritual things. Perhaps through her influence the church was established in Thyatira.

Lydia was truly a brave and courageous woman. She later received Paul and Silas into her house after their release from prison, where they had been sent because Paul had healed a certain maid who possessed a spirit of divination. Paul had rescued this girl from men who had been exploiting her as a fortune teller. When they saw their hope of gain gone, they had Paul and Silas arrested and dragged into the marketplace before the rulers. They were falsely accused, beaten with rods, and cast into prison, and the jailer was charged to keep them safely.

At midnight, in the inner prison, their feet in the stocks, Paul and Silas sang and prayed. "And the prisoners were listening to them." Suddenly a great earth quake shook the foundation of the prison and the tightly locked door swung open, "and every one's bands were loosened." They spoke the word of the Lord unto the jailer, and all that were in his house, "and he took them the same hour of the night, and washed their stripes; and was baptized, he and all his, straightway."

Upon their delivery from prison they hastened to Lydia's house. We can be sure that prayers had ascended for them, and that when they related the wonderful things that had happened there was a great rejoicing and thanksgiving.

Like Mary in Jerusalem, whose doors were opened to Peter after his imprisonment, Lydia had no fears and would always offer refuge to the persecuted Christians. "And when they had seen the brethren, they comforted them and departed."

Years later Paul wrote a letter to the church at Philippi, and said, "I thank my God upon every remembrance of you, always in every prayer of mine for you all; making request with joy for your fellowship in the gospel from the first day until now" (Phil. 1:3-5).

Perhaps Lydia was still with this band of Christians, and with them was encouraged and edified as they read this personal letter from Paul, the prisoner. He expressed his high hopes for their faithfulness, their unity and their spiritual growth. How their faith must have been strengthened as they remembered Paul's assurance, "God shall supply all your needs according to his riches in glory by Christ Jesus" (Phil. 4:19).

After eighteen centuries Lydia continues to be a sacred memory to Christians everywhere.

STUDY SUGGESTIONS

What was Lydia's native city? (Acts 16:14b)

What was her occupation? (Acts 16:14a)

Who wore purple in those days? (Luke 16:19)

Where did she now live? (Acts 16:12a)

Was it unusual for a woman to devote her time to business in this era?

What is said of her devotion? (Acts 16:14c)

Discuss her hospitality. What did the Jewish law require in regard to hospitality? (Lev. 14:33, 34)

What are the apostolic injunctions concerning hospitality? (Rom. 12:13; 1 Tim. 3:2; Tit. 1:8; 1 Pet. 4:9) Is this a neglected virtue among Christians today?

Granted there is less need for it today, should the spirit of hospitality be neglected?

Priscilla (Prisca)

Acts 18:1-8; 18:24-28
1 Cor. 16:19
Eph. 5:22

"Greet Priscilla and Aquilla, my helpers in Christ Jesus" (Rom. 16: 3).

A WOMAN of influence in the New Testament church was Priscilla. She and her husband, Aquilla, made tents. Their home was the meeting house for the church wherever they went; it was a haven of hospitality for Paul and other gospel preachers.

Driven from Italy by the edict of Claudius in A.D. 49, they came by boat to Corinth, where the apostle Paul found them sewing canvasses for tents. "And he went to see them; and because he was of the same trade he stayed with them, and they worked, for by trade they were tent makers." There are many facts in the Scriptures that indicate the prominence of Priscilla. Though she and her husband labored together, her name is mentioned first in three out of five places; this is evidence that she was the leader in these Christian activities.

Working Together

We can picture them, Priscilla, Aquilla, and Paul, in a "canvasmaker's shop," which was probably attached to the house in which they lived, talking about the gospel as they worked. Paul was a single man, and to have "boarded" him indicates Priscilla's and Aquilla's hospitality. Priscilla was an energetic and wise helpmeet to her husband.

When Paul departed from Corinth and sailed from Syria, they were with him. "And they came to Ephesus and he left them there." Paul went into the synagogue and argued with the Jews. They asked him to stay for a longer period, but he declined and again sailed for Syria.

At Ephesus the cause of Christ prospered under the influence of this Christian woman and her husband. They opened their house to the church for worship, and when Paul returned more than a year later he found a well organized congregation in Ephesus. The influence of this devoted couple rated next to Paul and Timothy in this congregation.

Priscilla, a Teacher

A very inspiring and encouraging aspect of Priscilla's life was that though she was a capable homemaker, and an assistant in her husband's trade, she found time to be a student and teacher of the gospel of Jesus Christ. Schooled in the Old Scriptures as a Jewess, and enlightened by what the Lord's apostle revealed, she grasped the full import of the gospel. She was thus in a position to teach others, which is proved by an incident involving "the eloquent Apollos" at Ephesus.

Apollos was a native of Alexander, and he was an eloquent man who was well versed in the scriptures. Being learned and fervent, he "taught accurately the things concerning Jesus, though he knew only the baptism of John." As he spoke out so boldly and earnestly, Priscilla and Aquilla were quick to recognize the limitation of his knowledge. "But when Priscilla and Aquilla heard him, they took him and expounded to him the way of God more accurately."

Famous for her hospitality, she may have invited Apollos to stay in her home, and there in privacy instructed him more perfectly. Apollos owed much of his knowledge to them and after this it is said that "he mightily convinced the Jews, and that publicly, shewing by the scriptures that Jesus was Christ."

Her Courage

Priscilla lived at a time when it was not easy nor safe to be a

Christian, but she was courageous and willing to make sacrifices for Christ and His church. Paul said, "Greet Prisca and Aquilla, my fellow workers in Christ Jesus, who risked their necks for my life, to whom not only I but also all the churches of the Gentiles give thanks; greet also the church in their house." Truly, when she sheltered the saints she was risking her neck, for others were losing their heads for even less.

The last time we read of this devout Christian is in Paul's second letter to Timothy. Paul's martyrdom is approaching; he sends salutation to Priscilla and Aquilla. Affectionately he calls her "Prisca," indicating a warm friendship with this fine woman.

There are many wonderful things to be learned from the life of Priscilla. She made her home devout and peaceful, and used it to shelter Christians. Being a true companion to her husband did not prevent her teaching the work of God. She was his helper in business and religion. Hers is an example of a life consecrated to self-sacrifice in the cause of Christ.

STUDY SUGGESTIONS

At what place do we first read about Priscilla? (Acts 18:5-8)

Why had she and her husband left Italy? (Acts 18:2)

What was their trade? (Acts 18:3)

Who found them in Corinth? (Acts 17:33; 18:1b)

Tell of their labors together.

Where do we hear of Priscilla and Aquilla next? (Acts 18:19)

Relate an incident that is evidence that she knew the scriptures, both Old and New Testaments. (Acts 18:24-28)

Discuss Apollos' point of error. (Acts 18:25, 26)

Tell how you think Priscilla and Aquilla taught him, and where.

After this, what is said of the power of his preaching? (Acts 18:28)

Where did she and Aquilla go from Ephesus? (Rom. 16:3)

What word did Paul send to them? (Rom. 16:3)

How had they risked their lives for Paul? (Rom. 16:4a)

How did Paul, with others, regard them? (Rom. 16:4b)

Why is her name usually mentioned before her husband's?

Is this an indication she was not in subjection to her husband? (Eph. 5:22)

Discuss her cooperation with her husband in religion and business.

Discuss her hospitality. (Rom. 16:5a; 1 Cor. 16:19c; Acts 18:3b)

What of the love bestowed upon strangers? (Heb. 13:1, 2)

Discuss her Bible knowledge. (Acts 18:24-26)

Where do Christian women wield the greatest power? (Titus 2:3-5)

What did Priscilla gain by taking the apostle Paul into her home? (Heb. 13:21)

Phebe

Rom. 16:1-2
1 Tim. 3:12

"I commend unto you Phebe our sister, who is a servant of the church that is at Cenchrea" (Rom. 16:1)

A LMOST 1,900 years ago, the apostle Paul wrote a very graphic but concise description of a certain Christian woman. Our introduction to Phebe is in the last chapter of the Roman letter, and here Paul has said much in two short verses.

Cenchrea was a port of Corinth on the east end of the isthmus in the Saronic Gulf, and it was here that Paul wrote the letter to the Roman Christians. Presumably Phebe carried the epistle from there to Rome, as private correspondence was sent by a friend or an envoy. Whether Phebe traveled by land or sea this was quite a long journey. The preferred manner of travel seemed to be the overland route, which would take her through Achaia and Macedonia, the scenes of Paul's missionary journey. We can well imagine what a sincere welcome she received in every congregation along the way, for not only did she come as a Christian traveler in need of hospitality, but she no doubt bore news concerning their beloved Paul.

Just how many made up the church at Cenchrea we have no way of knowing. Phebe is the only one mentioned by name. She must have been a woman highly esteemed for her work's sake. It is likely that she was financially able to travel, which, in addition to her influence, position, and Paul's high regard for her would possibly explain why she was the one selected to carry this inspired document to the Imperial City.

A SISTER IN CHRIST

Paul addressed this letter to "all that be in Rome, beloved of God, called to be saints," (Rom. 1:7a), and it is to these saints that he commends Phebe. He first refers to her as "our sister"; his sister and sister of the saints at Rome, to whom she was bringing the letter. She had the same relationship to the Roman Christians that she sustained to those in Cenchrea. Jesus on one occasion said, "For whosoever shall do the will of God, the same is my brother, and my sister, and mother" (Mk. 3:35). Therefore, by Paul's bestowal of the term "sister," we may safely conclude that Phebe was "doing the will of God."

Next he calls her "a servant of the church which is at Cenchrea." Again the words of our Savior gave to this woman a place of honor in the church where she served, for he said, "and whosoever will be chief among you, let him be your servant" (Matt. 20:27).

Many have called Phebe a deaconess. Some have even said she was a minister, even as Paul and Timothy, and others.

> "Woman has a wonderful work to perform in the church of God, and exerts a powerful influence for good in her own private sphere; but if she is to go into the pulpit to preach publicly, the word of God has failed to make plain that part of the Lord's will."
>
> (E. G. SEWELL)

The scriptures do not tell us if Phebe was appointed to some special work; the emphasis is on the service rendered and not on the office she held.

There are so many avenues of service for a woman, which an elder or deacon could not perform. In the instance of sickness in a home, afflicting the mother or perhaps children, food and medicine and other assistance are needed. This is particularly a woman's sphere. She can investigate the needs and make her report to the elders. Perhaps the situation is so urgent and immediate she must act on her own.

A sister who prepares the Lord's table each Sunday is a servant. A sister who assists in the necessary details of a baptismal service, seeing that proper garments are at hand, certainly constitutes a servant of the church. She may be called a deaconess, perhaps, if she has been appointed to this particular phase of work.

The sister whose home is ever a center of hospitality to entertain strangers, and an avenue of recreation for the young people in the congregation, is truly a servant of the church.

GREATNESS IN SERVICE

What a labor of love Paul attributes to Phebe in the brief statements, "she hath been a succourer of many." It was not easy to be a Christian in those days. It often meant loss of property, danger to life. Sacrifice was the common lot of those early Christians. She came to the aid of the oppressed and unprotected.

We hear our Lord commending the Phebes of the world, when he invited, "Come, ye blessed of my Father, inherit the kingdom prepared for you from the foundation of the world; for I was an hungered and ye gave me meat; I was thirsty and ye gave me drink; I was a stranger and ye took me in; naked, and ye clothed me; I was sick and ye visited me; I was in prison, and ye came unto me.—Inasmuch as ye have done it unto one of the least of these my brethren, ye have done it unto me" (Matt. 25:34-40).

Finally, Paul adds to his description of this woman that she was "a succourer of myself also." Her home may have been the apostle's home for a season. She may have cared for him when he was ill, or attended him when he was "in weariness and painfulness, in watchings often, in hunger and thirst, in fastings often, in cold and nakedness" (2 Cor. 11:27).

In those days when there were no formal meeting houses for the church, the homes became the meeting place; as was Mary's in Jerusalem, and the home of Lydia, as well as of Priscilla. Perhaps Phebe's home was the meeting place for the church at Cenchrea.

The church at Rome is instructed to receive her as "becometh saints," and Paul asked them to assist her "in whatsoever business she hath need of you." Her generous service in the church at Cenchrea obligated the church at Rome to receive her with respect and confidence, rendering any service she might require.

Did Phebe remain in Rome and perhaps lay down her life for the gospel? Or did she deliver the letter to the church at Rome and return to her home at Cenchrea? These things we do not know, but we perceive that she is an outstanding example of a woman's work in the church. As her ministry inspired those of the first century, it is still a source of inspiration and encouragement to women of the 20th century.

STUDY SUGGESTIONS

Who was Phebe? (Rom. 16:1-2)
To whom did Paul commend Phebe?
Why did she go to Rome?
Who established the Roman church? (Acts 2)
To whom do you think 1 Tim. 3:11 refers? If this refers to deaconesses, state her qualifications. If this refers to wives of deacons, would not this bar women from the office?
Enumerate work women can do to advance the cause of Christ.
Is it not true that the only restriction placed upon woman is 1 Tim. 2:12?
Discuss every congregation's need of a Phebe.

Drusilla and Bernice

Acts 12:1, 2; 24:1-27;
25:13-23; 26:30

"After some days Felix came with his wife Drusilla, who was a Jewess; and he sent for Paul and heard him speak upon faith in Christ Jesus" (Acts 24:24).

W OMEN BOTH lovely and otherwise adorn the pages of Holy Writ. Both the Old and New Testaments depict for all ages beautiful womanhood as God would have it. Evil women come into Biblical history, teaching clearly the heavy price paid for worldly pleasure and ambitious lust.

Two shameful sisters are briefly mentioned in the Acts of the Apostles. First Drusilla, and then her older sister, were privileged to be present and hear the Apostle Paul, as a prisoner, make his plea in the judgment hall at Caesarea. Josephus, the Jewish historian, records that these sisters were the daughters of Herod Agrippa I. Their father was Herod the King, who "stretched forth his hands to vex certain of the church. And he killed James, the brother of John, with the sword."

They were granddaughters of Herod the Great, who had sought to destroy the Child Jesus, and it was their uncle, Herod Antipas, who at the request of his illegal wife, had beheaded John the Baptist.

Drusilla was the younger sister, whom history records as being very beautiful and hated by Bernice. Luke, the inspired writer, introduces us to her along with Felix, her husband.

When she was about fourteen years of age she was married to King Aziz of Emesa, and was still in her teens upon her appearance in the book of Acts. Contrary to Jewish law, Drusilla had left Aziz to marry a Gentile. Her union with Aziz had been on the condition that he embrace Judaism. When Felix, Procurator of Judea, became passionately fond of her, Drusilla left her husband to marry this foreigner and idolator, and dwelt with him in Caesarea.

Paul's imprisonment was no doubt widely known, and Drusilla was probably very curious to see this notable Christian prisoner. Very probably Paul's second appearance before Felix was to please his young wife. Paul earlier had been accused before Felix by the high priest and the elders from Jerusalem. Tertullus, an orator who had accompanied these elders also accused Paul, but Felix demanded that Lyssas, the chief captain, be produced as a witness. "And after certain days, when Felix came with his wife Drusilla, which was a Jewess, he sent for Paul and heard him concerning the faith in Christ Jesus."

What a glorious privilege did God the Father extend to this sinful young woman. Not willing that any should perish, he calls all to repentance. She heard Paul's sermon concerning the faith in Christ Jesus; and knowing his audience, Paul reasoned with Drusilla and Felix concerning righteousness. Her desertion of Aziz was a breach of the law, of course. He also spoke of temperance, and judgment to come. An insatiable desire for power and luxury had induced Drusilla to commit an act for which she would surely have to answer before God.

However, there is nothing to indicate that Paul's words produced the slightest remorse in this sin-hardened woman. The Scriptures have shown many times, that when a woman gives herself unreservedly to carnality she is worse than a man. Drusilla's Jewish background should have been fertile soil for Paul's message; not so, but Felix trembled and dismissed Paul, saying, "Go thy way for this time; when I have a convenient season I will call upon thee." The words in the very next verse state, "He hoped also that money should have been given him of Paul, that he might loose him. . . ."

Thus, the proud and haughty Drusilla rejected faith in Jesus Christ. A woman attired in all her regal finery and sparkling jewels held her head high as she marched from the judgment hall, and turned a scornful back on the words of life.

History further tells us her period of power and glory was short-lived. In two years Felix was succeeded by Festus, and he and Drusilla went the way of all those who abuse their power and authority. Some eighteen or twenty years later, Drusilla and her only son, Agrippa, were buried beneath the burning lava of Mt. Vesuvius.

What a dreadful biography is this one. She had forsaken her lawful husband to live in sinful wedlock, rejected the gospel message, and died violently. These sins will meet her in the judgment.

Paul, still a prisoner in Caesarea, came again to plead his case; this time before Bernice, the older and evil sister of Drusilla. History records that both in Rome and Caesarea her incestuous conduct was notorious. She was publicly known as the official consort of her brother, Herod Agrippa II. "So on the morrow, Agrippa and Bernice came with great pomp. They entered the audience hall with military tribunes and the prominent men of the city." How Bernice must have revelled in all this pomp and show.

Festus had declared Paul's innocence to them. One word from her to her weak and despicable brother could have probably brought Paul freedom. She heard Paul tell of his conversion, and heard him declare Christ the Lord. "That the Christ must suffer, and that he should be the first to rise from the dead, and should show light unto the people and the Gentiles."

Paul declared that Christ had sent him, "To open their eyes, and to turn them from darkness to light, and from the power of Satan unto the power of God, that they might receive forgiveness of sins, and inheritance among them which are sanctified by faith that is in me." Bernice was given generous opportunity to avail herself of redemption, but in no way did the persuasive message affect Bernice. She departed the same sinful woman—harder even than her brother, who replied, "Almost thou persuadest me to be a Christian."

The king rose up, the governor, and Bernice, and they that sat with them; and when they were gone aside they talked between themselves, saying, "This man hath done nothing worthy of death or bonds." Yet they did nothing to release him.

History records that Bernice continued as one of the most shameless women in the Bible. At one time she was the mistress of Titus, before he became emperor, then she passes into obscurity. How different the end of these two sisters and the end of Paul's earthly sojourn. We read in 2 Tim. 4:7 his triumphant message, "I have fought a good fight; I have finished my course, I have kept the faith."

Paul brought to Drusilla and Bernice the power of the gospel, but they quickly rejected it and continued in their evil, sensuous ways.

STUDY SUGGESTIONS

Name the father and grandfather of these sisters. (Acts 12:1; Matt. 2:16)
Read and discuss the Herods' background. (Bible dictionary suggested)
To whom was Drusilla married? (Acts 24:24a)
What of her nationality? (Acts 24:24b)
What of her father's wickedness and miserable death? (Acts 12:1, 3; Acts 12:21-23)
To whom was Drusilla first married?
What great man was she privileged to hear? (Acts 24:24c)
Give three divisions of the sermon. (Acts 24:25a)
How was her husband affected by the power of the gospel? (Acts 24:25b)
How did he reject his convictions? (Acts 24:25c)
Of whom was Bernice the daughter? (Acts 12:1)
Of whom was she the sister? (Acts 25:13)
What does history tell of her character? (Josephus suggested)
    a. She was married to uncle, Herod, King of Chalcis
    b. She was married to King Ptolemy of Sicily
    c. Mistress of Titus
    d. Consort of her brother, Agrippa II
What governor was visited by this brother and sister? (Acts 25:13)
Describe the audience in the judgment hall. (Acts 25:23)
What were the highlights of Paul's speech? (Acts 26:1-23)
What were some things Paul said that should have aroused Bernice to thoughts of a better life? (Acts 26:18)
How did these things affect Agrippa? (Acts 26:28)

Lois and Eunice

2 Tim. 1:5; 3:15
Prov. 22:6
1 Sam. 1:28
1 Cor. 4:17a
1 Thess. 3:2

"When I call to remembrance the unfeigned faith that is in thee, which dwelt first in thy grandmother, Lois, and in thy mother, Eunice; and I am persuaded that in thee also" (2 Tim. 1:5).

A MONG THE personal letters of the apostle Paul are two written to a young preacher named Timothy. Paul expressed his regard for this fellow worker when he called him, "my dearly beloved son." Brief but revealing bits of information in these letters give us a picture of a devout family group of the New Testament.

HOME ENVIRONMENT

Young Timothy is the product of two spiritual generations. He was closely associated with the aged apostle, traveling and laboring with him, and was entrusted with missions of vast importance to the church of Christ. Paul makes it very plain that it was the mother and grandmother of Timothy who had prepared for such responsibilities, and he pays sincere tribute to these women in writing, "When I call to remembrance the unfeigned faith that is in thee, which dwelt first in thy grandmother Lois, and thy mother Eunice; and I am persuaded that in thee also."

Thus these two women stand among the great women of the New Testament. Their immortality comes entirely through their noble motherhood, for they will be ever remembered because of their Timothy, "a child who knew the Holy Scriptures."

This family is also brought to our attention in the Book of Acts, where Luke records that Timothy was the son of a certain Jewish woman of Lystra. His father was a Greek, and his name is not mentioned; his spiritual background and instruction came from the maternal side of his family. The marriage of a Jew to a Gentile was unusual, and the influence of the father was indicated in the fact that Timothy had not been circumcised according to the law.

Paul came to Lystra on his first missionary tour, and this family no doubt heard him expound the "Holy Scriptures, which are able to make thee wise unto salvation." Paul converted them, at which time Timothy was about fifteen years old. His home training had prepared him for the gospel message that Paul and Silas preached at Lystra. There is every indication that Paul baptized these three generations; the son, the mother, and the grandmother.

Some have thought that Timothy's father was dead and that his mother, Eunice, had to work to support the three of them. Lois was therefore able to exert the same influence upon Timothy, through scriptural teaching, that she had upon Eunice when she was young. In this way, faith passed from child to grandchild.

WOMAN'S WORK

Eunice and Lois clearly tell us that the most important work in a mother's life is the early training of her child. Someone has said that "the time to begin the child's training is to begin with the grand parent." The record of this son and grandson is an imperishable proof of this statement.

"Train up a child in the way he should go; and when he is old he will not depart from it." This and similar other scriptures found a place in the heart of Lois and Eunice, as they tried to live up to Deut. 6:6-9, "And thou shalt teach them diligently unto thy children, and shalt talk of them when thou sittest in thy house; and when thou walkest by the way; and when thou liest down; and when thou risest up. And these words which I command thee this day shall be in thy heart and thou shalt bind them for a sign upon thine hand, and they shall be as frontlets between thine eyes, and thou shalt write them upon the post of thy house and on the gates."

It was said by Alexander Campbell, "The discreet and affectionate mother lives forever in the heart of her children. There never was a man both good and great that did not owe it to his mother." One is not surprised when Paul again visited Lystra, to find that Timothy joined the apostle on his second preaching tour. He must have planned and talked with Eunice and Lois many hours concerning this great venture for the Lord Jesus. And like Hannah of old, when she left little Samuel in the house of God in Shiloh, these women, too, were ready and willing to say, "I have lent him to the Lord; as long as he liveth he shall be lent to the Lord." So this consecrated mother and grandmother sent forth one who was ready to sacrifice his all for Christ.

Through Paul, the Holy Spirit places the stamp of divine approval upon Timothy's home training, in saying, "And that from a child thou hast known the holy scriptures which are able to make thee wise unto salvation through faith which is in Christ Jesus." This statement is a lasting memorial to these faithful mothers.

Lois is the only woman in the Bible given the title of "grand-mother," and to know more of her and her daughter, Eunice, is to more fully perceive the character of Timothy. In Paul's letters to Timothy there are many passages listing admirable qualities which he could have possessed only through the influence of his devout upbringing. "Therefore, I send to you Timothy, my beloved and faithful child in the Lord." Paul trusted and commended Timothy, as in his presentation of him to the church at Thessalonica; "And we sent Timotheus, our brother, and minister of God, and our fellow laborer in the gospel of Christ, to establish you, and to comfort you concerning your faith." Surely his was a Christ-like personality.

The faith of Lois and Eunice was a rich heritage, handed down from one generation to the next. How the world needs such women, whose ardent love for Christ overflows into the hearts of their children.

STUDY SUGGESTIONS

Who is the Bible grandmother? (2 Tim. 1:5)
Who was her daughter? (2 Tim. 1:5)
Who was her grandson? (2 Tim. 1:2a)
Where did they live? (Acts 16:1)
What was their nationality? (Acts 16:1b)
When did Eunice begin to teach Timothy the Bible? (2 Tim. 3:15a)
What great blessing was handed down to this boy? (2 Tim. 1:5)
What of his influence at home? (Acts 16:2)
Discuss the influence of grandmothers for good. (Titus 2:3a, 4)
How was her faith handed down? (Rom. 10:17; 2 Tim. 2:1-5)
Where and when is the time and place to begin child training?
How were these women honored in Timothy?
What lessons may be learned from the relationship between Lois, Eunice, and Timothy.
When does "blood relationship" count. (2 Tim. 2:1-5)
How do we all become related to Christ? (Matt. 12:48-50)

Widows

"I caused the widow's heart to sing for joy" (Job 29:13).

Ex. 22:22
Deut. 10:18; 14:29; 16:11;
    24:17; 25:5-10
Prov. 15:25
Acts 6:1
1 Tim. 5:3-16
Jas. 1:27

God's Care for the Widow

FROM THE EARLIEST Bible times women who lost their husbands were looked upon with sincere pity. They were under the special care of the Lord, as is shown in Exodus 22:22, where afflicting a widow is directly forbidden. God's wrath will be executed upon that individual who takes advantage of her. The various facets of widowhood were covered by direct commandments throughout the old Testament, as by the prophet's pronouncement of woe upon those who do not relieve the need and distress of the widow and the fatherless (Isa. 1:23). It was of concern to the Apostles, through which the Holy Spirit said, "Pure religion and undefiled before God and the Father is this: to visit the fatherless and widows in their affliction, and to keep himself unspotted from the world."

She was not left to the mercy of an indifferent world, but was provided with financial, social, and moral protection, as is promised in Proverbs 15:25: "The Lord will destroy the house of the proud; but he will establish the border of the widow."

Throughout Deuteronomy there are many laws to assure justice and judgment to the bereaved woman. "Cursed be he that perverteth the judgment of the widow." She had to have material support, and there were several provisions made. The tithe of the third year was divided with her, for instance; and Ruth who gleaned in the field of Boaz was protected and provided for by the law. Job cries out against the wickedness of those who selfishly sent "widows away empty" (Job 22:9).

Those who aided these women went not without reward, for in Jeremiah 7:6, God promised "If ye oppress not—the widow, then will I cause you to dwell in the place, in the land that I gave to your fathers, for ever and ever." It is a fearful thing that one should not "heed the cause of the widow," for the Psalmist proclaims that God himself "relieveth the widow; but the way of the wicked he turneth upside down" (Ps. 146:9).

Socially and morally the widow was enjoined to rejoice before the Lord in the observance of feast and sacrifices. She is cautioned in Timothy to trust in God, continuing in prayers and supplications night and day.

Under the levirate law of Deuteronomy 25, protection was given to the woman whose husband was dead, and it gave unto her the assurance of motherhood. This law was cited on one occasion by the enemies of Christ. The Sadducees, desiring to trap Jesus, brought the case of the woman with seven husbands (Matt. 22:23-24). This in all probability was a hypothetical case, but her marriage was in keeping with old levirate law, placing upon a man the obligation to marry his brother's widow. This custom was observed long before the written law in Deuteronomy.

THE WIDOW WHO GAVE ALL

Mark and Luke both tell the story of the widow with the two mites (Mk. 12:41-44; Lk. 21:1-4). Jesus, who had been walking and teaching in the temple court, sat down opposite the treasury. The treasury was the chest into which the people cast the contributions which the law of Moses required that they bring when they came to Jerusalem to the annual festivals (Deut. 16:16-17). As he sat, "He beheld how the people cast money into the treasury; and many that were rich cast in much."

In contrast, there came a "certain poor widow" and cast into the chest her two mites. She could not give less, and her poverty prevented her giving more. Her devotion caught the Savior's approval. He called his disciples to him and praised her generosity, saying, "This poor widow hath cast more in than all which have cast into the treasury."

She gave her all, though that was but little in itself. She gave her living, when she had only her widow's hands to earn more.

Jesus made a distinction between an offering and a sacrifice. "For all of these have of their abundance cast in unto the offering of God; but she of her penury hath cast in all the living that she had." This widow immortalized her name by her sacrifice. "For if there first be a willing mind, it is accepted according to that a man hath, and not according to that he hath not" (2 Cor. 8:12).

"For ye know the grace of our Lord Jesus Christ, that, though he was rich, yet for your sakes he became poor, that ye through his poverty might be rich" (2 Cor. 8:9).

In this meaningful story women may learn the things which commend them unto Christ. In the sacrificial life the beauty of Jesus is reflected. Contrast the faith, love, and devotion that were the compelling forces in this widow who gave her all, to the desires and cravings of the modern woman for mere things.

Christians are urged, "that ye present your bodies a living sacrifice, holy and acceptable unto God, which is your reasonable service" (Rom. 12:1).

OTHER WIDOWS

One of the early recorded miracles of Jesus is told by Luke (Lk. 7:11-19). The only son of the widow of Nain was dead. Jesus, meeting this funeral procession when he came to the gate of the city, had compassion upon this woman who had already lost her husband, and was now about to bury her son. He told her to "weep not," and commanded the young man to arise. Immediately he began to talk, and Jesus "delivered him to his mother."

In one of Jesus' parables is the importunate widow (Lk. 18:1-8). This is the story of a widow who went to the judge and unsuccessfully begged him to avenge her of her adversary. In no wise discouraged by his refusal, she persisted until he agreed to help her. He agreed "lest by her continual coming she weary me." So by this parable Jesus taught the need of persistent prayer. Paul urged all Christians to "pray without ceasing" (1 Thess. 5:16-18).

Mothers, let us spend more time on our knees, and less time on the streets; more time in the kitchen and less in the movies; more conversation concerning God's Work, and less about the sordid news of the day.

GREEK WIDOWS

Early in the history of the church at Jerusalem, Luke records a discrimination against the Grecian widows. Those who are called Grecians were Jews who had lived in countries where the Greek language was spoken, but were sojourners in Jerusalem.

The disciples had put their property in a common fund. Out of this, every individual was to have his need supplied. There arose a murmuring of the Grecians against the Hebrews because their widows were neglected in the daily ministration.

Again we witness God's care for widows, in his directions for the selecting of wise and good men to care for these needy Christians.

YOUNGER WIDOWS

When Paul wrote the first Corinthian letter, the church was then in straits and difficulties. He advised the unmarried to remain single, and expressed the wish that all in the church were like himself, unmarried (1 Cor. 7:8, 9).

Paul did not mean that marriage should cease among mankind, nor did he wish the church to be composed of single people. His advice was for the distress prevalent at that time.

The widow who remarried was to be married "to whom she will, only in the Lord" (1 Cor. 7:39). Later, Paul wrote his beloved Timothy "that the younger widows were advised to marry, bear children, and guide the house; give none occasion to the adversary to speak reproachfully" (1 Tim. 5:14).

Thus they were to avoid idleness, meddling, and tattling. The older women were to assist and teach these young women to be "keepers at home" (Titus 2:4, 5). "Teach them to be lovers of their husbands and children." The welfare of the church depends upon the home, and the home depends upon women who love their homes and families.

WIDOWS INDEED

"Honour widows that are widows indeed" (1 Tim. 5:3). This widow is not a young, frivolous, pleasure-mad woman. Paul says that this type of woman is dead while she lives.

The younger women are to be provided for by their relatives, "and let not the church be burdened, that it may relieve them that are widows indeed" (1 Tim. 5:16). There were certain conditions on which the church was to support or honor widows. It was required that she be sixty years of age, the wife of one man, and that she possess a reputation for good works. She shall have reared children, exercised hospitality, visited the sick and needy, and diligently followed every good work (1 Tim. 5:10).

This woman has no relatives to support her. "She is a widow indeed and desolate, trusteth in God, continueth in supplications and prayers night and day" (1 Tim. 5:5).

As God charged Israel to care for the widows, (Deut. 14:29), so is the Lord's church charged with the responsibility to care for the "widow indeed." A widow who has children and grandchildren is not desolate. Her children are most solemnly commanded to care for their widowed mothers and grandmothers. "Let them first learn to show piety at home, and to requite their parents; for that is good and acceptable before God" (1 Tim. 5:4).

Not only has God given the family its organization, but he has assigned its purpose. As the mother and the father are to rear, train and nurture the child, so are the children to "honor father and mother" (Ex. 20:12). Too often this responsibility is neglected. The aged parents are disregarded and unwanted. There is a haunting fear of becoming a "burden to the children." For this reason there is obviously a lack of teaching on the responsibility of children to parents.

STUDY SUGGESTIONS

Name some widows of the Old Testament. (1 Kings 17:9-24; Luke 4:26; 2 Kings 4:1-7; 1 Sam. 25; Gen. 38:6; Ruth 1:2-20)

Discuss God's provision for widows. (Deut. 26:12; Deut. 16:11; Ruth 2:8, 14-16)

Name some reasons why Paul commanded the young widows to marry (1 Tim. 5:11-13).

What is commanded? (1 Tim. 5:14)

What is the responsibility of the elder woman to the younger? (Titus 2:4)

Should they marry a non-Christian? (1 Cor. 7:39)

What is meant by "only in the Lord"?

How does one get into the Lord? (Rom. 6:3; Gal. 3:27)

How serious is the sin of marrying out of the Lord?

Describe "widows indeed." (1 Tim. 5:5)

To whom should widows look for honor (support) in their old age? (1 Tim. 5:4)

Discuss, "let not the church be charged." (1 Tim. 5:16).

Does the establishment of homes for aged Christians violate 1 Timothy 5:16? Read Gal. 6:3. Think.

What is said of the individual who does not provide for those of his own house? (1 Tim. 5:8)

Discuss the early church's care for widows. (Acts 6:1-7)

Who cared for many widows? (Acts 9:36-39)

Discuss Jas. 1:27.

Jezebel of Thyatira

Rev. 2:18-25
2 Cor. 6:14-18

"These things saith the Son of God . . . I have a few things against thee, because thou sufferest that woman Jezebel, which calleth herself a prophetess . . ." (Rev. 2:18-25).

THYATIRA, a city of ancient Lydda, in western Asia, was located on a river and a key highway of commerce. It was a Macedonian colony founded about the 3rd century. The town gained prestige from its guild of weavers and dyers of wool and linen textiles.

Lydia, a cloth merchant from Thyatira who was converted by Paul at Philippi of Macedonia, was probably the one who carried the gospel to her native city. No doubt she was instrumental in the establishment of the church to which the message in this part of Revelation was addressed. The Son of God instructed John the apostle to write unto the church in Thyatira. "I know thy works, and charity, and service, and faith and thy patience, and thy works; and the last to be more than the first."

God is ever mindful of our labor of love, and here a group of Christians are highly commended for "faith which worketh by love" (Gal. 5:6). Here in this congregation is manifested a love of God, and love one to another. They are faithful in their service to widows, orphans, and the poor in general. They were faithful under affliction and persecutions which were the lot of Christians.

The people in this congregation had not become weary in well doing, which should characterize the members of the church of Christ. They had continued to grow in grace and the knowledge and love of Jesus Christ. It is not unlikely that this living, active group of Christians was the result of the labors of one devout woman, Lydia, the seller of purple.

THAT WOMAN JEZEBEL

The Son of God, who told the apostle to write those fine words of commendation for the faithful at Thyatira, told him also to write words of condemnation to a woman who called herself a prophetess. First there was censure for those who permitted "that woman Jezebel to teach and seduce my servants."

Just who this false teacher was is not known. Some have said she was the wife of one of the elders who allowed her to teach. Whoever she was, it is certain that she was a woman of power and influence in Thyatira. There is a parallel to Jezebel, the wife of Ahab (2 Kings 9:10). She also called herself a prophetess, and set herself up as a teacher. She was a promoter of idolatry, and so was the Jezebel of the New Testament.

God sent Elijah to Ahab to warn and pronounce judgment upon him, because he permitted Jezebel to seduce the Israelites. Ahab indicated repentance and God's judgment was averted for awhile. Thus Jezebel had time to repent, but she did not; instead she taught her sons the sins of idolatry.

Likewise, mercy was extended to the evil and wicked Jezebel of the New Testament, but she heeded not, and God pronounced terrible judgment upon her and her children.

The bed of her sin became the bed of her sickness and anguish. Her children were to be put to death. Her followers would be victims of a great tribulation, "and all the churches shall know I am He which searcheth the reins and hearts; and I will give unto everyone of you according to your works."

The terrible influence of a wicked woman is evident in this narrative. Some insist this was not a real woman, but a name and doctrine symbolizing the idolatry that had invaded the church at Thyatira.

God gives to woman a warm, gentle nature. Women who have learned to train and develop these innate gifts can bless humanity more than man ever can. But once a woman surrenders her virtue, she sinks deeper into immorality than it is possible for a man to sink. If she possesses a strong personality her influence for evil is extensive for time and eternity.

> "Come ye out from among them and be ye
> separate, saith the Lord, and touch no
> unclean thing; and I will receive you
> and will be to you a Father, and ye
> shall be to me sons and daughters, saith
> the Lord Almighty."

STUDY SUGGESTIONS

Who was Jezebel of Thyatira?
Would her position as an elder's wife, as some conjecture, make her influential?
How did she speak of herself?
Discuss her false doctrine and its dangers.
Is the church in danger today from women like Jezebel?
Compare her to Jezebel, Ahab's wife.

Heirs Together of The Grace of Life

"Likewise ye husbands dwell with them according to knowledge . . . and as being heirs together of the grace of life" (1 Pet. 3:7).

Gen. 1:11, 20, 24
Tit. 2:1, 3-5
Gen. 2:7, 21-23
1 Cor. 11:8, 9, 13
2 Pet. 1:3-8
1 Tim. 2:9-15
2 John

THE FIRST narrative of human beings in Genesis is a family history, and the beginning of the nation of Israel was one Hebrew family. The position of the mother in the patriarchal family, though secondary to the husband, was worthy and often revered. Her primary function was that of wife and mother, yet we see her in her tent life, as a homemaker. She wove the fabrics of the house "of hair"; she made clothing for her family and prepared the food. It was her lot to impart religious and spiritual training to the youth of the family.

Other women in Old Testament times were tireless drudges whose station was little better than that of cattle or slaves, but by New Testament days womanhood was moving on a plain somewhat more equal with that of man. Jesus honored woman by his courteous understanding and sympathetic ministry.

DIVINE PATTERN

The apostle Paul wrote the Corinthian Christians and said, "But I would have you know, that the head of every man is Christ; and the head of the woman is the man; and the head of Christ is God." The relationship stated in this verse is the order established by Jehovah in the beginning. The woman who refuses to acknowledge the headship of man is in rebellion against Jehovah.

When a woman becomes a wife she becomes "one" with her husband. This oneness with him is a relationship that she sustains to no other man, and all her other human affiliations are secondary to this. The divine order is God, Christ, man, and then woman. God is the head of Christ, not implying inferiority; wives are to be "in subjection to your own husbands" in everything. This does not teach abasement, nor inferiority. She is still an individual and responsible personality.

WOMEN IN PARABLES

Women are pictured in the parables of our Lord along with men. The woman with leaven is in Jesus' parable about the kingdom of God. The wise and foolish virgins are the subject of another parable, one which certainly indicates that women share in the responsibility for the spread of the kingdom on earth.

"Two women shall be grinding together, the one shall be taken, the other left." How very important for women to know the importance of their being ready for the day when Christ shall come. The responsibility is equal to that of man's.

WOMEN IN MIRACLES

In the Savior's ministry, healing of women figures equally with that of men. Matthew, Mark, and Luke all tell the story of three sick women who came to Jesus and were healed. One, Peter's mother-in-law, had a high fever; another had suffered for twelve long years of an incurable issue of blood. The third woman had for eighteen years endured the tragedy of being too twisted and bent to walk upright.

These women were healed by a touch or a word from our Lord; they owed Him their lives and their health. It is small wonder that they expressed their gratitude in service to the Son of God.

WOMEN WHOSE CHILDREN WERE HEALED

The Syro-Phoenician woman, whose daughter "was grievously vexed with a devil," came entreating Jesus to heal her child. Her faith, though severely tested, never wavered, and today we read the loving, merciful words of Jesus to her, "O woman, great is thy faith." From that hour her child was healed.

The first person Jesus raised from the dead was the son of the widow of Nain. He had compassion upon her, as he always did upon women in distress.

True, these women are not even called by name in the Bible, but they are recorded by the Holy Spirit that we may know the significant place held by women in the plans and purposes of God.

WOMAN'S MINISTRY IN THE HOUSE OF GOD

In the 35th chapter of Exodus is the account of God's employing the whole congregation of Israel, male and female, sons and daughters, to raise and adorn His house. The men worked and brought offerings; the women spun and brought their ornaments. "And all the women who were wisehearted did spin with their hands, and brought that which they had spun, both of blue, and of purple, and of scarlet, and of fine linen. And all the women whose heart stirred them up in wisdom spun goats' hair." A vivid picture of women who worked to beautify their place of worship. Today "wisehearted women" can use their talents and materials toward the same purpose.

This example of ancient woman's ministry in the house of God is further illustrated in the willingness with which they gave up their ornaments, even their mirrors, into the tabernacle service. It has been suggested that these "women—assembling at the door of the tabernacle" were devout, pious women, whose offering of the mirrors indicated sacrifice of their pride to the service of God.

"Many women were there," who had followed Jesus to the cross, says Matthew. Devout women watched the place of his burial. Brave and courageous women stayed close to Jesus throughout his dark hours upon the cross. These women prepared the spices to anoint His body, and were back at the sepulchre before sunrise. Christ's first appearance was to a woman, and because of her steadfast love and devotion, Mary Magdalene was the first to announce his resurrection.

In the ten days prior to the descent of the Holy Spirit, the disciples were waiting in Jerusalem as Jesus had instructed them before his ascension. There in an upper room, "these all continued with one accord in prayer and supplication, with the women, and Mary the mother of Jesus, and with his brethren." Significantly, the women are named along with the apostles in the roll call of this prayer meeting.

After ten days the ascended Christ kept the promise made to the apostles, "Howbeit, when he the Spirit of Truth is come, he will guide you into all truth; for he shall not speak of himself, but whatsoever he shall hear, that shall he speak; and he will show you things to come."

The Spirit-filled apostles preached the gospel of the risen Christ on that Day of Pentecost, A.D. 33, and the church of God was born. Women were among those who became obedient to the gospel, including Sapphira who made this noble start, but then failed so miserably, and died so tragically.

Philip's daughters were unmarried, and were prophetesses. He, being an evangelist, was selected to assist in the business and benevolent affairs of the young church at Jerusalem. He carried the gospel message to Samaria, and the last we hear of him is in Caesarea.

It is probable that these daughters were active in the churches in Jerusalem, Samaria, and Caesarea. Because of their spiritual endowments they could be of great assistance to their father. They probably assisted him in Samaria, as he preached and baptized. "But when they believed Philip's preaching concerning the kingdom of God, and the name of Jesus Christ, they were baptized, both men and women." Perhaps these daughters were influential in assisting the Samaritan women to an understanding.

Their home in Caesarea was also a haven of hospitality for Paul and his company. In the days when Christianity was young, women were teachers and dispensers of hospitality.

There is a beautiful picture of love and devotion earlier in this same chapter. Paul and his companion had spent seven days in Tyre, where they found disciples. Upon their departure, these followers, with wives and children, accompanied them to the outskirts of the city where they all kneeled down on the shore and prayed. Paul wrote to Timothy about women professing godliness. These women were instructed in true adornment, which was not a matter of elaborate coiffure, expensive raiment, or valuable jewelry, but the living of a good life. Good works are the true ornament of the godly woman.

Again the Holy Spirit designates women's rank with man. "But I suffer not a woman to teach, nor to usurp authority over the man, but to be in silence." She is not to teach over a man, or to take precedence over him.

The picture of the New Testament church is one of activity, men and women laboring together to promote God's kingdom upon earth. Each individual had a work to perform.

Euodias and Syntyche were workers in the church at Philippi, as Phebe was a servant of the church at Cenchrea. These women, said Paul, "labored with me in the gospel." They were worthy of help, "Whose names are in the Book of Life."

God's woman, so vividly portrayed from Genesis to Revelation, is man's assistant and helper in the home and the church. Every inspired command to man includes the woman. The one exception is the charge of headship or authority. In the home she is subject to her husband, in the church to the elders. The unity and fellowship of woman with man is the picture of Sarah's daughters, "whose daughters you are, as long as you do well."

Aged Women

Titus, according to Paul, must "speak things which becometh sound doctrine." Sound doctrine for the aged women is that they be holy in their behavior.

Here is an inspired recipe for a happy old age. Godly women, maintaining the Christian graces of faith, love, and patience, are the product of a sound doctrine. They will not be slanderous about friends and neighbors. They will not be given to much wine; and foolish, trivial things hold no attraction for them. Their days will not be spent in idleness as they seek to do all to the glory of God.

The aged woman is both qualified and commanded to be a teacher of good things. She is to teach the younger women to

"love their husbands and children, to be
sensible and chaste, home lovers, kind
hearted, and willing to adapt themselves

to their husbands; a good advertisement for
the Christian faith."
("Letters to Young Churches")
by J. B. PHILLIPS

Every congregation should plan for the aged women to teach the
younger women. The rising tide of broken homes, juvenile delinquency, and conflicting interests can be held in check if this kind of
teaching is prevalent. The world needs grandmothers like Lois.

"The right sort of woman, nobly planned,
To warn, to comfort, and command."
(WORDSWORTH)

LET US LOVE

The aged apostle John, in his letter to the elect lady and her children, has given to all Christian women a picture of noble motherhood.
In the very salutation he expresses sincere affection for this lady and
her children, "whom I love in the truth," he said.

Christ had stressed love for himself and his followers, and the
Holy Spirit, through the apostles; he emphasized love as a sign of
true discipleship. John's next statement, "And not I only, but also
all they that have known the truth," indicated that she was well known
in the church. She had a good report of all Christians in that vicinity,
and it is likely that her house was the meeting place for the church.
The apostles had in all probability preached there many times, and
had been recipients of the elect lady's hospitality.

This brief epistle, the second by the apostle whom Jesus loved,
seems to have been a reply to a letter written him by this honorable
lady. Her letter had caused him to rejoice greatly, for the cause of
Christ was prospering in the place where she lived, and in her own
household.

"I was overjoyed to find some of your
children living the life of truth,
as the Father Himself instructed us."
(*Letters to Young Churches*—PHILLIPS)

Perhaps some of her own children had been drawn away by the
adversary, for the letter contains strong warning against false teachers and evil associations. "If there come any unto you and bring not
this doctrine, receive him not into your house, neither bid him Godspeed. For he that biddeth him Godspeed becomes a partaker of his
evil deeds." Surely, in this short missive a great challenge is presented to the woman of today. Just as truly as this woman who
lived approximately A.D. 90 must walk in the truth, and bring her

children up in truth and love, so must the women of the 20th century. Every good mother should heed the inspired exhortations given to this Christian woman. She should, through study and prayer, have that spiritual perception which discerns between good and evil.

He urged this family to continue in Christian love and to set their faces sternly against those who would pervert the gospel.

The apostle John has placed great responsibility upon woman. She is not only responsible for her own household, but also for the household of God.

"My Lord, my Truth, my Way,
My sure, unerring Light,
On thee my feeble steps I stay,
Which thou wilt guide aright."
(Hymn, by JOHN WESLEY)

Phillips, in his *Letters to Young Churches*, rephrases John's words to the elect lady and gives us a very personal glimpse into the life of the beloved apostle.

"I have a lot that I could write to you, but somehow I find it hard to put down on paper. I hope to come and see you personally, and we will have a long talk together—and how we shall enjoy that. Your sister's children send their love."

Through his brief evaluation of this particular Christian woman, John sustains the teaching of another apostle, who said, "Ye are heirs together of the grace of life."

Ministering Women

Luke 8:3; 24:10

"Having then gifts given differing according to the grace that is given to us . . . let us wait on our ministering" (Rom. 12:7).

JOANNA, the wife of Chuza, Herod's steward, was among the many women who accompanied Jesus and the twelve on his later Galilean ministry. She was one of the certain women which had been healed of evil spirits or of sickness. She was drawn to the Savior who had brought healing to her body and new life to her soul.

Her husband was house-steward of Herod Antipas. Though he is not named as a disciple of Christ, he *must* have been very favorably disposed toward Him. His wife was permitted to give of herself, her time and her substance to Jesus and his disciples. Her ministry never faltered, and she is last mentioned at the empty sepulchre, where she had gone to embalm the Savior's body. She was among that faithful group who tell the apostles the words of the angel. "He is not here, but is risen."

Though the mention of Joanna is brief, we have the beautiful picture of a truly converted woman, her faith manifested by her works and her labors of love.

A JOYFUL MINISTRY

Susanna is the next mentioned in this group who accompanied Jesus and the twelve on this preaching tour. The service she rendered on this occasion has immortalized her name.

Many others, women whom Jesus had healed, followed him and ministered unto him of their substance. Mary Magdalene was in the Lord's train of grateful, clinging followers.

These ministering women who followed Jesus in his Galilean tour defied the custom in Palestine. The rabbis did not believe that women should be taught the law. They gained a knowledge of the Christ as they journeyed with him through Galilee; and like Mary of Bethany, their ministering to the Lord of their substance, "shall be spoken of as a memorial of them."

STUDY SUGGESTIONS

How may Christian women minister unto Christ? (Matt. 25:40)
What portion of material blessings belong to God? (1 Cor. 16:20)
Are women more liberal than men? Why?
What priceless gift did woman give to the world? (Gal. 4:45)
Discuss woman's opportunities to serve and labor for the Master. (Heb. 6:10)
Read Ephesians 2:10. How had God ordained that we should walk? Name some good works.

STUDY SUGGESTIONS

Read carefully (1 Pet. 3:1-7). Discuss the wife's relationship to her husband. How does the average woman of today regard subjection?
Define feminine escapism. Does the American woman who has left home to compete with men escape subjection?
Has woman's emancipation given more stability to the home, church, and nation?
Do you think broken homes, juvenile delinquency, mental illness, are the result of a disregard of God's plan?

Discuss the divine pattern versus the modern pattern.

Is it a part of the divine plan that a man support his family? (1 Tim. 5:8)

Is it a part of the divine plan that the woman be a keeper at home? (1 Tim. 5:14)

Name some failures of the modern home.

Do children feel that a mother prefers this thing called a job to them? Could this lead to emotional upset?

How does Peter advise husbands to dwell with their wives? (1 Pet. 3:7)

How is the woman the weaker sex?

Discuss her gentleness, sympathy, kindness and understanding.

What do you consider the greatest need of the world today?

What do you think of J. Edgar Hoover's appeal that women of America be restored to the homes?

What service does a Christian wife and mother render to the church?

Name home activities that could be termed work of the church.

Read and discuss the women in Jesus' parables. What does this show about the Lord's regard for woman?

Did home activities contribute anything to the Lord's service in his earthly ministry? Give some examples.

Describe the activities of the Christian woman in the early church.

     a. Mary—used her house. (Acts 12:12-17)

     b. Dorcas—worked with her hands. (Acts 9:36)

     c. Priscilla—homemaker and teacher. (Acts 18:1-3, 24-26; 1 Cor. 16:19)

     d. Euodia and Syntyche—laborers in the gospel. (Phil. 4:3)

     e. Eunice and Lois—keepers at home. (2 Tim. 1:1-5, 3:15)

     f. Phebe—servant of the church. (Rom. 6:1-2)

Discuss the womanly, Christian character of 2 John.

What did she contribute to the cause of the Lord?

What is the most important job a woman can do today?

Would you not consider noble motherhood the highest career for her?

Read 1 Tim. 2:12. Discuss.

Is teaching an unlimited prohibition in this passage? If unlimited, could a mother teach her children?

Is dominion over man limited or unlimited? If limited, when is she to have dominion?

Do the words "over a man," qualify "teach" and "dominion"?

"She does not teach over a man—nor have dominion over a man" (*God's Woman*—by C. R. Nichol)

Printed in the United States
56050LVS00003B/64-114